USING ENGLISH

DOROTHY DANIELSON *California State University, San Francisco*

REBECCA HAYDEN *University of California Extension, Berkeley*

PRENTICE-HALL, INC.

Englewood Cliffs, New Jersey

USING ENGLISH

YOUR SECOND LANGUAGE

Library of Congress Cataloging in Publication Data

Danielson, Dorothy.

  Using English.

    1. English language—Text-books for foreigners.
I. Hayden, Rebecca E., joint author. II. Title.
PE1128.D32   428'.24   72-10362
ISBN 0-13-939678-0

USING ENGLISH: YOUR SECOND LANGUAGE
Dorothy Danielson and *Rebecca Hayden*

Cover and text design by Maurine Lewis

Printed in the United States of America

10 9 8 7

Prentice-Hall International, Inc., *London*
Prentice-Hall of Australia, Pty. Ltd., *Sydney*
Prentice-Hall of Canada, Ltd., *Toronto*
Prentice-Hall of India Private Ltd., *New Delhi*
Prentice-Hall of Japan, Inc., *Tokyo*

Using English: Your Second Language is intended as a main or supplementary textbook for college students or adults who have completed basic courses in English as a second language and are well on their way to effective communication in speech and writing. Students with a fairly high level of proficiency in English should be able to cover the material in a 40 to 50 hour course of study; students who still need considerable oral and written practice of basic structures will possibly need twice that amount of time.

Although we expect that most intermediate and advanced students will be reasonably proficient in the language, we have nonetheless aimed at fairly complete coverage. The earlier units—on questions, attached statements and rejoinders, commands and requests—have more of an oral than written emphasis and, on this basis, might be considered more elementary. Later units—on clauses and punctuation—emphasize written work and might be considered more advanced and sophisticated. Beyond that, we have made no assumptions about the order of difficulty of the various units.

The units can be taken up in the order in which they appear in the book, or material throughout the book can be selected for study as the need arises. Admittedly there are some disadvantages to the self-contained type of unit—mainly the necessity to include in one place both simple and difficult material on relative clauses, indefinite articles, verb tenses, and so on; however, the flexibility gained seems worth the price. Parts of the book can be assigned to complement other reading and writing assignments, and problem areas can be either reviewed quickly or studied in depth. The material to be reviewed in each unit will naturally depend on the degree of proficiency of the students. In addition to review, however, each unit will surely contain expansion of the known and quite possibly the challenge of the unknown.

Within each unit, examples are followed by explanation and drill. The drill is usually short (a "minidrill") when it is used mainly to reinforce a point or to see whether the student comprehends and can use the structure; it is somewhat longer when it constitutes part of the explanation. The latter is often the case when the material is essentially for list learning—for example, verbs followed by *to* or *for* + indirect object.

With quite advanced students, the teacher may bypass the examples and explanations and go directly to the minidrill, proceeding rapidly until students reach material that is difficult for them. With less advanced students, however, the examples, explanations, and minidrills may not always be sufficient. When this is the case, supplementary drills, preferably drills that relate to the immediate experience of the students, can be added.

Exercises at the end of each unit are for the most part cumulative. The degree of control in these exercises varies, but the student has considerable freedom to create his own sentences and to express his own ideas.

The book also has devices to enable students to use it as a handy reference. In shaded sections at the bottom of appropriate pages, there are, for example, lists of contractions, irregular nouns, irregular and two-word verbs, as well as guides to the pronunciation and spelling of plural nouns and third-person singular verbs. Section numbers in the margins and two indexes—one for words and one for topics—simplify the finding of information.

Because the list of those who have given valuable suggestions and assistance through criticism or experimenting with the material is unbelievably long, we cannot possibly thank each one individually. However, we should like to single out for special thanks David P. Harris, director of the American Language Institute, Georgetown University, and members of his staff for criticism of an early version of the manuscript; David DeCamp, University of Texas, for his suggestions after reading a still earlier version; Martha Kornblum of Queens College and Ronald Wardhaugh, director of the English Language Institute, University of Michigan, for their thoughtful reviews of the final manuscript.

We are indebted to Allis Bens, director of the American Language Institute, California State University, San Francisco, and members of her staff for trying out much of the material; and to Alice C. Rowbotham, former head of Independent Study, University of California Extension, for encouraging us to develop a short course based on several units of the book. We express appreciation to colleagues at California State University, San Francisco, for insights gained in discussions of analysis and presentation of material; to former graduate students, now young colleagues teaching English as a second language, for their interest in the book and for encouraging us to complete it; and to the many students from all over the world for the pleasure, challenge, and enrichment they have given us.

We are most appreciative of the consideration of families, friends, colleagues, and editors, especially Larry Danielson, Ray L. Grosvenor, Aurora Quiros Haggard, Jagdish Jain, Maurine Lewis, William H. Oliver, Lois Wilson, and Thurston Womack. Last but most of all, we wish to thank Daniel Glicksberg, California State University, San Francisco, who brought his formidable critical faculties to bear on two meticulous readings of our very detailed and technical manuscript, offering innumerable notes on content and format.

CONTENTS

1 YES/ NO QUESTIONS

AND RESPONSES   *1*

1·1 IS/ ARE/ WAS/ WERE/ Questions and Short Responses   *1*

1·11 IS . . . GOING/ HAVE . . . GONE/ CAN . . . GO Questions and Short Responses   *4*

1·14 DO/ DOES/ DID Questions and Short Responses   *6*

1·17 Long Responses   *7*

1·19 YES/ NO Questions versus Choice Questions   *8*

1·21 Negative Questions and Responses   *8*

Exercises   *10*

2 WH-QUESTIONS

AND RESPONSES   *13*

2·1 WH-Questions: Functions   *13*

2·6 WH-Words and Phrases   *14*

2·12 WH-Questions: Special Situations   *16*

Exercises   *21*

3 TAG

QUESTIONS   *24*

3·1 Statement + Tag   *24*

3·11 Repeated Statement + Tag Question   *27*

3·13 Tag Question versus Contrastive Question   *28*

Exercises   *30*

4 ATTACHED STATEMENTS/

REJOINDERS   *33*

4·1 Attached Statements   *33*

4·14 Rejoinders   *37*

Exercises   *39*

5 COMMANDS/ REQUESTS/ INVITATIONS/ SUGGESTIONS/ DIRECTIONS   *42*

5·1 Affirmative Commands and Requests   *42*

5·3 Standard Requests and Responses   *44*

5·6 Negative Commands and Requests   *45*

5·10 Requests for Permission   *46*

5·15 Invitations   *47*

5·17 Suggestions   *48*

5·19 Directions   *49*

5·21 Reported Commands/ Requests/ Invitations/ Suggestions   *50*

Exercises   *53*

6 OBJECTS/ PASSIVE AND

CLEFT SENTENCES   *56*

6·1 Indirect Objects   *56*

6·4 Passive Sentences   *58*

6·11 Cleft Sentences *61*
6·13 Object Complements *62*
Exercises *63*

7

VERBS *66*

7·1 Simple Present versus Continuous
Present *66*
7·6 Present Continuous versus Present
(Continuous) Perfect *68*
7·10 Present Perfect versus Simple Past *72*
7·16 Simple Past versus Continuous Past *78*
7·18 Simple Past versus Past Perfect *79*
7·20 Future/ Future Continuous/
Future Perfect *80*
Exercises *82*

8

AUXILIARIES *85*

8·1 Possibility and Probability *85*
8·5 Necessity *86*
8·7 Permission *87*
8·9 Ability and Capability *87*
8·11 Obligation *88*
8·13 Suggestion *88*
8·15 Preference *89*
8·17 Repeated or Habitual Past Activity *89*
Exercises *90*

9

ADVERBIALS *92*

9·1 Position of Adverbials *92*
9·17 Special Usage *97*
9·42 Expression of Purpose *104*
9·45 Modifiers of Adverbs and Adjectives *105*
Exercises *107*

10

**ARTICLES AND
PREARTICLES** *111*

10·1 The Indefinite Articles: A/ AN/ SOME *111*
10·17 The Definite Article: THE *117*

10·20 A/ AN/ THE before Nouns Referring to a
Group *120*
10·24 Prearticles *122*
Exercises *131*

11

**ARTICLES WITH
PROPER NOUNS** *136*

11·1 No Article versus THE before
Place Names *136*
11·11 A/ AN versus THE before Proper
Nouns *140*
Exercises *142*

12

**TWO-WORD VERBS
AND OTHER
COMBINATIONS** *148*

12·1 Two-Word Verbs: Structure and
Meaning *148*
12·2 Separable Two-Word Verbs *149*
12·14 Nonseparable Two-Word Verbs *156*
12·23 BE and HAVE Combinations *161*
Exercises *163*

13

**ADVERBIAL
CLAUSES** *169*

13·1 Position and Function of Adverbial
Clauses *169*
13·3 Clauses of Time *169*
13·9 Clauses of Place *171*
13·11 Clauses of Distance, Manner, and
Frequency *172*
13·13 Clauses of Reason or Cause *172*
13·22 Clauses of Result *174*
13·29 Clauses of Purpose *176*
13·34 Clauses of Contrast and Concession *177*
13·42 Adverbial Clauses and Participial
Phrases *180*
Exercises *182*

14 **COMPARISONS** *185*

14·1 THE SAME AS/ DIFFERENT FROM/ LIKE/ UNLIKE/ SIMILAR TO *185*

14·16 AS . . . AS/ -ER THAN/ MORE . . . THAN/ -EST OF ALL/ MOST . . . OF ALL *188*

14·45 SIMILARLY/ ON THE OTHER HAND *196*

Exercises *198*

15 **NOUN CLAUSES** *200*

15·1 Position of Noun Clauses *200*

15·2 WH-Clauses *200*

15·15 IF or WHETHER Clauses *204*

15·22 THAT-Clauses *207*

Exercises *213*

16 **RELATIVE CLAUSES** *215*

16·1 Position and Function of Relative Clauses *215*

16·3 Restrictive Clauses *215*

16·20 Nonrestrictive Clauses *221*

16·30 Relative Clauses in Writing *224*

Exercises *226*

17 **HOPES/ WISHES/ CONDITIONALS** *229*

17·1 HOPE versus WISH *229*

17·8 Conditional Sentences *232*

Exercises *235*

18 **VERB FORMS AS COMPLEMENTS** *236*

18·1 THAT-Clause/ TO + Verb *236*

18·17 THAT-Clause/ Verb-ING *241*

18·27 Passive and Perfect Infinitives and Verb-ING Forms *243*

18·31 Adjective + Verb-ING or TO + Verb *245*

18·33 Verb-ING and Verb-ED as Adjectives *245*

18·35 HAVE Someone DO Something/ HAVE Something DONE *246*

18·38 SEE/ HEAR/ FEEL Something MOVE/ MOVING *247*

18·40 HELP/ MAKE/ DO/ LET + (Pro)Noun + Simple Verb Form *247*

Exercises *248*

19 **PUNCTUATION** *250*

19·1 End-of-Sentence *250*

19·2 Between Sentences *250*

19·6 Adverbial Phrases and Clauses *251*

19·8 Relative Clauses *252*

19·10 Within the Sentence *253*

19·18 Capitalization *255*

19·20 Dialogs *256*

19·24 Quotations, Footnotes, and Bibliography *257*

19·31 Letters *259*

Exercises *263*

ENGLISH SPEECH SOUNDS *266*

SUBJECT INDEX *268*

WORD INDEX *274*

IS/ARE/WAS/WERE Questions and Short Responses

1·1   This painting **is** by Picasso.

Is that painting by Picasso, too?

These paintings **are** by Braque.

Are those paintings by Braque, too?

Hiroshige **was** a Japanese painter.

Was Hiroshige a landscape painter?

There **were** some art exhibits last month.

Were there some art exhibits the month before?

- Notice that the verb is in the first position in the questions above.
- Native speakers use both rising and falling intonation on questions of this type. The rising intonation seems to be more common. *Examples:*

Was Hiroshige a painter?   or: Was Hiroshige a painter?

1·2   **Is this painting** by Picasso?   Yes, **it is.**

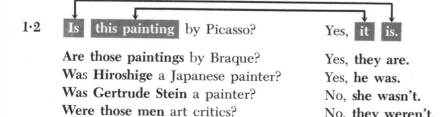

Are those paintings by Braque?   Yes, **they are.**
Was Hiroshige a Japanese painter?   Yes, **he was.**
Was Gertrude Stein a painter?   No, **she wasn't.**
Were those men art critics?   No, **they weren't.**

- Pronouns replace noun subjects in short responses; a form of **be** is repeated in the response.

1·3   Are  a painter?   Yes, **I** am.

Are **you** painters?   Yes, **we** are.
Is **he** a sculptor?   Yes, **he** is.

- **You** becomes **I** or **we** in the answer.
- There are no contractions in short affirmative responses consisting of only a pronoun + a form of **be.** *Examples:*

  Yes, **I** am. (NOT: Yes, I'm.)   Yes, **we** are. (NOT: Yes, we're.)
  Yes, **he** is. (NOT: Yes, he's.)   BUT: Yes, we're late.

1·4   Are they sculptors, too?   No, they **aren't.**

Is she a poet?   No, she **isn't.**
Are you a poet?   No, **I'm not.**

- Contractions are customary in short negative responses. **I** + **am** + **not** becomes **I'm not.** With other pronouns, however, two types of contractions are possible. *Examples:*

  No, **she isn't.**   No, **she's not.**
  (See the shaded area for more information on contractions.)

1·5   Were there some art exhibits last month?   Yes, there were.

Is **there** a museum on Third Street?   Yes, **there** is.
Are **there** many theaters in this area?   No, **there** aren't.

- **There** is in the subject position in these questions; **there** is also repeated in the response.

1·6   There are many theaters in this area.

Isn't **there** a **theater** in the next block?

- Notice that the verbs in the preceding examples are both singular and plural; the verbs do not agree with **there** but with the noun or pronoun.
- Notice the contraction of **there** and **is** (**there's**).

1·7 DRILL In this drill, one person asks the question and another answers according to his knowledge or opinion. Ask someone whether . . .

1. there is a good movie in town →
   Is there a good movie in town? → *Yes, there's a good film at the Metro.*

2. there are many movie theaters in the downtown area →
   Are there many theaters in the downtown area? → *Yes, there are quite a few.*
   OR: *No, there's only one.* OR: *I don't really know.*

3. there is a theater that shows mainly foreign films

4. the theaters are usually crowded on weekends

5. the theaters are closed on Sundays and holidays

6. there was a Charlie Chaplin film on television last night

1·8 Is **this** the museum director?   Yes, **it** is.

Was **that** Mrs. Lee?   No, **it** wasn't.
Are **those** your friends?   No, **they** aren't.
Are **these** your children?   Yes, **they** are.

- Notice in the short responses that **this** and **that** become **it**, and **these** and **those** become **they**. It is used even when talking about people (for example, the museum director and Mrs. Lee).

CONTRACTIONS

Contractions are customary in conversational English. They are generally acceptable in all but very formal writing and speaking.

Pronoun + **be** or auxiliary:

...m	he's	she's	it's	we're	you're	they're
...ll	he'll	she'll	it'll	we'll	you'll	they'll
...ve	he's	she's	it's	we've	you've	they've
...d	he'd	she'd	—	we'd	you'd	they'd[1]

be or auxiliary + **not**:

...sn't	aren't	wasn't	weren't	hasn't	haven't	hadn't
...oesn't	don't	didn't	can't	couldn't	won't	wouldn't
...houldn't	mustn't	needn't	oughtn't			

auxiliary + **have**:

...ould've	would've	should've	might've	must've

In spoken English, **is** frequently contracts with a preceding noun, and the vowel in **are** is often dropped. These pronunciations are not ordinarily represented in written English.

Written English	Spoken English
My vacation **is** in June.	"My vacation's in June."
Their vacations **are** in July.	"Their vacations're in July."

...d = **had**, as in **I'd** (he'd/ she'd/ we'd/ you'd/ they'd) better go, or **would**, as in **I'd** (he'd, etc.) rather go.

1·9   **My brother** is an engineer.

Is **yours** an engineer, too?   Yes, **he** is.

Is **hers** also an engineer?   No, **he** isn't.

Mr. Nader's office is on the fourth floor.

Is **yours** on the fourth floor, too?   No, **it** isn't.

Is **hers** on the second floor?   Yes, **it** is.

Are **theirs** on the first floor.   Yes, **they** are.

■   When the subject of a question is a possessive pronoun like **yours, mine, ours, hers, his, theirs,** the pronoun in the short response depends on the person or thing being talked about. For example, in the first set of the preceding examples, the pronoun in the response is **he** because the person being talked about is "my brother." What would the pronoun in the short response be if the person being talked about were "my sister" instead of "my brother"? What is being talked about in the second set of examples?

1·10   DRILL   Give short responses according to your knowledge or opinion.

1. Is February 22nd a legal holiday in the United States? → *Yes, it is.*

2. Is that George Washington's Birthday? → *Yes, it is.*

3. Was there another famous American President born in the month of February?

4. Was it Abraham Lincoln?

5. Is Abraham Lincoln's Birthday on February 12th?

6. Is yours on February 12th, too?

7. Were your parents born in February?

8. Are their birthdays holidays?

9. Is July 4th a holiday in the United States?

10. Is that Independence Day?

11. Are there any religious holidays in the United States?

12. Are those holidays Christmas Day and Easter Sunday?

IS . . . GOING/ HAVE . . . GONE/ CAN . . . GO Questions and Short Responses

1·11

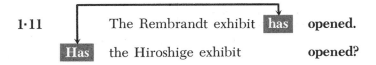

The Rembrandt exhibit **has** **opened.**

Has the Hiroshige exhibit **opened?**

They **are**   **going to see** the exhibit next Saturday.
Are you   **going to see** it next Saturday, too?

You **should** **have asked** them to go with you.
Should we   **have asked** them to go with us?

I **can** **meet** you there.
Can you   **meet** me there?

- The first word (auxiliary) of a verb phrase introduces the question. The other words of the verb phrase remain after the subject.

- Questions with **I** and **we** are natural when the speaker is uncertain or is asking for advice or permission or extending an invitation.

Natural	*Unnatural*
Have I told you about Marjorie?	Have I lived here long?
Are we going to see her tomorrow?	Are we talking to Marjorie now?
Shall we dance?	Are we dancing now?

1·12   **Has** the Rembrandt exhibit opened?   Yes, it **has.**

Have you seen it?   Yes, I **have.**
Had you seen it before?   No, I **hadn't.**
Are they going next Saturday?   Yes, they **are.**
Can we meet them there?   Yes, we **can.**

- The same auxiliary occurs in the question and the response.

1·13   DRILL In this drill, one person asks the question and another gives a short response. *Situation:* A Rembrandt exhibit has recently opened at a local art museum. Ask someone whether he/she . . .

1. has seen the exhibit yet →
 Have you seen the exhibit yet? → *No, I haven't.*   OR: *Yes, I have.*

2. is going to see it soon →
 Are you planning to see it soon? → *No, I'm not.*

3. has thought about going next Saturday

4. would like to go with you

5. can get in cheaper with a student card

6. would give you a ride to the museum

Ask someone whether you . . .

7. can take pictures in the museum →
   Can I take pictures in the museum? → *No, you can't. (Cameras aren't allowed.)*

8. should plan on spending several hours at the museum

9. could go with him/her

10. could get in free

11. should read something about Rembrandt before you go

12. can borrow a book on Rembrandt from the museum library

DO/ DOES/ DID Questions and Short Responses

1·14   The meeting **begins** at eight o'clock tonight.
Does the lecture **begin** at eight o'clock tomorrow night?

They **plan** to attend the lecture.
Do   you **plan** to attend the lecture?

They **attended** the last lecture.
Did they **attend** the lecture before that?

- **Do, does,** or **did** occurs in the first position. The simple form of the verb follows the subject. *Example:*

  Does John **plan** to attend the lecture?   (NOT: Does John plans. . . .)

1·15   **Does** the lecture begin at eight o'clock?   Yes, it **does.**

Do   they plan to attend the lecture?   Yes, they **do.**
Did they attend the last lecture?   No, they **didn't.**

- **Do, does,** and **did** occur in both the question and the short response.

1·16   DRILL   In this drill, one person asks a question and another gives a short response. *Situation:* Your English teacher gave you a long assignment yesterday. Ask someone whether he/she . . .

1. did the assignment last night →
   Did you do the assignment last night? → *Yes, I did.*   OR: *No, I didn't.*

2. found the assignment difficult

3. usually studies in the library

4. usually studies with a friend

5. went to the library last night

Ask someone whether (name or names of people in the group) . . .

6. usually comes to class on time →

Does (Joe) usually come to class on time? → *Yes, he does.*   OR: *No, he doesn't.*

7. usually study together

8. usually sits in the front row

9. usually sit in the last row

10. speaks Chinese

11. speak Spanish

12. speaks English at home

Long Responses

1·17   Does that bus go downtown?   Yes, it goes as far as First Street.

Is there a bus stop here?   No, but there's one across the street.

Is the bus service good?   Yes, it is. In fact, it's very good.

- Long responses are seldom a mere repetition of information in the question. The response usually contains a *qualification,* a *contradiction,* or *additional information.*

- Sometimes the speaker answers **yes** or **no** and then gives other information. *Examples:*

Are you going to take the bus downtown?   No, I'd rather walk.
Do you often walk to the office?   Yes, I need the exercise.

- Giving other information is especially common in responses to requests or invitations in question form. (See also §5.10 through 5.16.) *Examples:*

Would you like to play golf on Saturday?   I'm sorry, but I can't make it.
Could we play next Saturday?   Yes, that would be fine.

1·18   DRILL   Answer *yes* or *no,* and give other information. Tell about yourself.

1. Have you studied English long?

2. Did you study English in high school?

3. Did you study any other languages in high school?

4. Were all your high school courses taught in English?

5. Do you ever speak English at home?

6. Do you speak English with your friends?

7. Have you read any books in English lately?

8. Do you read any magazines regularly?

YES/ NO Questions versus Choice Questions

1·19   — Would you like **tea or coffee?** (Please state your choice.)
— Coffee, please.

— Would you like **cream or sugar?** (Do you want anything in your coffee?)
— No, thank you. I like it black.

■ The intonation pattern is important in distinguishing a choice question from a **yes/no** question. The first example ("Would you like tea or coffee?") clearly asks the person addressed to make a choice. He cannot say just **yes** or **no** but must state his preference ("Coffee, please"). He can, of course, refuse both ("I don't care for either, thank you").

■ The second example asks whether the person addressed wants anything at all in the coffee.

1·20   DRILL   Look at the cue on the left; then ask the question, and give an appropriate response.

Yes/No	1. Do you want cream or sugar? → *Yes, a little of both, please.*
Choice	2. Would you like milk or cream in your coffee? → *Cream, please.*
Yes/No	3. Would you like lemon or sugar in your tea?
Choice	4. Do you take lemon or cream in your tea?
Choice	5. Do you want your coffee black or with cream?
Choice	6. Do you want to have lunch at twelve o'clock or at one o'clock?
Choice	7. Do you want to go to the Elephant Room or the Campus Inn?
Yes/No	8. Shall we ask Fred or Jack to join us?

Negative Questions and Responses

1·21

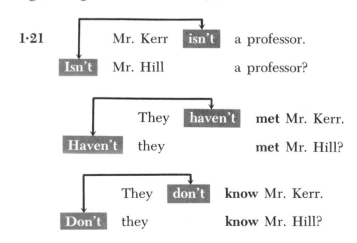

Mr. Kerr **isn't** a professor.
Isn't Mr. Hill a professor?

They **haven't** met Mr. Kerr.
Haven't they met Mr. Hill?

They **don't** know Mr. Kerr.
Don't they know Mr. Hill?

■ Contractions are quite customary in negative statements; notice the position of the contraction in the questions.

■ Uncontracted **not** conveys an emphatic or a very formal tone in both statements and questions. *Examples:*

He has **not** met Mr. Kerr.
Has he **not** met Mr. Kerr?

■ Negative statements, in a sense, are the opposite of affirmative statements. Mr. Kerr *is* or *isn't* a professor. *Examples:*

Mr. Kerr **isn't** a **professor.** He's a **doctor.**

However, negative questions are very much like affirmative questions; they differ only in degree or point of emphasis. *Compare:*

Is Mr. Kerr a professor?
(I really don't know. Please tell me.)

Isn't Mr. Kerr a professor?
(Something makes me think he is. Please tell me if I'm wrong.)

■ Answers to negative questions are like answers to affirmative questions; they depend on the situation, not on the form of the question.

1·22   DRILL   Complete the sentences, following the pattern of the first two examples. (In oral practice, stress the pronoun in the answer.)

Joe:	*Jim:*
1. She isn't here.	I know that, but *isn't hé here?*
2. She wasn't at home.	I know that, but *wasn't hé at home?*
3. She can't go with us.	I know that, but
4. She isn't going to the meeting.	I know that, but
5. She didn't give us her address.	I know that, but
6. She hasn't paid for her dress.	I know that, but

1·23   DRILL   Complete the answers.

1. Wasn't there a concert last night?	Yes, *there was.*
2. Wasn't the concert sold out?	No, *I don't think so.*
3. Didn't they go to the concert?	Yes, *they went with us.*
4. Isn't there a concert tonight?	Yes,
5. Aren't there any tickets left?	Yes,
6. Doesn't the box office open at one o'clock?	No,
7. Haven't you got a ticket?	No,
8. Can't we get tickets before the performance?	Yes,

1 Make *yes/no* questions based on the information in the following sections; then give long or short responses, as appropriate.

PART A: *Is/ Are/ Was/ Were Questions* (Refer to §1.1 through 1.10.)

Rembrandt, a great Dutch painter, was a very versatile artist. He was both an excellent portrait painter and draftsman, and he is famous for his portraits and etchings. His landscape etchings are especially beautiful, one of the most famous being *The Three Trees*. His pen-and-ink drawings of everyday scenes are also outstanding; in fact, many of them are little masterpieces.

Examples:

Was Rembrandt a German painter?
No, he wasn't. OR: *No, he wasn't. He was a Dutch painter.*

Was Rembrandt one of the greatest Dutch painters?
Yes, he was. OR: *Yes, he was a very famous Dutch painter.*

PART B: *Have/ Can/ Could/ etc. Questions* (Refer to §1.11 through 1.13.)

Rembrandt's paintings have increased in value over the years, and today very few people can afford to purchase a Rembrandt painting. One of his paintings would now sell for over a million dollars. For example, in 1966, his painting *Titus* sold for over $2,000,000. This painting, which is a portrait of Rembrandt's son, was purchased as a gift for the Los Angeles County Museum. Since then, *Titus* has occasionally appeared in exhibits at other museums featuring a collection of Rembrandt's works.

PART C: *Do/ Does/ Did Questions* (Refer to §1.14 through 1.16)

Rembrandt lived in the seventeenth century. He studied art for several years in Amsterdam; then he returned to Leiden, his home town, where he quickly established himself as a painter. Later he returned to Amsterdam, and there he eventually became famous and wealthy. However, his popularity declined in later years, and he died in poverty in 1669. Today his paintings are again in demand, but only very wealthy individuals or large museums have the means to purchase a famous work by Rembrandt.

2 Read the following sentences; then make *choice* questions and give appropriate responses, as we have done for the first sentence. (Refer to §1.19.)

1. Rembrandt was *Dutch/ German.* →
   Was Rembrandt Dutch or German? → *He was Dutch.*

2. He was born in *Sweden/ Holland.*

3. He lived in the *seventeenth/ eighteenth* century.

4. He was primarily *a sculptor/ a painter.*

5. He studied art in *Amsterdam/ London.*

6. He lived in *luxury/ poverty* during the last years of his life.

7. His paintings have *decreased/ increased* in value over the years.

8. One of his famous paintings would sell for about *a thousand/ a million* dollars today.

3 (1) Change the questions into statements; (2) arrange the statements into a paragraph (suggestions are given for making the sentences in the paragraph seem more related or connected).

GROUP A (EXAMPLE):

1. Isn't the population of Ceylon homogeneous?° 2. Is about 70 percent of the population Sinhalese? 3. Are the Sinhalese known as the "lion people"? 4. Are the Sinhalese Buddhists? 5. Did their ancestors come to Ceylon in the sixth century B.C.? 6. Did they conquer the ancestors of the Veddas? 7. Are the Veddas an aboriginal† people? 8. Do they now live in remote mountainous regions? 9. Are the Hindu Tamils the largest minority group? 10. Did they later come from southern India? 11. Do other minority groups include the Moslem Moors, the Eurasians, and the Burghers? 12. Are the Burghers descendants of the Dutch and Portuguese colonists?

Statements: 1. The population of Ceylon is not homogeneous. 2. About 70 percent of the population is Sinhalese. 3. The Sinhalese are known as the "lion people." 4. The Sinhalese are Buddhists. 5. Their ancestors came to Ceylon in the sixth century B.C. 6. They conquered the ancestors of the Veddas. 7. The Veddas are an aboriginal people. 8. They now live in remote mountainous regions. 9. The Hindu Tamils are the largest minority group. 10. They later came from southern India. 11. Other minority groups include the Moslem Moors, the Eurasians, and the Burghers. 12. The Burghers are descendants of the Dutch and Portuguese colonists.

Suggestions for writing the paragraph: (1) Combine Statements 1 and 2, connecting them with *however* (preceded by a semicolon and followed by a comma). (2) Combine Statements 3 and 4; change Statement 3 to "who are known as Sinhalese" and place it (surrounded by commas) in the middle of the sentence between "The Sinhalese" and "are Buddhists." (3) Combine Statements 5, 6, 7, and 8: first, combine Statements 5 and 6, dropping "they" from Statement 6 and connecting the two parts by *and;* then change Statements 7 and 8 to "an aboriginal people who now live in remote mountainous regions" and add that (preceded by a comma) to the sentence resulting from Statements 5 and 6. (4) Combine Statements 9 and 10; change Statement 10 to "who later came from southern India" and place it (surrounded by commas) after "The Hindu Tamils." (5) Combine Statements 11 and 12, changing Statement 12 to "who are descendants of the Dutch and Portuguese colonists" and placing it (preceded by a comma) at the end of Statement 11.

Sample paragraph:

The population of Ceylon is not homogeneous; however, about 70 percent of the population is Sinhalese. The Sinhalese, who are known as the "lion people," are Buddhists. Their ancestors came from northern India in the sixth century B.C. and conquered the ancestors of the Veddas, an aboriginal people who now live in remote mountainous regions. The Hindu Tamils, who later came from southern India, are the largest minority group. Other minority groups include the Moslem Moors, the Eurasians, and the Burghers, who are descendants of the Dutch and Portuguese colonists.

° **Homogeneous** = the same or similar.
† **Aboriginal** = native to or original.

GROUP B

1. Is Nepal one of the small independent countries shut off from the rest of the world by the Himalayas? 2. Are several of the world's highest mountains located in Nepal? 3. Is Mount Everest included among them? 4. Did Nepal not open its borders to foreigners before 1950? 5. Was travel in the mountains strictly forbidden before then? 6. Since that time, have more and more travelers gone there each year? 7. Have there been numerous expeditions to conquer the high mountains? 8. Was the most famous expedition the conquest of Mount Everest by Sir Edmund Hillary and Tenzing Norgay in 1953?

Suggestions for writing the paragraph: (1) Combine Statements 2 and 3 into one sentence; reduce statement 3 to a phrase, "including Mount Everest" (set off by commas), and place it after "Several of the world's highest mountains." (2) Combine Statements 4 and 5 into a compound sentence connected by *and* (preceded by a comma); and begin this sentence with "Before 1950" (followed by a comma) and drop the "before then" at the end of Statement 5. (3) Combine Statements 6 and 7 into a compound sentence connected by *and* (preceded by a comma). (4) In the last sentence, add the phrase *of course* (set off by commas) after "The most famous expedition."

4 Write out long responses to the following questions, applying them to a country with which you are familiar (you may wish to consult an encyclopedia). Then develop a paragraph of 75 to 100 words from this information. The paragraph should be somewhat similar to the one in Group A, Ex. 3.

1. Is the population of the country heterogeneous° or largely homogeneous?

2. Are the people in the majority group native inhabitants of the country or did they come from another place?

3. Are there several minority groups? Are some groups larger than others or are they about the same size? Do the people in these groups differ from one another, and from the majority group, in race, national origin, or religion?

° **Heterogeneous** = not the same or similar; composed of different types or elements.

WH-Questions: Functions

2·1   **Who** called Ray?   **Lois** called him.

What was wrong?   **Nothing** was wrong.

- In these questions, the **wh**-words ask for information about the subject and are in subject position.

2·2   **Who(m)** did Lois call?   She called **Ray.**

When did Lois call Ray?   She called him **last night.**

- In these questions, the **wh**-words ask for information about someone or something in the predicate. Predicate-type questions are similar to **yes**/**no** questions except that the **wh**-word replaces something in the predicate. *Compare:*

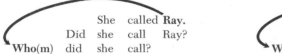

	She	called	**Ray.**
	Did	she	call	Ray?
Who(m)	did	she	call?

		He	is	**in Los Angeles** this week.
		Is	he	in Los Angeles this week?
Where		is	he		this week?

Is **do** (**does**/ **did**) used in a predicate-type question? Is **do** (**does**/ **did**) used in a subject-type question?

2·3   DRILL   Read the situation sentences and complete the questions. *Situation:* Last week Lois received a birthday card from Paolo. Paolo is in Italy now. He sent the card from Venice.

1. Who *received* a birthday card from Paolo?

2. Who(m) _____ a birthday card from?

3. When _____ a birthday card from Paolo?

4. What _____ from Paolo?

5. Who _____ in Italy now?

6. Where _____ Paolo now?

2·4   **Who** called you just now?   **Helen.**
          What did she want?   She wanted to know where Bill was.
          Where is Bill?   I don't know.
          What happened to Frank?   He moved to Arizona.

- **Wh**-questions ask for specific information. Although the information in the response can be given in a full sentence, a word or phrase is often sufficient.

2·5   **DRILL**   Decide which of the following answers can be reduced to a word or phrase. Under-line the word or phrase.

   1. *What* is John's hobby?   Photography is his hobby.
   2. *Whose camera* is this?   It's Jack's.
   3. *Who* took these pictures?   Jack took them.
   4. *When* did he take them?   He took them last week.
   5. *Which picture* do you like best?   I like this one.
   6. *How much* does a camera like Jack's cost? I have no idea.
   7. *What happened* to your slide projector?   My sister borrowed it.
   8. *When* will she bring it back?   I think in about a week.
   9. *What kind of camera* does she have?   She has an expensive Japanese camera.
  10. *Where* did she buy it?   She bought it at Fuji's Camera Mart.

WH-Words and Phrases

WHO/ WHOM/ WHOSE/ WHAT/ WHICH

2·6   **Who** borrowed your dictionary?   **Jane.**
          Who(m) did you lend your dictionary to?   Jane.
          Whose dictionary is that?   It's his.

- **Who/ whom/ whose** ask for information about persons. **Who** is the subject form; **whom** is the object form, but **who,** rather than **whom,** is very common in conversational English. *Compare:*

    Who shall we send the letter to?   (conversational)
    Whom shall we send the letter to?   (middle ground)
    To whom shall we send the letter?   (formal)

    Whose is the possessive form. **Whose** occurs alone or before nouns that refer to either persons or things. *Examples:*

    This is **hers.**   **Whose** is this?
    Janet is **his secretary.**   **Whose secretary** is Kay?
    This is **her desk.**   **Whose desk** is this?

2·7   **What** are you looking for?   **A dictionary.**
       Which (one) do you want?   (I want) **the large English dictionary.**

- **What** and **which** ask about things, but in certain contexts they may refer to persons.
  Compare:

Identification:	**Who** is **it?**	It's **John Crane.**
	(at the door or on the phone)	
Occupation:	**What** is he?	He's **the gardener.**
Selection:	There are two women over there. **Which** is Mrs. Hill?	**The one** in the red dress.

2·8   **What word** did you look up?   **Xenophobia.**
       Which word means fear or hatred of strangers?   Xenophobia.
       Which one means fear or hatred of England?   Anglophobia.
       What kind of person is an Anglophile?   A person who admires England and the English people.

- **Which** or **what** can occur before words referring to either persons or things. *Examples:*

Which man is German?	Which words are Italian?
Which one is Dutch?	Which ones are Spanish?
What men are you talking about?	What words are you talking about?

- **Which** implies a choice or singling out from a specific group; **what** is usually more general. *Compare:*

  — **Which** men are German?
  — **What** men are you talking about?
  — The men in that group over there.

2·9   DRILL   Fill in the blanks with *who(m)/ whose/ which/ what,* as appropriate.

1. _____ of you is Martha Smith?   I am.

2. _____ is your occupation?   I'm a secretary.

3. _____ was the man who spoke to you?   That was Mr. Moore.

4. _____ does Mr. Mozart do?   He's the office manager.

5. _____ of these desks is his?   This one.

6. _____ desk is this?   It's mine.

7. _____ do you work for?   Mr. Thompson.

8. _____ office is his?   That one.

WHERE/ WHEN/ WHY/ HOW

2·10   **Where** did he go?   To Boston.
      When did he go?   Last night.
      Why did he go?   To visit his family.
      How did he go?   By plane.

- These interrogatives ask questions about place, time, reason or purpose, and manner. All questions with these interrogatives are of the predicate type and require the *do*-auxiliary: **How did he go?** (NOT: How went he?)

- **How** also occurs in many **wh**-units; for example, **how often** (frequently), **how far** (distance), **how long** (time–duration).

2·11   DRILL   Ask questions about the words in *italics*. Use appropriate *wh*-words or phrases.

1. *Joe* drove Don to the airport. → *Who drove Don to the airport?*
2. Don left *last night*. → *When did Don leave?*
3. He went *to Chicago.*
4. He went to Chicago *to visit his friends.*
5. Last year he stayed with *Bill Parker.*
6. This year he is staying with *Liz and Ben Chen.*
7. *Joe's car* was in the garage for repairs.
8. Joe borrowed *John's car.*
9. Alice and John went to the airport *by bus.*
10. *Both the No. 16 bus and the No. 18* go to the airport.
11. They took *the No. 16 bus.*
12. The No. 16 bus runs *every half hour.*

WH-Questions: Special Situations

COLOR/ SIZE/ SHAPE

2·12   **What color** is her new dress?   It's **red.**
      What size dress does she wear?   She wears **a size 10.**
      What shape are the buttons?   They're **round.**

- **What** occurs frequently with nouns such as **color, size, shape,** and **type.**

2·13   DRILL   Ask questions about the *italicized* parts beginning with *what color, what size,* or *what shape.* Then give appropriate responses.

1. She bought *a green* dress. →
   What color dress did she buy? → *She bought a green one.*
2. She wears *a size 10* dress.

3. The buttons on the dress are *square*.

4. She wanted to buy *some white* shoes.

5. The salesman showed her *a size 7*.

AGE/ HEIGHT/ WEIGHT/ OCCUPATION

2·14 **What** is her occupation?   She's a teacher.

How old is she?   She's twenty-seven.

How tall is she?   She's five feet three.

How much does she weigh?   She weighs 115 pounds.

2·15 DRILL Ask questions about the occupation, age, height, and weight of the people in Column 1 and then give the information requested. *Examples:*

What is Robert Brown's occupation?   *He's an architect.*
(OR: *What is Robert Brown?*)

How old is he?   *He's twenty-eight.*

1 Name	2 Occupation	3 Age	4 Height	5 Weight
Robert Brown	architect	28	5'11"°	176 pounds
Marjorie Moore	lawyer	27	5'2"	105 pounds
Daniel Gross	businessman	40	5'10"	250 pounds
Virginia Tully	accountant	52	5'4"	135 pounds

LENGTH/ WIDTH/ DEPTH/ HEIGHT

2·16 **How long** is the box?   It's 3 feet long.

How wide is it?   It's 2 feet wide.

How deep is it?   It's a foot deep.

How high is the table?   It's 36 inches high.

How tall is that building?   It's 40 feet high.

2·17 DRILL Ask questions about the length, width, depth, and height of the items in Column 1 and then give the information requested. *Examples:*

How deep is the swimming pool?   *The maximum depth is ten feet.*
How long is the fence?   *It's 26 feet long.*

1 Item	2 Length	3 Width	4 Depth	5 Height
swimming pool	30'	20'	10' (max.)	
fence	26'	14"		16"
Suez Canal	107 miles	197'	43' (min.)	
Panama Canal	51 miles	110'†	41' (min.)	

° 5' = 5 feet; 11" = 11 inches.

† This width refers to the lock chambers of the canal; the canal is wider in other sections.

QUANTITY

2·18   **How much tea** did she have?   Two cups.
       How many cups of coffee did she make?   Eight.
       How many sandwiches did she make?   Two dozen.

   ■   **How much** occurs before noncount nouns (**coffee, tea,** etc.); **how many** occurs before
        plural count nouns (**cups, sandwiches,** etc.).

2·19   DRILL   Ask questions about the amount or number of items; give responses based on the
        information in the quantity column (an inventory of office supplies). *Examples:*

   How much blue ink do we have?   *We have 12 bottles.*
   How many boxes of paper clips do we have? *We have 25 boxes.*

Item	Quantity
ink	12 bottles of blue ink
glue	6 2-ounce jars
carbon paper	10 boxes (100 sheets per box)
white paper	15 boxes (100 sheets per box)
envelopes	20 boxes (50 per box);
pencils	5 boxes (10 per box)
ballpoint pens	50 red; 20 black; 15 blue
typewriter erasers	2 boxes (15 per box)
paper clips	25 boxes

MONTH/ DAY/ DATE

2·20   **Which** was the coldest month?   January.
       Which month was the warmest?   July.

2·21   DRILL   Ask questions based on information in the table; give responses. *Examples:*

   Which was the coldest month?   *January.*
   Which month had an average temperature of 50 degrees?   *March.*
   Which month had two inches of rain?   *January.*

Month	Average temperature	Rainfall
January	41° (Fahrenheit) °	2″
February	43° F	1″
March	50° F	2½″
April	57° F	3″

2·22   **What day** is today?   It's Monday.
       What is the date today?   It's the 24th of July.

° 41°F is equivalent to 5° Celsius (formerly Centigrade). The formula is: $C° = \frac{5}{9}(F° - 32)$.

2·23 DRILL Ask questions based on the information given in the table; give responses. *Examples:*

What day is the baseball game?	*Saturday.*
What is the date?	*July 23rd.*
What is the date of the library tour?	*July 26th.*

Baseball game	Club picnic	Committee meeting	Library tour	Class reunion	Political rally
Saturday July 23	Sunday July 24	Monday July 25	Tuesday July 26	Wednesday July 27	Thursday July 28

TIME

2·24 What time is it?   It's two o'clock.

- There are a variety of possible responses to that frequent question "What time is it?"

On the hour
11:00 It's eleven o'clock. It's eleven.
It's eleven sharp. It's eleven P.M.

1 to 29 minutes past an hour
11:05 It's five minutes past eleven. It's five past eleven.
It's five minutes after eleven. It's five after eleven.
It's 11:05 ("eleven 'oh' five").

Alternatives for 15 minutes past an hour
11:15 It's quarter past eleven. It's fifteen after eleven.
It's eleven fifteen. It's quarter after eleven.

30 minutes past an hour
11:30 It's half past eleven. It's eleven thirty.

29 minutes to 1 minute to an hour
11:35 It's twenty-five minutes to twelve. It's eleven thirty-five.
It's twenty-five to twelve.

Alternatives for 15 minutes to an hour
11:45 It's quarter to twelve. It's fifteen to twelve.
It's eleven forty-five. It's a quarter of twelve.

Alternatives for 12:00
It's noon. It's midnight.

2·25 DRILL Give one or more ways of telling the following times.

10:00 *It's ten o'clock.* OR: *It's ten.*	10:40
10:15	10:45
10:27	11:00
10:30	12:00

WEATHER

2·26 **How**'s the weather in San Francisco in August?   It's usually foggy.
         What kind of weather does New York have then?   It's usually hot and humid.
         What's the weather like in New York in the fall?   It's very pleasant.

■ The weather is a popular topic of conversation in the United States, as it seems to be in most parts of the world where there are marked daily or seasonal changes. What is good weather to some may be bad weather to others—it is largely a matter of taste. Generally speaking, Americans consider moderately warm, sunny days as pleasant and extremely hot, cold, or wet days as unpleasant. Here are some of the adjectives Americans use in talking about the weather.

Temperature	Sky covering	Moisture in air	Movement of air
warm	clear	misty	breezy
balmy	sunny	foggy	windy
hot	overcast	rainy	calm
scorching	cloudy	stormy	still
cool	hazy	humid	blustery
crisp	smoggy	dry	stormy°
cold	foggy	raw	
freezing	misty	damp	

2·27 DRILL   Ask questions about the weather based on the information below; other students can give responses. *Example:*

Monday: very foggy →

What was the weather like on Monday? → *It was very foggy.*

Friday (last Friday): warm and sunny all day

Saturday: hot in the afternoon

Sunday: cool and overcast

Monday: very foggy in the morning

Tuesday: cloudy all day

Wednesday: cool and rainy

Thursday: very stormy

Friday (today): cool and clear

° **Stormy**—usually wind and rain, sometimes accompanied by lightning, or heavy snow falling; **smoggy**—condition resulting from smoke and fumes; **foggy**—cloud covering very close to or touching the ground; **hazy**—unclear because of either smoke or fog; **misty**—very light moist covering, like a veil.

1 Look at the questions in the left-hand column; find the information in the right-hand column; and then answer in full sentences. *Example:*

What is glass made of? → (c) *soda, lime, and sand* →
Glass is made of soda, lime, and sand.

1. What is glass made of?
2. What is done with the mixture of soda, lime, and sand?
3. At what temperature does the mixture become liquid?
4. What kind of matter is removed?
5. What is the hot liquid allowed to do?
6. What is done with the cooled substance?
7. How is most glassware made today?
8. How was glassware formerly made?
9. Where was the art of glass blowing practiced thousands of years ago?
10. What is a common substitute for glass today?

a) modeled into different shapes
b) all foreign matter
c) soda, lime, and sand
d) heated to a very high temperature
e) by blowing the cooled liquid through a tube
f) in China, Egypt, and Babylon
g) to cool
h) plastic
i) by machine
j) at 2600 degrees

GROUP B

1. When was the National Park Service established?
2. Who establishes national parks?
3. How many national parks are there?
4. How many people visit the parks each year?
5. What is Old Faithful?
6. Where is Old Faithful located?
7. How often does this geyser shoot steaming water into the air?
8. How high does the steaming water go into the air?

a) over sixty million people
b) in Yellowstone National Park
c) in 1916
d) a famous geyser°
e) Congress
f) more than thirty national parks
g) every hour
h) 150 feet into the air

° A hot spring that sends jets of steaming water into the air intermittently.

2 One group will ask questions; the other group will give answers based on the ads below.

CHEVROLET. '71 Vega. Bright yellow. 28,000 mi. Top condition. Automatic. $1600. Owner moving out of town. Call evenings. 931-2438.

FIAT '67. Red convertible. Good tires. Brakes need relining. 90,000 mi. $850. Owner going to Europe to get new car. 777-1300.

ROLLS-ROYCE. '60. Silver gray. Excellent condition. Owner too old to drive. Best offer. 592-9292.

Situation: A friend calls to say that he has just come across some cars advertised for sale in the "want ads" section of the paper, and he thinks you might be interested. Ask him to give you the following information for each car. You should ask him about only one car at a time. If the ad does not give the information, the person answering should say so.

Type of car (What kind . . . ?)   Mileage (How many miles . . . ?)
Cost (How much . . . ?)   Condition (What condition . . . ?)
Color (What color . . . ?)   Owner's reason for selling (Why . . . ?)

3 Change these *wh*-questions to statements, using the information given below to replace the underlined *wh*-words. Then arrange the sentences in a paragraph. Punctuate the sentences appropriately. Group A is done for you.

Information about Central College Library—Group A

Color code	*Other information*
blue: reference room	
yellow: main catalog room	750,000 books listed in the main catalog
red: reserved book room	more than 10,000 books in the reserved book room; books checked out for only two hours
green: study areas	more than 5,000 students a day use these areas

GROUP A

1. *What* does the library at Central College use to indicate the different areas? 2. *What color* is used in the reference room? 3. *What* is the color in the main catalog area? 4. *How many* books are listed in the main catalog? 5. *What color* is the reserved book room? 6. *How many* books does it contain? 7. For *how long* at a time may these books be checked out? 8. *What color* are the three large study areas? 9. *How many* students study in these areas each day?

Statements: 1. The library at Central College uses color to indicate different areas. 2. Blue is used in the reference room. 3. Yellow is the color in the main catalog area. 4. The main catalog lists 750,000 books. 5. The reserved book room is red. 6. It contains more than 10,000 books. 7. These books may be checked out for only two hours at a time. 8. The three large study areas are green. 9. More than 5,000 students study in these areas each day.

Suggestions for writing the paragraph: (1) Combine Statements 2 and 3 by joining them with a semicolon; a semicolon (;) ties them more closely together than a period would. (2) Now continue the sentence resulting from (1) with Statement 4, writing it (preceded by comma) as "where 750,000 books are listed." (3) Combine Statements 5 and 6, writing Statement 6 as "which contains more than 10,000 books" (set off by commas). (4) Combine Statements 8 and 9 by joining them with a semicolon.

Sample paragraph:

    The library at Central College uses color to indicate different areas of the library. Blue is used in the reference room; yellow is the color in the main catalog area, where 750,000 books are listed. The reserved book room, which contains over 10,000 books, is red. These books may be checked out for only two hours at a time. The three large study areas are green; more than 5,000 students study in these areas each day.

Information for Group B

Alexander Graham Bell invented the telephone.

First thought about transmitting speech by electrical waves in 1865; took over 10 years to put idea into practice; first words transmitted in 1876.

Soon thereafter organized the Bell Telephone Company; also established Volta Laboratory; first phonograph record developed there.

Invented a number of other things, including the audiometer for testing hearing.

Carried on father's work in education of the deaf.

GROUP B

1. *Who* is known primarily as the inventor of the telephone? 2. *When* did he first think of transmitting speech by electric waves? 3. *How long* did it take him to put the idea into practice? 4. *When* was it, to be exact, that he managed to transmit the first words? 5. *When* did he organize the Bell Telephone Company? 6. *What* did he also establish? 7. *What* was developed there? 8. *What* did he invent in addition to the telephone? 9. *What else* did he invent? 10. *Whose work* did he carry on in improving the education of the deaf?

Suggestions for writing the paragraph: (1) Combine Statements 2 and 3 into a compound sentence connected by *but* (preceded by a comma). (2) Combine statements 4 and 5 by joining them with a semicolon. (3) Combine Statements 6 and 7, writing Statement 7 (preceded by a comma) as "where the first successful phonograph record was developed." (4) Combine Statements 8 and 9 by reducing Statement 9 to "including the audiometer for testing hearing" (set off by commas) and placing it after "other things." (5) Now combine the sentence resulting from 4 with Statement 10, connecting them with *and* (preceded by a comma or semicolon).

4 Your task is to find out about another student's home town.

1. Write out 5 to 10 *wh*-questions that you can use to get the information you need.

2. Ask the person these questions and jot down the answers.

3. Write out the answers in full sentences.

4. Develop a paragraph from the statements, as you did in Ex. 3.

TAG QUESTIONS

Statement + Tag

3·1   You know Mrs. Lesca, **don't you?**   You know Mrs. Lesca, **don't you** ?

- Most tag questions can be spoken with either a rising or a falling intonation. However, the meaning is different. *Compare:*

  You like her, **don't you?**
  (I can't tell whether you like her or not. Tell me.)

  You like her, **don't you** ?
  (You really seem to like her. Am I right?)

3·2   Mrs. Lesca **is** Italian, **isn't** she?   Yes, she is.

She **can't** speak Italian, **can** she?   Yes, she can.
Her brother **lives** in Italy, **doesn't** he?   No, he doesn't.

- When the statement is affirmative, is the tag affirmative or negative? When the tag is affirmative, is the statement affirmative or negative?
- Notice that both the tag question and the short response contain a pronoun and a form of **be** or an auxiliary (**can, does,** etc.). The response can be either **yes** or **no,** depending on the situation.

(handwritten at top) When no aux appears in 1st part, forms of DO in tag

(handwritten arrows pointing to "used to go" and "didn't")

3·3   Mrs. Lesca **used to go** to Italy every year, **didn't** she?   No, she didn't.

She **has to get** her passport renewed, **doesn't** she?   Yes, she does.
She **needs to get** a smallpox vaccination, **doesn't** she?   No, she doesn't.
She **had** a typhoid shot, **didn't** she?   Yes, she did.

- What kind of tags do **used to, have to,** and **need to** have? Do not confuse **used to . . .** (habitual past) with **be used to . . .** (be accustomed to). *Compare:*

  She **used to** travel by ship, didn't she?   Yes, she did.
  She **is used to** traveling, isn't she?   Yes, she is.

- In American English, **have** (meaning possession, ownership, or relationship) ordinarily has a **do (does/ did)** tag, as in "She **had** a typhoid shot, **didn't** she?"

3·4   — Mrs. Lesca **is** in Rome now, **isn't** she?
— **Is** she? I thought she was in London.
— She **hasn't been** to Switzerland yet, **has** she?
— **Hasn't** she? I thought she went there first?

- The response to a tag question may be a short question indicating surprise, uncertainty, or disbelief. The question is affirmative if the tag is negative; the question is negative if the tag is affirmative.

3·5   You'd **better** find out, **hadn't** you?   { I guess I had.
                                                       { Yes, I'd better.

You **will come** with us, **won't** you?   { Yes, I will.
                                              { Certainly, thank you.

- A variety of responses are possible for suggestions, requests, and invitations. See also §5.1 through 5.18.

3·6   **DRILL**   In this drill, one person adds a tag; another gives an appropriate response. Use a rising intonation for the first seven items and a falling intonation for the last five. (What does a rising intonation on a tag indicate? A falling intonation?)

1. You don't have a cold, *do you?* → Yes, I do.
2. You haven't had a cold in a long time, *have you?* *(handwritten)*
3. You used to have a lot of colds,
4. You aren't going out,
5. You shouldn't be out in the cold air,
6. You need a warm coat,
7. You have enough money for a taxi,

(handwritten right margin) used to / has to / needs to / have ⟩ do

(handwritten bottom left) Be ⟩ Tag Be / Should etc

(handwritten bottom center) Have — do / Haven't had — have you

8. You don't like to take medicine, *do you?* *No, I don't.*

9. You aren't used to being sick,

10. You haven't seen a doctor,

11. You know a doctor,

12. You'd better be careful,

3·7 **Ray** wants to make a phone call, doesn't **he?**

He doesn't want to speak to me, does **he?**
There's someone using the other phone, isn't **there?**
That's Jim on the phone, isn't **it?**
This isn't Jim speaking, is **it?**
Those are your friends, aren't **they?**

■ Nouns become pronouns in tag questions; pronouns and **there** are repeated. What do **this, that, these,** and **those** become?

3·8 DRILL The questions in this drill are about U.S. currency. One person gives the initial statement or question; another responds and completes the tag questions—anyone who knows the answer can give it.

1. — There's a picture of someone on this ten-dollar bill. →
   — That's Alexander Hamilton, *isn't it?* → — *Yes, it is.*

2. — Whose picture is on this five-dollar bill?
   — That's Abraham Lincoln,

3. — Who is on this one-dollar bill?
   — Let me see it. This is George Washington,

4. — Whose picture is on a fifty-cent piece?
   — There's one with a picture of John F. Kennedy,

5. — Tell me who is on this quarter.
   — That's George Washington,

6. — What's on the other side?
   — There's a picture of an eagle,

7. — Who is on this dime?
   — Let me see it. This is Franklin Delano Roosevelt,

8. — What kind of metal is in these coins?
   — Those are both silver,

3·9

It's a nice day, **isn't it?**　　　　　　$\begin{cases} \text{It's absolutely gorgeous.} \\ \text{Yes, it certainly is.} \\ \text{It certainly is.} \end{cases}$

You like warm weather, **don't you?**　　$\begin{cases} \text{I love it.} \\ \text{Not particularly.} \end{cases}$

- Tag questions with a falling intonation are often used to begin or keep a conversation going. The responses vary, depending on the situation and the speaker.

3·10　**DRILL**　In this drill, one person adds a tag; another gives an appropriate response. Use a falling intonation on the tags.

1. New York is a fascinating city, *isn't it?* →
   Yes, it certainly is.　OR: *I don't think so.*
2. Central Park is beautiful in autumn, *isn't it?* →
   Yes, it is.　OR: *Yes, it's quite spectacular.*
3. The view from the Empire State Building is magnificent,
4. During the rush hours, the subway is very crowded,
5. The people don't seem very friendly there,
6. There are always so many things to do,
7. There are always thousands of tourists there,
8. New York City is exciting,

Repeated Statement + Tag Question

3·11　— Mrs. Penworthy wants to run for President.

— She **wants** to run for President, **does** she?

— She has a great personality.
— She **has** a great personality, **does** she?
— We think you should be her campaign manager.
— Oh, you **do, do** you?

— There aren't many people campaigning for her.

— Oh, there **aren't, aren't** there?

— You can't refuse to help her.
— Oh, I **can't, can't** I?

- The speaker uses this kind of a tag question to make a comment on the previous statement. The tag may express surprise, friendly interest, humor, anger, or sarcasm, depending on the situation and the intention of the speaker.

- The repeated statement and the tag are either both affirmative or both negative. The repeated statement can be shortened to a subject and an auxiliary.

3·12   DRILL   Add tags that indicate anger, surprise, sarcasm, or humor.

1. Mr. King makes $1,000 a month. → *Oh, he does, does he?*
2. He brings Mrs. King flowers every payday. → *Oh, he brings her flowers, does he?*
3. Mrs. King says he's a saint.
4. He has tried hard to get a job.
5. There are ads for salesmen in the paper.
6. It would be a great opportunity for him.
7. That isn't the best way to look at it.
8. You should be more positive.
9. You could be successful if you worked at it.
10. You could go right to the top.

Tag Question versus Contrastive Question

3·13   — You haven't read *David Copperfield,* **have you?**
    — Yes, I have. **Have you?**

- Although **have you?** and **Have you?** look alike, they differ in several ways. The subject in the tag refers to the same person; the subject in the contrastive question refers to a different person. *Compare:*

  Mary is here, isn't **she?** (same person)
  Mary is here. Is **he?** (different person)

  In the tag, emphasis is on the verb; in the contrastive question, emphasis is on the subject. Also, the subject in a tag is always a pronoun, whereas in a contrastive question it can be either a noun or a pronoun. *Compare:*

  Mary is here, **ísn't** she? (emphasis on verb; **she** and **Mary** = same person)
  Mary is here. Is **hé?** (emphasis on subject; **he** is contrasted with **Mary**)

In the written form, a comma separates the statement and the tag; a period usually separates the statement and the contrastive question. *Compare:*

May is here, isn't she? (tag follows comma)
Mary is here. Is he? (period)

Unlike the tag, the contrastive question can be either affirmative or negative after an affirmative statement. *Compare:*

Mary **is** here, **isn't** she?   Mary **is** here. **Isn't** he?
                                      Mary **is** here. **Is** he?

3·14   DRILL   One person adds a tag question to the statement; another person gives a short response followed by a short separate question; then the first person responds to that question.

1. You have read some novels in Spanish, *haven't you?* →

    No, I haven't. Has Carlos? → *No, I don't think so.*

2. You can speak Spanish, *can't you?* → *No, I can't. Can you?* → *Yes, I can.*

3. You can't speak Spanish,

4. Your parents don't speak Spanish,

5. Your parents can speak English,

6. You speak English at home,

1 Add tags; and give appropriate responses.

1. There are thirty days in November, *aren't there?* → *Yes, there are.*

2. There are thirty-one days in April,

3. There are 52 weeks in a year,

4. Nine times six is fifty-four,

5. The square root of 100 is 10,

6. There are 5,280 feet in a mile,

7. There shouldn't be much rain in July,

8. It shouldn't be very cold in May,

9. We'll need to wear overcoats in January,

10. *Occurred* has two *c*'s and two *r*'s,

11. It is accented on the first syllable,

12. We'd better look it up in the dictionary,

13. *Refute* and *refuse* mean the same thing,

14. We'd better look the words up in the dictionary,

15. *Says* rhymes with *days*,

16. *Said* doesn't rhyme with *bed*,

17. Shakespeare wrote *Hamlet*,

18. You have read *Hamlet*,

19. Mozart wrote the *Emperor* piano concerto,

20. You are majoring in music,

2 Ask affirmative or negative tag questions about the geographical location of the mountains listed below; give responses. *Examples:*

Mount Olympus is in Greece, isn't it?   *Yes, it is.*
The Andes Mountains are in North America,   *No, they aren't. They're in South*
aren't they?   *America.*

Mountains	*Geographical location*
Mount Fuji	Japan
the Matterhorn	Switzerland
Mount Kilimanjaro	Africa
the Ural Mountains	Russia
Mount Olympus	Greece
the Andes Mountains	South America
Mount Whitney	California
the Caucasus Mountains	southeastern Europe
Mount Etna	Sicily
the Himalayas	Asia
Mount Everest	Nepal

3 Using the information below, make tag questions; give responses. *Examples:*

John and Alice Wu live on 64th Street, don't they?   *Yes, they do.*
The number is 124 64th Street, isn't it?   *Yes, it is.*
They used to live at 60 Park Street, didn't they?   *No, they didn't.*
Carlos Lopez doesn't live on Louis Avenue anymore, does he?   *Yes, he does.*

Name	*Current street address*	*Previous street address*
John and Alice Wu	124 64th Street	94 Park Street
Carlos Lopez	22 Louis Avenue	1230 Fulton Street
Roger and Jane Hill	485 Charles Street	25 Peach Street
Suzanne Tanner	981 Laurel Drive	200 Tenth Avenue
Richard and Ronald White	560 Lincoln Road	1980 Oak Way
James and Emily Leeds	2232 Spring Street	910 Euclid Terrace
Amir Kashfi	777 Sunset Boulevard	18 Bay Place
Fred and Marge Loomis	604 Bay View Drive	1024 North Street

4 Using the information in Columns 1, 2, 3, and 4, make affirmative or negative tag questions; give responses. *Examples:*

Marco Polo was born in 1254, wasn't he?   *Yes, he was.*
Captain Cook and Admiral Byrd were both American naval officers, weren't they?   *No. Admiral Byrd was American, but Captain Cook was English.*
Ferdinand Magellan discovered a new sea route around Africa to India, didn't he?   *No, he didn't.*
Magellan didn't discover the Philippines, did he?   *Yes, he did.*

(1)	*(2)*	*(3)*	*(4)*
Marco Polo	1254–1324	Venetian traveler	Traveled in Asia
Christopher Columbus	1451–1506	Italian explorer in service of Spain	Discovered America
Vasco da Gama	1469–1524	Portuguese navigator	Discovered a new sea route around Africa to India
Ferdinand Magellan	1480–1521	Portuguese navigator	Discovered the Straits of Magellan and the Philippines
Sir Francis Drake	1540–1596	English naval officer	First Englishman to sail around the world
Captain James Cook	1728–1779	English naval officer	Explored Australia, New Zealand, Hawaii, and Antarctica
Robert Falcon Scott	1868–1912	English naval officer	Explored Antarctica
Admiral Richard Byrd	1888–1957	American naval officer	Explored Antarctica

5 Look up more information on one of the explorers listed in the preceding exercise.

1. Using that information, write 5 to 10 tag questions about the explorer's life.

2. Change the questions to statements, omitting *yes* or *no*.

3. Develop a paragraph of 75 to 100 words from the statements in 2. You will probably want to combine statements and add connecting words in order to get a smooth, coherent paragraph. (See examples in Ex. 3 at the end of Chapter 1 and in Ex. 3 at the end of Chapter 2.)

ATTACHED STATEMENTS/

REJOINDERS

Attached Statements

4·1   Michiko is from Tokyo.   Morimi is from Tokyo.

Michiko is from Tokyo,   **and** $\begin{cases} \textbf{Morimi is too.}^{*} \\ \textbf{so is Morimi.} \end{cases}$

Michiko and Morimi live in Tokyo.   Keiko lives in Tokyo.

Michiko and Morimi live in Tokyo, **and** $\begin{cases} \textbf{Keiko does too.} \\ \textbf{so does Keiko.} \end{cases}$

- Attached statements are particularly common in spoken English. Attached statements are possible whenever the predicate of the second sentence is closely modeled on the predicate of the first sentence. **And** is the connector when both sentences are affirmative.

- Notice that the word order after **and so** is a form of **be** (or auxiliary) + *subject*.

- Notice that in the attached statement part of the predicate is usually omitted. *Example:*

  Michiko is an exceptionally intelligent student, **and Morimi is too.**
  (NOT: . . . and Morimi is an exceptionally intelligent student too.)

4·2   DRILL   Assume the following remarks about Gerald apply also to Helen.

1. Gerald is a junior, and *Helen is too.*
2. Gerald is majoring in chemistry, and so *is Helen.*
3. Gerald attends a chemistry lecture at 10 o'clock every morning, and so
4. Gerald has a chemistry lab on Tuesday and Thursday afternoons, and so
5. He was an *A* student last semester, and
6. He received a scholarship last year, and so

---

*ALSO: . . . **and Morimi is, too.** In short statements, a comma before **too** is generally considered optional.

7. Last night Gerald had to study for a test, and so

8. He plans to get a Ph.D. in chemistry, and

9. Gerald's father used to teach chemistry, and so

10. His father would rather do research, and

4·3   DRILL   Convert these sentences, which now have compound subjects, into sentences with affirmative attached statements.

1. Mr. King and Mr. Chase are lawyers. →
   Mr. King is a lawyer, and Mr. Chase is too.
   OR: *Mr. King is a lawyer, and so is Mr. Chase.*

2. Mr. Lee, Mr. Nye, and Mr. Rex are Mr. King's clients. →
   Mr. Lee and Mr. Nye are Mr. King's clients, and Mr. Rex is too.
   OR: *Mr. Lee and Mr. Nye are Mr. King's clients, and so is Mr. Rex.*
   OR: *Mr. Lee is Mr. King's client, and Mr. Nye and Mr. Rex are too.*
   OR: *Mr. Lee is Mr. King's client, and so are Mr. Nye and Mr. Rex.*

3. Mr. King and Mr. Chase received their law degrees from Harvard Law School.

4. Mr. King and Mr. Chase employ students from local law schools.

5. Tony Berges, Sam Burke, and Nelson Riddle are law students.

6. Tony Berges and Nelson Riddle attend the Haley College of Law.

7. Tony, Sam, and Nelson work in Mr. King's office.

8. Sam and Nelson worked in Mr. Chase's office last year.

9. Tony and Nelson will graduate from law school next June.

10. Tony, Sam, and Nelson want to be corporation lawyers.

4·4   Henry Wong wasn't born in Hong Kong.   His brother wasn't born in Hong Kong.

Henry Wong wasn't born in Hong Kong, **and** $\begin{cases} \text{his brother wasn't either.} \\ \text{neither was his brother.} \end{cases}$

■ What is the connector when both sentences are negative? What is the word order after **and neither?**

4·5   Henry Wong $\begin{cases} \textbf{seldom} \\ \textbf{never} \\ \textbf{hardly ever} \\ \textbf{rarely} \end{cases}$ speaks Chinese, **and** $\begin{cases} \textbf{his brother doesn't either.} \\ \textbf{neither does his brother.} \end{cases}$

■ Sentences with adverbs like **never, seldom, hardly ever,** and **rarely** are followed by negative attached statements.

4·6   DRILL   Assume that the following remarks about Frank also apply to Henry.

1. Frank doesn't like history, and *Henry doesn't either.*
2. Frank isn't doing well in history, and neither *is Henry.*
3. Frank didn't get a passing grade on the last test, and neither
4. Frank can't expect to pass the course unless he studies more, and neither
5. Frank hasn't been spending enough time in the library, and
6. Frank can't concentrate on his studies, and neither
7. Frank won't have to take a history course next semester, and
8. Frank shouldn't spend so much time playing tennis, and neither
9. Frank doesn't participate in campus activities, and
10. Frank isn't interested in campus politics, and neither

4·7   DRILL   Convert these sentences, which now contain compound subjects, into sentences with negative attached statements.

1. Mrs. Steele and Miss Hill aren't professional librarians. →
   Mrs. Steele isn't a professional librarian, and Miss Hill isn't either.
   OR: *Mrs. Steele isn't a professional librarian, and neither is Miss Hill.*
2. Mrs. Steele and Miss Hill didn't graduate from library school.
3. Mrs. Steele and Miss Hill seldom work on Saturday afternoon.
4. Mrs. Steele and Miss Hill never work evenings.
5. Mrs. Steele and Miss Hill don't receive as large a salary as the head librarian.

4·8   **Neither** Frank **nor** his brothers **are** interested in opera.

Frank isn't interested in opera, **and neither** are his brothers.

Neither Frank's parents **nor** his grandmother **is** interested in rock music.

Frank's parents aren't interested in rock music, **and neither** is his grandmother.

- Compound subjects connected by **neither ... nor** can be restated as a sentence with a negative attached statement.
- Notice that the verb agrees with the noun following **nor.** In conversation, you may hear "Neither Frank's parents nor his grandmother are interested . . . ," but in formal writing a singular verb is customary.

4·9   DRILL   Convert these sentences with compound subjects into sentences with negative attached statements.

1. Neither the head librarian nor Mrs. Steele attended the last library conference. →
The head librarian didn't attend the last library conference, and neither did Mrs. Steele.

2. Neither the main library nor the branch libraries are open on Sunday.

3. Neither the main library nor the branch libraries have a large enough staff.

4. Neither the branch libraries nor the main library has a children's librarian.

5. Neither the main library nor the branch libraries are going to be open on Friday evening during the summer months.

4·10   Maya speaks Russian.   Boris doesn't speak Russian.
Maya speaks Russian,   **but Boris doesn't.**

OR:

Boris doesn't speak Russian.   His parents speak Russian.
Boris doesn't speak Russian,   **but his parents do.**

■ **But** indicates contrast or contradiction. Notice that it connects affirmative and negative sentences.

Although and **however** can be used in place of **but.** (See §13.36 and 13.40 for additional information on **although** and **however.**)

Nicholas **can't speak** Russian **although** his brother can.
Olga **was born** in the United States; **however,** her parents weren't.

4·11   DRILL   Complete the following statements with appropriate forms of *be* or an auxiliary.

1. Polly didn't know how to do the first problem, but Pat *did.*

2. Polly had to work a long time on the second problem, but Pat

3. The first problem required a knowledge of calculus, but the second

4. Pat has taken calculus, but Polly

5. Polly doesn't like math courses, but Pat

6. Polly needs a math course to graduate, but Pat

7. Pat got an *A* on her last examination, but Polly

8. Polly had to take a makeup test, but Pat

4·12   **This book** is in Russian, but **that one** isn't.
These newspapers are in Russian, but **those** aren't.
The first magazine isn't in Russian, but **the second (one)** is.

■ **This/ that** + *noun* often becomes **that one/ this one** in attached statements. **These/ those** + *noun* becomes **those/ these.** **The first** (second, etc.) + *noun* becomes **the second one** or **the second** (third, etc.).

4·13 DRILL Complete the following statements with *this one, that one, these, those, the second (one)*, etc., and appropriate forms of *be* or an auxiliary. *Situation:* Kevin and Frances are discussing a math assignment.

1. — The last assignment was easy, but *this one isn't.*
2. — The first two problems are easy, but
3. — The first two don't require a knowledge of calculus, but
4. — These problems will take a long time to do, but
5. — Those equations are simple, but
6. — That answer is correct, but

Rejoinders

4·14 *Jim:* This problem was difficult.
Bob: **But that one wasn't.**
Tom: I got the second one right.
Jim: **So did I.** But I missed the third one.
Tom: **I did too.**
Sam: I couldn't do the fourth problem.
Jim: **Neither could I.**
Bob: I didn't think it was so hard.
Tom: **I didn't either.**

■ Rejoinders are responses to statements. In making a rejoinder, another speaker often models his response on the statement of the first speaker.

■ These particular rejoinders are the same as attached statements with **and** and **but** usually omitted.

4·15 DRILL Make rejoinders to the following statements according to your own knowledge, experience, or taste.

1. He hasn't read Shakespeare's sonnets. → *Neither have I.*   OR: *I haven't either.*
2. She's very fond of poetry.
3. They aren't interested in modern art.
4. He seldom attends symphony concerts.
5. Ray is especially fond of Italian opera.
6. We're baseball fans.
7. He prefers soccer to baseball.
8. She would like to be rich and famous.
9. Tom doesn't want to be a failure.
10. Bob would like to be the first person to land on Mars.

4·16   *Sally:*   Ellen is very pretty.
Betty: I think **so** too.
Nancy: I don't think **so.**

■ In this type of rejoinder, the person responding uses **so** instead of repeating the statement of the first speaker ("I think so too" rather than "I think she is pretty too.") Here are some *other examples:*

You have a wonderful family.	I'm glad you think so.
Elizabeth is very charming.	I think so too.
Ellen is a very intelligent girl.	Do you think so?
Is Ellen related to Jim Pine?	I believe so.
I think Jim is conceited.	I don't think so.
That was certainly a rude remark.	I should say so.
He shouldn't say things like that.	I don't think so either.
Do you think he's still talking to Jane?	No, I don't think so.

In the preceding examples, notice that the information is *not* repeated after **so:** "I'm glad you think so." (NOT: I'm glad you think so you have a wonderful family.)

4·17   DRILL   Respond to the following statements and questions with remarks like "I think so" and "I don't think so."

1. Your handwriting is better than mine.

2. You're a better typist than I am.

3. Your papers always look neater than mine.

4. Tolstoy's *War and Peace* is a great novel.

5. Did Ernest Hemingway write any plays?

6. He thinks Picasso is a great artist.

7. Are we going to have an exam next week?

8. She doesn't think we're going to have a test next week.

9. Are the textbooks for this course expensive?

10. The food in the school cafeteria is quite good.

1 Convert the following sentences into sentences with attached statements.

1. Hope and Paul are interested in photography. →
   Hope is interested in photography, and so is Paul.

2. Hope and Paul want to be professional photographers.

3. Neither Hope nor Paul has a camera with a telescopic lens.

4. Hope and Paul have each ordered a camera with a telescopic lens.

5. Hope and Paul haven't sold any pictures yet.

6. Walter and Robert are interested in mountain climbing.

7. Robert and Walter know several famous mountain climbers.

8. Neither Robert nor Walter has climbed the Matterhorn.

9. Walter and Robert have done most of their climbing in the United States.

10. Neither Robert nor Walter has had the opportunity to climb the famous mountains of Europe.

11. Elizabeth, Suzanne, and Lois are gourmet cooks.

12. Elizabeth and Suzanne are especially interested in French cuisine.

13. Lois and her husband are connoisseurs of Italian pasta.

14. Neither Suzanne nor Elizabeth can make pasta as well as Lois can.

15. Elizabeth, Suzanne, and Lois haven't mastered Chinese cooking yet.

16. Elizabeth and Suzanne are now studying with a Chinese chef.

17. Suzanne and her husband are especially fond of Chinese food.

18. Suzanne and her husband and Elizabeth and her fiancé often dine at Chinese restaurants.

19. Suzanne and Elizabeth never miss an opportunity to pick up a new recipe.

20. Suzanne, Elizabeth, and Lois seldom try out new recipes on their guests.

2 Complete the following dialog with remarks like *so do I, I don't either*, or *I think so*.

A: Let's go out to dinner tonight.
B: That's a marvelous idea.
C:
B: I'd like to go to a Chinese restaurant.
C:
A: I would, too. Let's go to the Shanghai Restaurant.
C: I think the Shanghai is too expensive.
B:

A: Is Mei-Ling's open on Monday night?

B:

C: I think Mei-Ling's is too expensive.

B:

A: Well, I guess Mei-Ling's is out. What about the Peking Palace? I don't think it's very expensive.

C:

A: Let's go there then.

B: I don't like the atmosphere.

C:

A: You are hard to please. I don't think we can agree on a Chinese restaurant.

B:

C: How about an Italian restaurant? I have heard Eduardo's is great!

A: So have I.

B:

C: Let's go then. I can be ready in ten minutes.

A:

B:

3 Convert these sentences, which now contain attached statements, into sentences with compound subjects.

   1. Ray doesn't agree with Harold and Doug, and Dean doesn't either. →
      Ray and Dean don't agree with Harold and Doug.
      OR: *Neither Ray nor Dean agrees with Harold and Doug.*

   2. Ray wants to hire more salesmen, and so does Dean.

   3. Ray expects sales to increase a lot this year, and Dean does too.

   4. Harold doesn't believe sales will increase at all this year, and neither does Doug.

   5. Doug is never very optimistic about sales, and Harold isn't either.

   6. Ray is always optimistic about the future, and so is Dean.

   7. Doug will go to a conference in Frankfurt this fall, and his wife will go with him.

   8. Doug has never traveled so far away before, and neither has Ginny.

   9. Doug very seldom takes any time off from business, and Harold doesn't either.

  10. Their wives think they should learn to relax, and so do their children.

4 Complete the paragraphs by filling in the blanks.

    1. I hear Mark is looking for a roommate. What do you think of Richard? Mark and Richard have a lot in common. First of all, they are both advertising students. Mark is a senior, _____. Mark studies a lot, _____. Richard doesn't have much money, _____. Don't you think they would get along well together?

    2. Bianca and Claudia are twins. They are alike in many ways. Bianca's eyes are blue, _____. Bianca has blond hair, _____. With a few exceptions, they like to do the same things. Bianca likes to ride horses, _____. Claudia doesn't like to ski, _____. Neither of them likes to play bridge. In fact, Bianca doesn't like any card games, _____.

5 Write brief paragraphs, patterned after the paragraphs in Ex. 4.

    1. You might begin the first paragraph with a statement like "I hear John is looking for a business partner" or "I hear Harry is looking for a wife." (See no. 1, Ex. 4.)

    2. You might begin the second paragraph with a statement like "Herb and Ralph are first cousins" or "Bette and Dolores are sisters-in-law." (See no. 2, Ex. 4.)

COMMANDS/REQUESTS/INVITATIONS/
SUGGESTIONS/DIRECTIONS

Affirmative Commands and Requests

5·1
— Come on, everybody. Let's get going.
— Please wait for me.
— Okay, but hurry.
— Will someone help me carry these picnic baskets?
— Joe, you help her.
— Sure. Jim, give me a hand, will you?
— Let me take that basket.
— Wait! Take this basket too, will you?
— Would you put them in the car, please?
— Would you mind putting them in the other car?
— Why don't you come with us?
— Sorry, I can't. Have a good time! Do be careful on the freeway.

■ Commands and requests range from direct orders (**Wait!**) to friendly entreaties (**Have a good time!**). They also include suggestions (**Let's get going**) and invitations (**Why don't you come with us?**). "Why don't you come with us?" is an affirmative invitation or suggestion even though the form is "don't you come."

■ The situation and tone of voice can influence the relative abruptness or politeness of commands and requests. For example, the usually polite "Would you mind putting them in the other car?" could be quite rude if the speaker used a sarcastic or annoyed tone. In general, the following features modify commands and requests:

Politeness
The addition of **please** makes the request more polite.

Please wait for me.

A question tag usually softens the request.

Give her a hand, **will you?**

To many people, **would** seems softer and more polite than **will.**

Would someone please help me?

Would you mind . . . or **Do you mind . . .** are, in general, polite and deferential. Notice that verb-**ing** follows **mind.**

Would you (Do you) mind putting them in the car?

Emphasis

Do makes requests more emphatic.

Do be careful.   **Do** have a good time.

You, someone/somebody, or **everyone/everybody** is sometimes added for emphasis or to single out the person or persons addressed.

John, **you** help her.   **Someone** help her.   Come on, **everybody.**

■ A distinction is usually made between **Let's** and **Let us.** This distinction becomes clearer when a tag question is added or the request is put in the form of a question. *Compare:*

Let's go, shall **we?**   **Shall** we go?
(The person speaking is making a suggestion. The 's includes the speaker and the person or persons addressed.)

Let **us** go, will **you?**   Will **you** let **us** go?
(The person speaking is asking someone to allow him and another person, or a group of persons, to go. The person addressed is clearly not included in the **us.**)

5·2   DRILL   What would you say to the following people? What else could you say? Would the meaning be almost the same?

1. A friend is leaving, and you want him to wait for you. →

   Wait for me!   *Please wait for me.*
   Wait for me, will you?   *Will you please wait for me?*
   Why don't you wait for me?   *Would you please wait for me?*

2. You are afraid you are going to be late to class, and you want your friend to finish his coffee quickly.

3. You want the waitress to bring you more coffee.

4. You want a stranger in a cafeteria to pass the salt and pepper.

5. You want a bus driver to give you a transfer.

6. You want your next-door neighbor to turn down his TV.

7. Some children have thrown candy wrappers on your lawn. You want them to pick them up.

8. An elderly woman is about to step off the curb into the path of a speeding car.

9. A friend is leaving on his vacation.

10. Someone is blocking the door you want to enter.

Standard Requests and Responses

5·3

Please close the door.	Certainly.
Will you please help me move this chair?	Of course.
Would you put it over there?	All right.
Do you mind waiting for a minute?	Not at all.
Would you mind calling her for me?	I'd be glad to.
Please be quiet.	I'm sorry.

■ Responses, of course, vary with the situation. Sometimes there is no oral response. The person addressed just does what he is asked to do.

5·4

Close the door, will you?	Sure.
Help me move this desk.	Okay.
Come here.	Just a minute.
Let me use your pen.	Help yourself.

■ The requests and responses above are more informal than those in the preceding group. Although politeness is always in good taste, persons who know each other well or who are of the same age group are often direct and abrupt with each other. Also, persons in authority are sometimes direct and abrupt when speaking to subordinate workers.

5·5   DRILL   Give appropriate responses.

1. *Professor:* Would someone please open a window?
   Student:

2. *John:* Let me have the sports section, will you?
   Joe:

3. *Librarian:* Please put the magazines back on the shelf when you're through with them.
   Student:

4. *Mary:* Be sure to invite Joe to the party.
   Jane:

5. *Dr. Pepper:* Take one capsule after each meal.
   Patient:

6. *Mrs. White:* Would you please tell Mr. Peck that I was here to see him?
   Secretary:

7. *Mary:* Hey, you, leave your wet umbrella in the hall.
   Joe:

8. *Mrs. Nelson:* Would you mind coming to my house for the meeting?
   Mrs. Whipple:

Negative Commands and Requests

5·6 Please **don't** tell him.   Will you please **not** tell him?
Don't smoke in here.   Would you mind **not** smoking in here?
Don't let her worry about it.   Let's **not** worry about it.

■ The preceding examples are negative requests. The first two sentences in both columns mean approximately the same thing. The third sentence differs only in that **let her** and **Let's** have different meanings.

5·7 **Won't** you please tell him?   Will you please tell him?
Wouldn't you like to tell him?   Would you like to tell him?
Why don't we tell him?   Let's tell him.

■ The examples in the left column are *not* negative requests. They mean approximately the same thing as the sentences in the right column.

5·8 **Don't** interrupt me.   I'm sorry.   OR: Sorry.   OR: Okay.
Would you mind **not** smoking in here?   All right   OR: Okay.
Don't let her worry about it.   I won't.   OR: No way.

■ Negative requests and responses can be formal or informal depending on the situation.

5·9 DRILL Make negative requests for the following situations. Other students can give possible responses.

1. You are cold and your friends start to open a window. →
   Please don't open that window. → *Okay.*
2. The neighbor's dog has been barking all morning and you would like him to shut up.
3. The neighbor's children are making a lot of noise in the backyard.
4. You like your coffee black, and your friend is about to put some cream in your cup.
5. Your friend is thinking of letting an irresponsible person borrow his car.
6. Your friend is watching a TV program that you can't stand.
7. You have been trying to tell a story, but your friend keeps interrupting.
8. You are at a party with some friends. They want to leave, but you would like to stay longer.
9. Some children are throwing rocks at your car.
10. You are driving with a friend on the freeway. He is going so fast that you are frightened.
11. You are trying to study. Your roommate keeps talking to you.
12. You want to speak English. Your friends keep talking to you in your native language.

Requests for Permission

5·10 — Let's say it is very stuffy on a bus, and I'd like to open a window. What should I say to the person sitting next to me?

— I can think of several things you could say: **May** I open the window? **Could** I please open the window? **Would it be all right if** I opened the window? **Do you mind if** I open the window? **Would you mind if** I opened the window?

— Is it all right to say "**Can** I open the window?"

— Of course, it is. It's a matter of usage. **May** is more formal than either **could** or **can. Could** is always acceptable, but some people consider **can** unacceptable in some situations.

■ Notice that the verb after **Would you mind** . . . is past and the verb after **Do you mind** . . . is present. *Compare:*

Do you mind if I **leave** early?
Would you mind if I **left** early?

	Formal responses	*Informal responses*
5·11 Could I take the day off?	Certainly. I'd rather you didn't. Of course.	Sure. Go ahead. No way. Sure. Why not?
Do you mind if I take the day off?	Not at all. Of course not. I'd rather you didn't. I certainly do.	No, go ahead. No way. I sure do.

■ Again, responses vary according to the situation.

5·12	
Can't I take the day off?	Of course, you can.
Don't you really mind if I take the day off?	No, I don't mind.
I can take the day off, **can't** I?	Absolutely not.
You **don't** mind if I take the day off, **do** you?	Yes, I do mind.
You **wouldn't** mind if I took the day off, **would** you?	No, I wouldn't mind.

■ The above examples illustrate other variations, using negatives and tag questions.

5·13	
Would you mind if I **didn't** come to work tomorrow?	It's all right.
Do you mind if I **don't** finish this report today?	Not at all.

■ For permission *not* to do something, use **Do (Would) you mind if I don't (didn't)** . . . ?

5·14   DRILL   Ask for permission to do the following things. (Make your request fit the situation.)

1. smoke at a dinner party → *Do you mind if I smoke?*
2. borrow your friend's dictionary
3. leave your English class early
4. use a friend's pen
5. turn in an assignment late
6. open a window in the classroom
7. use your host's telephone
8. join people you don't know very well at a table in the cafeteria
9. park your car in a neighbor's driveway
10. ride downtown with an elderly neighbor

Invitations

5·15   — Come in, please. Won't you sit down? Could I get you some tea?
— Thank you. I'd love some.
— Please help yourself to lemon and sugar. Do try some of these cookies. They're delicious.

■ **Will/ won't** and **would/ wouldn't** mean approximately the same thing in invitations. *Compare:*

	Invitation	*Response*
Would **Wouldn't** }	you like some tea?	No, thank you.

This is not true of other types of invitations, however. *Compare:*

Don't try those cookies. They're stale.
Do try those cookies. They're delicious.

■ Intonation can be important in invitations. *Compare:*

— Would you like some tea or coffee?
(Do you want either one?)

— Yes, thank you. I'll take some coffee.

— Would you like your coffee black or with cream and sugar?
(Please make a choice.)

— Black, please.

- **Do** makes an invitation more emphatic.° *Example:*

  Do come to see us!

- The question form is usually not as forceful, insistent, or enthusiastic an invitation as the command form. *Compare:*

  Won't you have more tea?
  Please have some more tea.

5·16 DRILL Extend invitations for the following situations:

1. Enthusiastically encourage someone to accompany you and a friend to a concert. →
   Do come to the concert with us!

2. Extend a sincere but not insistent invitation to a friend to go to a movie with you.

3. Invite someone you like very much to come see you.

4. Ask someone if he would like to have something cold to drink.

5. Ask if the person would like iced tea, lemonade, or beer. (Make it a choice question.)

Suggestions

5·17   — How many ways can you think of to **suggest going out** for a cup of coffee?

— Let's see: Let's get some coffee. Let's get some coffee, shall we? Shall we go get some coffee? Why don't we go get some coffee? Would you like to go out for coffee? I **suggest that** we go get some coffee.

— When someone asks you to go out for coffee, does it mean that you have to drink coffee?

— No. It's just a way of saying "Let's go out to get something to drink." You both might end up ordering tea, Coke, or orange juice.

- Notice that verb-**ing** (**going**) or a **that**-clause follows **suggest.** The infinitive does *not* follow **suggest.**

- When someone says "Let's do this or that," he is including himself. He cannot use "Let's" if the suggestion does not include him. *Compare:*

  I **suggest** that **we** get some coffee.   **Let's** go get some coffee.
  I **suggest** that **he** get some coffee for us.   —
  ("Let's go get some coffee" means "Let's go out and get some coffee." "Let's get some coffee" can be used in the same situation.)

- Notice that the simple form of the verb always follows **suggest.** *Compare:*

  I **suggest** that **he go** to Max's Cafe.
  I **hope** that **he goes** to Max's Cafe.

  Some people use **should** + *verb* after **suggest.** *Example:*

  I suggest that we **should get** some coffee.

°In American English **do** (emphatic) seems more common in women's speech than in men's.

■ Suggestions stated in the form of questions can include or exclude the speaker. *Compare:*

Why don't **we** go now?	**Let's** go now.	I suggest that **we** go now.
Why doesn't **he** go now?	—	I suggest that **he** go now.

5·18   DRILL   Make suggestions for the following situations.

1. Suggest to a friend that the two of you go to a movie tonight. →
   Let's go to a movie tonight.   OR: *Why don't we go to a movie tonight?*
   OR: *I suggest that we go to a movie tonight.*

2. Suggest to your friend that you go out to dinner before the movie.

3. Suggest to your friend that you go to see a foreign film.

4. Suggest to your friend that he take his car.

5. Suggest to your friend that he pick you up at five-thirty.

Directions

5·19   — Can you tell me how to get to the Liberty Theater?
   — Certainly. Go to the next corner, turn left, and walk two blocks to Liberty Street.
   Turn right and continue until you see the theater.

■ Notice the types of command and request forms used in giving directions. How else
   could the request for information (**Can you tell me . . . ?**) be stated?

■ Do the following requests mean approximately the same thing? Would they be used
   in slightly different situations? *Explain.*

   Can you tell me how to get to the post office?
   Would you please tell me how to get to the post office?

5·20   DRILL   *A* will ask how to get to the places indicated; *B* will give directions. The directions
   will be determined by the actual situation.

1. the nearest post office →
   A: Can you tell me how to get to the nearest post office?
   OR: *Would you please tell me how to get to the nearest post office?*
   *B: Certainly. Take the No. 14 bus at the next corner, get off at Park Lane, turn to the
   right, and walk two blocks north.*
   OR: *Sure. Go straight ahead to Park Lane, make a right turn,° and continue on for
   about two blocks.*

2. the nearest drugstore or pharmacy or public library

3. the nearest supermarket or grocery store or bakery

4. the nearest beauty parlor or barber shop

5. the nearest bus stop or gas station

° ALSO: take a right turn.

Reported Commands/ Requests/ Invitations/ Suggestions

5·21   *Situation:* Lupe has just arrived in the United States. Although she has studied English for several years, she finds it difficult to understand Americans. One day she goes downtown on the bus with Mrs. Benson, an elderly American lady.

Bus driver: Have your fare ready.
Lupe: What did he say?
Mrs. Benson: He **said to have** the fare ready.

Bus driver: Hurry, will you?
Lupe: What did he say to that man?
Mrs. Benson: He **told him to hurry.**

Bus driver: Would you please move to the rear of the bus?
Lupe: What did he ask us to do?
Mrs. Benson: He **asked us to move** to the rear of the bus.

- Commands and requests can, for the most part, be reported by using a reporting verb such as **said, told, ask** and converting the request to a **to** + *verb* (infinitive) phrase.

  A noun or pronoun follows **told** and **ask** but not **said.** *Compare:*

  He **told him** to hurry.   He **asked him** to hurry.   He **said** to hurry.

- Notice how the pronouns change in reported speech.

  Conversation
  Mrs. Benson: Please give **me** two transfers.

  Reported Speech
  I asked the bus driver to give **me** two transfers.
  (Mrs. Benson is reporting.)

  Mrs. Benson asked the bus driver to give **her** two transfers.
  (Another person is reporting.)

- Negative commands and requests are reported in the same way. *Example:*

  Bus driver: **Don't crowd** me. And **don't stand** at the front of the bus.
  (The bus driver is asking the passengers **not** to crowd him and **not** to stand in the front of the bus.)

5·22   **DRILL**   Change to reported commands and requests. Use *said, told,* and *asked* as reporting verbs; you are doing the reporting.

1. *Passenger:* Driver, please tell me when to get off. →
   A passenger asked the bus driver to (please) tell her when to get off.
2. *Mrs. Benson:* Lupe, take the seat in the front of the bus.
3. *Mrs. Benson:* Please hold the transfers for me.
4. *Lupe:* Be sure to tell me where to get off.
5. *Mrs. Benson:* Don't worry, Lupe.

5·23 At noon Mrs. Benson and Lupe go into a restaurant.

Hostess: Do you mind if I seat you at that table by the door?

Mrs. Benson: Would you mind if we took that small table in the corner?

Hostess: I'm sorry, but that table is reserved. May I seat you in the next room?

Mrs. Benson: Certainly. That will be all right.

Lupe asks for an explanation. Here is what Mrs. Benson says:

The hostess asked if we minded if she seated us at that table by the door. I asked if she minded if we took the small table in the corner. She said that she was sorry but that that table was reserved. She asked if she could seat us in the next room. I told her that would be all right.

- Compare the verbs and pronouns in the conversation and in the reported dialog. Verbs in clauses following **asked, said,** and **told** are generally past, especially in writing, where the report is likely to be made at a much later date.

- Notice that **if** comes after **asked** in the reported dialog (The hostess asked **if** . . .). **That** comes after **told** and **said** but is optional (She **said** (that) she was sorry . . .). Notice that a pronoun follows **told** but not **said.** *Compare:*

  I **told her** that. . . .   (NOT: I told that. . . .)   She **said** that. . . .   (NOT: She said her that. . . .)

5·24 DRILL   Change to reported dialog. Use *asked.*

1. *Mrs. Benson:* I have forgotten my glasses. Would you please read the menu to me? →
   Mrs. Benson said she had forgotten her glasses and asked Lupe if she would (please) read the menu.

2. *Mrs. Benson:* May I order for you, Lupe?

3. *Lupe:* Do you mind if I have onions on my hamburger?

4. *Waitress:* May I take your order?

5. *Mrs. Benson:* Could we have a side order of French fried potatoes?

5·25 *Mrs. Benson:* Let's have some dessert, Lupe.

Waitress: Why don't you try one of our homemade pies?

Mrs. Benson: Did you understand, Lupe?

Lupe: Yes, I did. **You suggested** that **we have** some dessert, and **the waitress suggested** that **we try** one of their homemade pies.

- The simple form of the verb follows **suggested.** *Compare:*

  The waitress **suggested** that **they have** some homemade pie.
  Mrs. Benson **suggested** that **Lupe have** some apple pie. (NOT: . . . that Lupe has)

- "Why don't you try one of our homemade pies?" is an affirmative suggestion, even though the form (**don't try**) is negative. The suggestion can be repeated in the following ways:

  The waitress suggested that we try one of their homemade pies.
  The waitress asked us why we didn't try one of their homemade pies.
  (Again the suggestion is affirmative, although the form—**didn't try**—is negative.)

5·26   DRILL   Report the following suggestions that Mrs. Benson made to Lupe. Use *suggested.*

1. Why don't we have some apple pie, Lupe? →

    Mrs. Benson suggested that she and Lupe have some apple pie.
    OR: *Mrs. Benson suggested to Lupe that they have some apple pie.*

2. Let's have pie à la mode.

3. Let's have some coffee with our pie.

4. Why don't you have a glass of milk, Lupe?

5. Why don't we go to the fair in the park after lunch?

5·27   "Would you please tell me how to get to Laney Park?" Mrs. Benson asked the bus driver.

"Sure. Get off at Cherry Street and transfer to a westbound No. 21 bus," the driver replied.

"The driver said to get off at Cherry Street and transfer to a westbound No. 21 bus," Mrs. Benson explained to Lupe.

■ The sentences above are quotations as they would appear in writing. In Mrs. Benson's explanation to Lupe, what part is quoted dialog? Does the quoted dialog contain reported dialog? Does the driver's "Sure" appear in the reported dialog?

5·28   DRILL   Change the quoted dialog to reported dialog. Use *ask, said,* and *told* as reporting verbs.

1. "Would you please tell me how to get to the flower show?" Mrs. Benson asked the man in the information booth. →

    Mrs. Benson asked the man in the information booth (to tell her) how to get to the flower show.

2. "Certainly. Just take the path to the left," the man replied. →

    The man told her to take the path to the left.

    (Notice that "certainly" and "just" are omitted in the reported dialog. Can you think of a reason for omitting them?)

3. "Would you please tell me how to get to the health food exhibit?" Mrs. Benson asked an attendant.

4. "Certainly," the attendant replied. "Just go straight ahead to the west exit and turn to your right."

5. "Would you tell me how to make this delicious Vita-Min salad dressing?" Mrs. Benson asked the woman behind the counter.

6. "Take a clove of fresh garlic and rub it on the bottom and the sides of a small bowl," the woman told her. "Add ½ cup of salad oil and ½ cup of lemon juice. Season with sea salt, fresh ground white pepper, and organically grown salad herbs."

1   Make a list of things to do and not to do if a fire breaks out in a building. *Examples:*
Be calm.
Don't panic.

2   Make a list of safety rules for children walking or playing on city streets. *Examples:*
Don't play games in the street.
Stay in your front yard or on the sidewalk.

3   Make a list of things for foreigners driving cars in your country to do and not to do.
Example:
Get a guidebook and study the traffic regulations carefully.

4   Many commands appear as printed signs or symbols on doors, fences, streets and highways, or in parks or other public places. Where would you expect to find these signs?

NO SMOKING	KEEP OFF THE GRASS
DO NOT ENTER	NO TRESPASSING
NO LEFT TURN	KEEP OUT

Make a list of signs or symbols that you see on buildings, streets, etc.

5   As you watch television or read advertisements in magazines, make a list of commands and requests that you hear on television or see in magazines.

6   How many ways can you think of to invite someone to go to a play, concert, or opera with you? In what situations would you use the various invitations?

7   Make a list of things to do and not to do if you want to make a good impression on a certain person or a group of persons. For example, you might tell a student what to do and not to do in order to make a good impression on a certain professor. You might tell someone what to do and not to do to make a good impression on a prospective employer or friend.

8   Rewrite the passage, changing the quoted dialog to reported dialog.

The chemistry class was over, and Ahmad and his American friend Dan were gathering up their books and papers. "Could I talk to you for a few minutes?" Ahmad asked his friend. Dan looked at Ahmad and saw that he was really troubled about something. "Why don't we talk over a cup of coffee?" he suggested. Ahmad seemed hesitant, but he didn't say anything. "Come on," Dan urged. "Let's hurry so that we can get a quiet table in the corner."

9   Change the quoted dialog to reported dialog.

Denise and Carla, who had been attending college in Los Angeles, were going to go to New York during the summer to visit relatives. "Why can't we take a bus and see some of the country?" asked Denise. Carla thought this was a good idea. "Let's ask some of our American friends where we should go," she suggested.

10   Change all the questions to statements, and then arrange in paragraph form.

1. Did everyone have a suggestion when Denise and Carla told their American friends that they were going to take a bus to New York? (In changing this sentence, put the *when*-clause at the beginning of the sentence.)

2. Did Millie suggest that they take a southern route so that they would see the Grand Canyon and New Orleans?

3. Did Martin suggest that they go straight across the country so they could see the great plains and wheat fields of the Middle West?

4. Did Bruce suggest that they travel farther north so that they could see Yellowstone National Park in Wyoming?

5. Did Linda suggest that they go up the West Coast to Vancouver and across Canada?

6. Were Denise and Carla understandably confused by all these suggestions?

11   One of your closest friends will be in town next Saturday. He (or she) has written asking you for suggestions about how you and he (or she) might spend the day and evening together. Write a letter in which you include several suggestions based on the activities and places actually available to you. Use the model below if you wish.

(write your address)
(write the actual date)

Dear (*write your friend's name*),

I'm really looking forward to seeing you next Saturday, and I've thought a lot about what we might see and do. . . .

Sincerely, (*Love, As ever*, or
whatever closing remark
seems suitable)

12 Write out two sets of instructions on how to get to your house from a certain place (school, office, etc.). The first set will direct people driving cars; the second set will direct people taking public transportation (or walking if the distance is not too great). You might begin:

These instructions should get you to my house at (*your address*) without too much difficulty. . . .

13 Below is a recipe for a mustard salad dressing. Read it and then use it as a model for a recipe of your own.

Fill a measuring cup about one-fourth full with a light salad oil and pour in an eighth of a cup or more, according to your taste, of white wine vinegar; then squeeze in the juice of half a lemon. Add salt and freshly ground pepper; stir or shake the mixture vigorously. In a separate container put two or three heaping teaspoons of dry mustard (again according to taste), pouring in enough of the oil and vinegar mixture to moisten and smooth the mustard; then put the mustard mixture into the cup with the oil and vinegar. Next, season the mixture with shredded parsley or other herbs of your preference. Shake well before mixing with your salad greens.

14 Below are instructions on how to start a fire in a fireplace. Read them and use the passage as an example of instructions on how to do something. For example, tell someone:

1) how to park a car
2) how to wash and polish a car
3) how to make a dress
4) how to cash a check
5) how to shop for food economically
6) how to budget your time or money
7) how to get a job
8) how to find an apartment
9) how to prepare for an examination
10) how to get good grades
11) how to use the library card catalog
12) how to make friends
13) how to meet people
14) how to start a conversation with a stranger

Here is one way to start a good fire in a fireplace. First, crumple up several sheets of an old newspaper and place them under the grate in the fireplace. Then break up several pieces of kindling wood and place them on top of the grate. Next, place two or three logs so that they cross. Finally, strike a match and light the newspapers; in a moment, you should be enjoying the beautiful warm blaze of the fire.

OBJECTS/PASSIVE AND

CLEFT SENTENCES

Indirect Objects

6·1   — I'd like to ask a favor of **you.**

— Sure. What can I do for **you?**

— My professor gave **me** some difficult problems. Would you please explain them to **me?**

— Okay. Give them to **me** now. I'll see what I can do.

— Thanks. While you're looking them over, I'll get **us** some coffee.

- *Direct objects* are persons or things directly acted upon by an agent (I'll get **some coffee**). *Indirect objects* are the intended receivers of the things acted on (I'll get **us** some coffee). The boldfaced pronouns in the dialog above are indirect objects. What are the direct objects?

- Which indirect objects in the dialog occur between the verb and the direct object? Which occur after the direct object? Which preposition occurs after **ask?** Which prepositions occur after the other verbs?

- **To** and **for** have different meanings. **To** *someone* basically means movement toward the receiver and occurs with verbs such as **announce, bring, carry, deliver, describe, explain, get, give, hand, leave** (the decision, something in a will, etc.), **lend, mail, mention, offer, pass, present, read, report, return, say, sell, send, serve, suggest, take, teach, tell, throw, toss,** and **write.** *Examples:*

  Larry **sent** the book **to** Richard.   Larry **got** the book **to** Richard on time.

  For *someone* simply indicates the intended receiver and occurs with verbs such as **answer, build, buy, cash, close, do, find, fix, get, leave, make, open, outline, prescribe,** and **repair.** *Examples:*

  Richard **made** a bookcase **for** Larry.   Larry **got** the wood **for** Richard.

  For *someone* has another meaning—"instead of" or "in place of."

  Sue **wrote** a letter (to Richard) **for** Larry.

■ With many verbs, there are two possible positions for the indirect object. *Compare:*

I'd like to ask a favor **of you.**   I'd like to ask **you** a favor.
Please give these papers **to Sue.**   Please give **Sue** these papers.
Please make an appointment **for me.**   Please make **me** an appointment.

There are certain restrictions, however:

1) Pronoun indirect objects cannot precede pronoun direct objects.

   Richard made **it for him.** (NOT: Richard made him it.)

2) The preposition cannot be omitted when **for** someone means *in place of* or *instead of* someone. For example, the sentence "Someone made a desk for Larry" is ambiguous. We do not know whether Larry was supposed to make the desk and someone made it instead of him. "Someone made Larry a desk" is not ambiguous, however; Larry is clearly the receiver.

3) The preposition almost always is used with verbs such as **announce, answer, carry, cash, close, deliver, describe, explain, fix** (meaning "repair"), **leave** (the decision), **mention, open, outline, prescribe, repair, report, return, say,** and **suggest.**

   Please $\begin{cases} \textbf{explain} \text{ the question} \\ \textbf{leave} \text{ the decision} \\ \textbf{say} \text{ something} \end{cases}$ to me.   Please $\begin{cases} \textbf{answer} \text{ the question} \\ \textbf{cash} \text{ a check} \\ \textbf{repair} \text{ the clock} \end{cases}$ for me.

6·2   DRILL   Add *to* or *for*, as appropriate.

1. Someone gave a lot of heavy cotton string _____ Vicki. She decided to make a macramé belt _____ herself and a bag _____ her mother. She was going to mail the bag _____ her mother in Miami, but a friend who was going to Florida offered to take the bag _____ her mother _____ her.

2. The delivery boy left these flowers _____ Nancy. I can't imagine who would be sending flowers _____ her at this address. I can't possibly take them _____ her this afternoon. Could you take them _____ her _____ me? I'll find her address _____ you.

3. — Would you please do something _____ me?

   — Sure. What can I do _____ you?

   — Would you please carry this heavy box upstairs _____ me? If I get a hammer and a pair of pliers _____ you, do you think you can open it _____ me?

   — Sure. Who sent it _____ you?

   — My mother. She has decided to give some of her silver dishes _____ my sister and me. She has probably sent some things _____ me _____ my sister.

4. — Here's some money. Please buy a quart of milk _____ me.

   — All right. Is there anything else I can get _____ you?

6·3   DRILL   (1) Repeat the sentences, adding appropriate prepositions and using the words in parentheses as indirect objects; (2) wherever possible, place the indirect object directly after the verb and give the sentence again.

1. Betty and Sam sent a birthday card. (Mrs. Jones) →
   Betty and Sam sent a birthday card to Mrs. Jones.
   Betty and Sam sent Mrs. Jones a birthday card.

2. The postman delivered it. (her) → *The postman delivered it to her.*

3. Betty made a cake. (Mrs. Jones)

4. Sam and Betty delivered it. (her)

5. Mrs. Jones made some tea. (Sam and Betty)

6. She served it. (them)

7. She passed the sugar. (Betty)

8. Betty passed it on. (Sam)

9. Mrs. Jones told an amusing story. (them)

10. Betty asked Mrs. Jones a question and Sam answered it. (her)

11. Betty said something. (Mrs. Jones)

12. Mrs. Jones explained the joke. (them)

13. Mrs. Jones read a letter from her daughter, Joan. (them)

14. She mentioned Joan's engagement. (them)

15. Later Betty reported the news. (her friends)

Passive Sentences

6·4   — Who founded Harvard University?

— I don't know who founded it, but I know when it **was founded.** It **was founded** in 1636.

— Do you know when the University of Uppsala **was founded?**

— Yes, it **was founded** by an archbishop in 1477.

■ Sentences are called *active* when the subject is the agent or actor (that is, the person who produces or causes the action). They are called *passive* when the receiver of the action is in subject position. Which of the following sentences is active and which is passive?

The University of Uppsala was founded in 1636.
An archbishop founded the University of Uppsala in 1477.

Examine the sentences in the dialog for active and passive constructions. How do the verb forms differ?

■ Native speakers do not use active and passive sentences at random. The choice depends largely on the situation. In general, we can say that a person uses the passive when he does not know who the agent is or when he does not consider the agent especially important and does not wish to call attention to the agent.

6·5   DRILL   Ask and answer questions about the following universities.

1. Yale University (1701) →
   Q: *When was Yale University founded?*
   A: *(I believe) it was founded in 1701.*

2. Princeton University (1746) →
   Q: *When was Princeton University founded?*
   A: *(It seems to me) it was founded in 1746.*

3. Georgetown University (1789)

4. Indiana University (1820)

5. The University of New Mexico (1889)

6. The Massachusetts Institute of Technology (1859)

7. The University of Chicago (1891)

8. Columbia University (1754)

9. The University of Hawaii (1907)

10. When was the university or college you are attending founded?

6·6   **The stewardess** serves **lunch to the passengers** at one o'clock.
Lunch is served to the passengers at one o'clock.
The passengers are served lunch at one o'clock by the stewardess.

- Notice that the direct and indirect objects in the first sentence occur in the subject position in the second and third sentences. What happens to the subject of the first sentence? In the third sentence, is "the stewardess" an agent (one who brings about the action) or the receiver of the action? In what situation do you think a speaker would prefer to use the passive sentences rather than the active sentences?

- The passive is formed with **be** + *past participle.*

	is (are/ was/ were)	**served**
is (are/ was/ were)	**being**	**served**
is (are, etc.) going to	**be**	**served**
has (have/ had)	**been**	**served**
may	**be**	**served**
may have	**been**	**served**

Example:

Lunch { is / is **being** / is going to **be** / may **be** / has **been** } **served** by the stewardesses.

6·7   DRILL   Change the following sentences to the passive.

1. The stewardess always serves coffee to the passengers. →
   Coffee is always served to the passengers (by the stewardess).
   OR: *The passengers are always served coffee (by the stewardess).*

2. The stewardess is now serving coffee to the passengers. →
   Coffee is now being served to the passengers (by the stewardess).
   OR: *The passengers are now being served coffee (by the stewardess).*

3. The stewardess served coffee to the passengers a little while ago.

4. The stewardess has already served coffee to the passengers.

5. The stewardess is going to serve coffee now to the passengers.

6. The stewardess should serve coffee to the passengers soon.

6·8   The food **that is served to passengers in the first class section** is different from the food **that is served in the economy section.**

The food **served to passengers in the first class section** is different from the food **served in the economy section.**

■   Notice that the relative clauses in the first sentence become phrases in the second sentence. What words are omitted in the second sentence?

6·9   **After the passengers were (had been) served lunch,** they were much less restless.

Having been served lunch, the passengers were much less restless.

OR: The passengers, **having been served lunch,** were much less restless.

■   Notice that the clause becomes a participial phrase (a phrase beginning with verb-**ing**). For clear identification, the subject of the clause (**the passengers**) replaces the pronoun (**they**) in the main clause. Also notice that a comma follows the phrase as well as the clause at the beginning of the sentence. The phrase is separated from the main clause by a pair of commas if it occurs in the middle of the sentence.

■   Notice that the subject of the two clauses is the same (**passengers/they**) and that the subject (**passengers**) does not appear in the participial phrase. If the subjects are different, both the participial phrase and the main clause should contain subjects. *Examples:*

After **lunch** was served, **the trays** were removed.

Lunch having been served, **the trays** were removed.
(NOT: Having been served, **the trays** were removed.)

6·10   DRILL   Change the *italicized* clauses to phrases.

1. Few passengers pay attention to the safety precautions *that are demonstrated by the stewardess.* →
   Few passengers pay attention to the safety precautions demonstrated by the stewardess.

2. *After the safety precautions were demonstrated,* the equipment was put away. →
   The safety precautions having been demonstrated, the equipment was put away.

3. The glass of champagne *that is served before dinner* is free.

4. Soft drinks *that are served during the flight* are free, too.

5. The movie *that is shown after dinner* costs $2.00.

6. All flight bags *that are carried on the plane* must be placed under the seat.

7. *When the "No Smoking" sign was turned on,* all cigarettes were extinguished.

8. *After the stewardess had been praised by several passengers,* she became even more friendly and helpful.

9. *Since the passengers had been warned of bad weather,* they did not panic when the plane began to pitch and toss.

10. The stewardess, *who had been trained for such emergencies,* succeeded in calming the passengers.

Cleft Sentences

6·11 — Mr. Winter bought a Jaguar, but **what he should have bought was a Volkswagen.**
— He's going to Mexico City, but **where he would like to go is Puerto Vallarta.**
— **What he plans to do is drive as far as the border and take a plane.**

■ The boldfaced constructions, which we call *cleft sentences,* are formed like this:

	He wants		to sell		his old car to	a man	in Rye.
What	he wants		to sell	**is**	his old car.°
What	he wants	**to do is**	(to) sell		his old car to	a man	in Rye.
What	he wants	**is**	to sell		his old car to	a man	in Rye.
Where	he wants		to sell		his old car	**is**	(in) Rye.
The person	he wants		to sell		his old car to	**is** a man	in Rye.

6·12 DRILL Restate the italicized sentences or clauses. Begin your sentences or clauses with *what, where,* or *when.*

1. Mr. Winter bought a new car. *He should have bought a used one.* →
What he should have bought was a used one.

2. He bought the car at Oxford Motors, *but he should have bought it at Stanley Motors.* →
He bought the car at Oxford Motors, but where he should have bought it was Stanley Motors.

3. He bought a British car. *He should have bought an American car.*

4. The car has standard tires, *but he wants to get radial tires.*

5. The car has an AM radio, *but he wants to get an FM radio.*

6. The car has good ventilation, *but he wants to put in air conditioning.*

7. the car doesn't need a brake adjustment. *It needs a motor tuneup.*

8. He often parks his car in the driveway. *He should park it in the garage.*

°ALSO: **What** he wants to sell to a man in Rye **is** his old car.

Object Complements

6·13   What color did the Rogers paint their boat?
They painted it **white with a blue trim.**
What do they call their boat?
They call it ***The Jolly Rogers.***

- Notice, in the second and fourth sentences of the dialog above, that both an adjective phrase (**white with a blue trim**) and a noun phrase (***The Jolly Rogers***) follow the direct object, **it.** These phrases are called *object complements*—an appropriate name, because they complement or complete the predicate (verb + direct object). What are the direct objects in the first and third sentences? Do these sentences have object complements?

- Since the object complement completes the predicate, it must come after the direct object. *Examples:*

  They painted **the boat white.** (NOT: They painted white the boat.)
  They named **the boat *The Jolly Rogers.*** (NOT: They named *The Jolly Rogers* the boat.)

6·14   DRILL   Answer the following questions, using the adjective cues in parentheses. If a different verb is expected in the response, it is also given.

1. What color did the Rogers paint their house? (red) → *They painted it red.*
2. What have they done to the driveway? (have made/ wider) →
   They have made it wider.
3. What did her daughter do to her hair? (cut/ short)
4. Did the boys open the gate? (wide)
5. Did they remember to close the gate? (slammed/ shut)
6. How does Mr. Rogers like his new job? (finds/ interesting)
7. What do you think of Mr. Rogers? (consider/ lucky)
8. Do you consider yourself lucky? (answer as appropriate)

6·15   DRILL   Answer the questions, using the noun cue in parentheses.

1. What do John Rogers' classmates call him? (Einstein) →
   They call him Einstein.
2. Do his teachers consider him a poor student? (an excellent student) →
   No, they consider him an excellent student.
3. Who(m) did the senior class elect president? (John)
4. Who(m) did he appoint chairman of the social committee? (Fanny Price)
5. Did the debate team make John captain? (John's cousin)
6. What did the students name the debate club? (the Patrick Henry Debating Society)

1 Respond according to the pattern set in the examples. Use *one, any,* or *some* in your response.

1. I'll buy you *a newspaper.* → *Don't buy one for me. Buy one for John.*

2. Let me give you *some cookies.* → *Don't give any to me. Give some to John.*

3. I'll bring you *a sandwich.*

4. I'll make you *a cup of coffee.*

5. Let me fix you *some lunch.*

6. Let me give you *some more coffee.*

7. Let me prescribe *something* for you.

8. I'll do *some shopping* for you.

9. I'll make you *an appointment.*

10. I'll send you *a ticket.*

2 Read the first sentence and complete the second sentence; you will need to add appropriate information. The first two are completed to show you the type of sentence you should use.

1. The mayor is planning to raise our taxes. →
   What he should do *is lower our taxes and raise our salaries.*
   OR: What I would like him to raise *is my salary.*

2. The mayor wants to balance the budget. →
   What he should do *is fire half of the personnel staff.*
   OR: What I would like him to do *is to get rid of graft and corruption.*

3. Funds for parks and recreational facilities have been cut.
   What should be cut

4. The Athletic Club is going to circulate a petition protesting the budget cut.
   What the club should protest

5. The new concert hall will be built in the Civic Center.
   Where it should be built

6. Many people are writing letters to the mayor.
   The person to whom they should write

7. The city streets are very dirty.
   What we need

8. The city buses are so old that they are dangerous.
   What we need

9. The mayor goes to the golf course on Sunday morning.
   Where he should go

10. The mayor is too old to run for reelection.
    What he should do

3 Rewrite the paragraphs, changing the italicized verbs from passive to active constructions wherever possible.

1.   The Taj Mahal *was erected* by Emperor Shah Jahan as a tomb for his beloved wife, Mumtaz Mahal. The monument *was constructed* during the years 1630 to 1648 by some 20,000 workmen.

2.   Two twenty-story apartment houses *were built* by the ABC Construction Company in the last year. Two twenty-five-story apartment buildings *are* now *being built* by the ABC Company in the next block. Next year two thirty-story apartment houses *will be built* across the street from them by the ABC Company.

3.   The bus fare *is being raised* to thirty cents by the Rapid Transit Company next month. Two years ago the fare *was raised* from fifteen cents to twenty-five cents by the RTC. Next year the city *is going to be divided* into zones° and a rate fixed by the RTC for each zone. In this way the revenue *can be increased* by the RTC without an overall raise in the bus fare.

4.   The game of tennis as we know it today *was introduced* to guests at a garden party given by Major Walter Clopton Wingfield on his estate at Nantclwyd, Wales, in December 1873. The game *was adapted* by him from court tennis, the ancient game of kings, and *was patented* under the Greek name *Sphairistiké*. Sphairistiké *was introduced* into the United States in the spring of 1874 by Miss Mary Ewing Outerbridge. The first tournament *was held* by the Americans on Staten Island in 1880.

4 Rewrite the paragraphs below, changing sentences to passive constructions whenever possible.

1.   The Indians warmly greeted the Florentine navigator Giovanni da Verrazano as he entered New York harbor on April 17, 1524. Other explorers and traders soon followed him. In 1609, Henry Hudson, an Englishman in the service of the Dutch, made a trip up the river on the west side of Manhattan Island. The people later named the river the Hudson, in his honor. The reports of his journey encouraged trading, and in 1621 the Netherlands granted exclusive commercial rights in America to the Dutch West India Company. The settlers established New Amsterdam, now known as New York, in 1625 on the lower tip of Manhattan Island. The following year, Director-General Peter Minuit purchased Manhattan Island from the Indians for $24 in goods.

2.   Monticello, now a national shrine, is one of the many buildings that Thomas Jefferson designed. He designed the house to look smaller than it actually is and devised many novel features. He hid the servants' quarters and replaced the customary large central staircase with a small staircase in each wing of the house. He also introduced gadgets such as a hideaway bed and a dumbwaiter in a mantle.

°**Zones** = districts or designated areas.

5 Read the paragraph below; then write one in your own words in which you tell what Margaret can do to make her room more cheerful. For example, what color should she paint the walls, the ceiling, and the woodwork? What color would you suggest that she paint the desk and chair? What color should she dye the bedspread and curtains?

Margaret has moved into a rented room. The walls are a dirty tan. The woodwork and ceiling are dark brown. The desk and chair are gray, and the curtains and bedspread are a faded green. Margaret's landlady has told her that she can paint the walls, woodwork, ceiling, desk, and chair and that she can dye the bedspread and curtains in order to make the room more cheerful.

6 Using the information given below, write a brief report of the meeting of the International Club. Tell (a) when, where, and for what purpose the meeting was held, (b) who(m) the club members elected to the various offices, and (c) who(m) the new president appointed chairman of the various committees.

Name of organization:	the International Club
Time of the meeting:	the first week of the semester
Place of the meeting:	the student lounge
Purpose of the meeting:	to elect club officers for the coming year
Results of the election:	President: Kazuo Fujii Vice-President: Jorge Corea Secretary: Teresa Ting Treasurer: Frank Kalligeros
Appointments made by the new president:	Chairman of the Social Committee: Rosalina Ramos Chairman of the Fund Raising Committee: Abdul Hamimi Chairman of the Publicity Committee: Young Duck Kim

VERBS

7

Simple Present versus Continuous Present

7·1

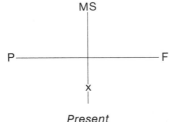

Present

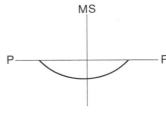

Continuous present

MS = moment of speaking; P = past; F = future.

I **see** Alan and Henry Chin.	Alan **is looking** this way **now.**
I **know** Alan **sees** us.	**Now** he's **waving** at us.

- In the sentences on the left, **see** and **know** express sense perception or mental perception in the immediate present. **See, hear, feel,** and **smell** are often used to express immediate sense perception. *Example:*

  I **see** (**hear**/ **feel**/ **smell**) something.

  Know, believe, feel, understand, think, like, want, and **prefer** are examples of verbs used to express mental perception. *Example:*

  He **knows** (**believes**/ **understands**/ **wants**) something.

- Verbs expressing sense or mental perception do not usually occur in the present continuous. *Examples:*

  He **sees** us. I **know** it. (NOT: He is seeing us. I am knowing it.)

  However, speakers also use **think** and **feel** in the continuous present to express a temporary condition in process. *Examples:*

How **is** he **feeling** now?
Are you **thinking** of going to see him at the hospital?

- In the sentences on the right, **is looking** and **is waving** indicate activity in progress **now** (the moment of speaking).

7·2   Alan **speaks** Chinese very well.   He **is** probably **speaking** Chinese with Henry **now.**

- In the sentence on the left, **speaks** expresses a general state or activity in the present; in the sentence on the right, **is ... speaking** indicates activity in progress **now** (the moment of speaking). Some verbs like **speak** can express either meaning. *Examples:*

    Henry **plays** the guitar.   He **is playing** for Alan now.
    Alan **takes** good pictures.   He's **taking** a picture of Henry now.

    Because **now** means both *at the present time* and *at the moment of speaking,* **now** can occur with simple present as well as present continuous verbs. *Compare:*

    Henry **takes** two lessons a week **now.**
    Henry **is playing now.** Listen.

7·3   Henry **usually practices** an   He **is taking** guitar lessons from
hour **every day.**   Carlos Santos **at the present time.**

- In the sentence on the left, **usually practices ... every day** indicates repeated activity in the present. (This type is sometimes called *habitual present.*) Time expressions like **every day (week, month, year), once in a while, from time to time, usually, sometimes, often, frequently,** and **never** often occur with verbs expressing repeated activity. These expressions do not ordinarily occur with the present continuous. *Example:*

    Henry **usually practices every day.**
    (NOT: Henry is usually practicing every day.)

- In the sentence on the right, **is taking ... at the present time** indicates activity in progress over a period of time regarded as present. Time expressions like **now** (meaning "at the present time"), **at the present time, this semester (month, week, year),** and **these days** occur with this type of continuous present. *Example:*

    Henry **is taking** two lessons a week **now** (at the present time/ this month/ these days).

7·4   — Should I say "Henry **lives** with his brother now" or "Henry **is living** with his brother now"?

    — You can say either one. Both mean approximately the same thing.

- **Work** and **live** can express about the same meaning in both the simple present and the present continuous. For some people, however, the continuous may suggest a more recent situation. *Compare:*

    Henry **lives** with his brother.
    (He has lived with him for several years.)

    Henry **is living** with his brother.
    (He has recently moved in with his brother.)

7·5   DRILL

1. Look around the room or out of the window. Tell what you see and hear. If you see people, tell what they are doing. If objects are in motion, tell what is happening. *Examples:*

    I see a man across the street. He is probably waiting for the bus.
    I see a clock on the wall. The second hand is moving.

2. Imagine you are in a cafeteria or restaurant at lunch time. Tell what you hear, see, and smell. How does the food taste? *Examples:*

    I see a lot of hungry people.
    I hear the clatter of dishes.
    I smell hot dogs and hamburgers.

    Now pick out several people and tell what they are doing. *Example:*

    A busboy is picking up the dirty dishes.

3. Look at Mr. Brown's schedule and then tell what he usually does every day at a certain time.

    Mr. Brown's schedule:

A.M.	P.M.
6:30: gets up	12:15: leaves for lunch
7:30: leaves the house	1:30: returns to office
8:15: arrives at the office	1:30–3:30: works on reports
8:30–9:00: answers correspondence	3:30: goes out for coffee
10:00–11:00: telephones clients	4:00–5:00: interviews job applicants
11:00–12 noon: meets with vice-president of the firm	5:00: leaves for home

    Examples: Mr. Brown usually gets up at 6:30 A.M.
    From 8:30 to 9:00, he usually answers correspondence.

Present Continuous versus Present (Continuous) Perfect

7·6

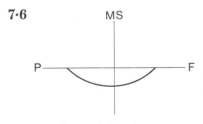

Present continuous

Present (continuous) perfect

Toby **is watching** an old movie on TV **now.**

He $\begin{Bmatrix} \textbf{has been watching} \\ \textbf{has watched} \end{Bmatrix}$ TV **for an hour.**

■ In the sentence on the left, **is watching ... now** indicates activity in progress at the moment of speaking. In the sentence on the right, **has been watching (has watched) ... for an hour** both indicate activity during a period of time extending to the moment of speaking. **Has been watching** emphasizes the continuous nature of the activity; **has watched** merely describes the activity that takes place during the period of time. In both cases, the period of time is over (**for an hour** = a period of time extending to the moment of speaking); the activity, however, may continue.

■ Time expressions like **for an hour** (**two days/a month/a year,** etc.) and **since eight (nine/ten,** etc.) **o'clock** frequently occur with the present (continuous) perfect. They do not occur with the present continuous, however. *Compare:*

He **has been watching** TV **since eight o'clock.**
(NOT: He is watching TV since eight o'clock.)

He **has watched** TV **for an hour.**
(NOT: He is watching TV for an hour.)

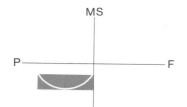

Present continuous perfect

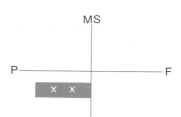

Present perfect

Toby **has been watching** an old movie on TV.

He **has seen** the movie at least twice before.

■ Both examples are present perfect. The one on the left, however, indicates *continuous* activity over a period of time (such as for the last hour) extending to the present; the one on the right conveys *repeated* activity in a period extending to the present.

■ Time expressions such as **three** (**four/ five,** etc.) **times before** and **twice** (**three times/ four times,** etc.) **this week** (**month/ year**) frequently occur with the present perfect to show repeated activity. These expressions do not ordinarily occur with the present continuous. *Example:*

He **has seen** them **three times before.**
(NOT: He is seeing them three times before.)

■ When time expressions such as **for an hour** refer to a period of time that is over, we must use the present perfect, not the continuous present. *Example:*

Toby **has been watching** TV **for an hour.**
(NOT: Toby is watching TV for an hour.)

If **for an hour** refers to a future period of time, a present continuous verb is possible. *Example:*

Toby **is watching** TV for an hour.
(Toby is going to watch TV for an hour.)

7·8

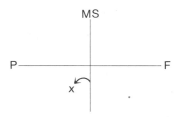

The hero **has already saved** the heroine.

He **has just shot** the villain.

- **Has already saved** and **has just shot** express *completed* activities closely tied to the present. The simple past instead of the present perfect is often used to express this type of activity (He **just shot** the villain). The speaker's sense of recency in a certain context probably influences the choice.

- Time expressions like **already, just,** and **recently** occur with this type of present perfect. **Still** and **yet** in a question or negative sentence indicate activity *not completed so far* (up to the moment of speaking). *Examples:*

  — **Has** the hero **kissed** the heroine **yet?**
  — No, he **still hasn't kissed** her.

VERB SUFFIXES

Third Person Singular

Group A	Final sound	Spelling 3rd sing.	Pronunciation
miss	/s/	misses	
close	/z/	closes	
push	/š/	pushes	/əz/
lurch	/č/	lurches	
rouge	/ž/ or /ǰ/	rouges	
judge	/ǰ/	judges	

After the sibilant sounds /s, z, š, č, ž, ǰ/, the spelling of the third singular suffix is **es** or **s** and the pronunciation is /əz/.

Group B	Final sound	Spelling 3rd sing.	Pronunciation
pat	/t/	pats	
hope	/p/	hopes	/s/
puff	/f/	puffs	
cook	/k/	cooks	

After voiceless consonants not included in Group A, the spelling is **s** and the pronunciation is /s/. (See the list of voiceless and voiced consonants on page 266.)

Group C	Final sound	Spelling 3rd sing.	Pronunciation
crowd	/d/	crowds	
call	/l/	calls	/z/
play	/ey/	plays	

After voiced consonants not included in Group A and after all vowels, the spelling is **s** and the pronunciation is /z/.

In writing, the letter **y,** when preceded by a consonant letter, changes to **i,** and **es** is added. *Examples:*

carry / carries   BUT: destroy / destroys
imply / implies   employ / employs

Notice the vowel changes in **say** and **do:**

say /sey/   says /sez/
do /duw/   does /dəz/

Add **s** and **es** suffixes to these verbs:

wish	stay	study	note
look	sell	laugh	deny

7·9 DRILL

1. Tell what book each person is reading at the *present time* and how many pages or chapters each person *has read so far*.

Name	Title of book	Pages or chapters read
John	*The Understanding of Music*	100 pages
Bill	*The Roots of Modern English*	220 pages
Helen	*Ecology for the Future*	150 pages
Bob	*The Urban Crisis*	3 chapters
Sue	*The Psychology of Women*	2 chapters

Example: John is reading The Understanding of Music. *He has read 100 pages so far.*

2. The following people have recently moved to a new address. Tell where each person is living now. Also tell how long each person has lived at the new address.

Name	New address	Length of time at new address
John Smith	101 Page Street	3 months
Tom Smith	101 Page Street	2 months
Ellen Rich	230 Elm Drive	4 months
Sue Rich	230 Elm Drive	6 weeks
Lana Thompson	890 Mason Road	2 weeks
Sharon Forsmark	512 Cherry Drive	1 week

Example:
John Smith is now living at 101 Page Street. He has lived there for three months.

Past and Past Participle: Regular Verbs

Group A	Final sound	Spelling -ed suffix	Pronunciation
crowd	/d/	crowded ⎫	
note	/t/	noted ⎭	/əd/

After final /t/ and /d/, the -ed suffix is spelled d or ed and pronounced as a separate syllable /əd/.

Group B	Final sound	Spelling -ed suffix	Pronunciation
talk	/k/	talked ⎫	
hope	/p/	hoped ⎪	
toss	/s/	tossed ⎬	/t/
rush	/š/	rushed ⎭	

After voiceless consonants except /t/, the -ed suffix is spelled d or ed and pronounced /t/.

Group C	Final sound	Spelling -ed suffix	Pronunciation
pull	/l/	pulled ⎫	
breathe	/th̬/	breathed ⎬	/d/
play	/ey/	played ⎭	

After voiced consonants except /d/ and all vowels, the -ed suffix is spelled d or ed and pronounced /d/.

In writing, the letter **y**, when preceded by a consonant letter, changes to **i**, and **ed** is added. However, **y** does not change to **i** when the **-ing** is added. *Examples:*

apply	applied	applying
study	studied	studying
try	tried	trying

Add -ed and -ing suffixes to these verbs:

stray	play	comply	destroy
imply	employ	convey	stay

Doubling Final Consonants (all groups)

A final consonant letter, with the exception of **x, y, h,** or **w**, is doubled if it meets these conditions:

1 The consonant is preceded by a single vowel letter.

stop	stopped	stopping
BUT: look	looked	looking

2 The consonant occurs in an accented syllable.

fít	fitted	fitting
omít	omitted	omitting
BUT: óffer	offered	offering

Add the -ed and -ing suffixes to these words:

spot	insíst	box	rot
defér	work	laugh	occúr

3. Think of three friends, relatives, or acquaintances who have recently got or changed jobs. Tell where they are working and how long they have worked there. Use only the present continuous and present perfect in this drill. *Example:*

   Denise is working for an advertising agency. She has worked there only a short time.

4. What are you studying this semester? Have you studied this subject (or these subjects) before?

Present Perfect versus Simple Past

7·10

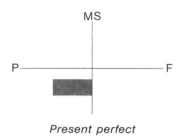

Present perfect

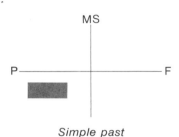

Simple past

Toby **has watched** TV **for two hours.**	**Last night** Toby **watched** TV **for two hours.**
He **has watched** TV **since seven o'clock.**	**Two nights ago** he **watched** TV **from six to eleven-thirty.**

- Compare the sentences on the left and the right. With the present perfect (**has watched**), the period of time (**for two hours** and **since seven o'clock**) extends to the moment of speaking. With the simple past (**watched**), the period of time (**for two hours** and **from six to eleven-thirty**) is definitely cut off from the present.

- Time expressions like **last night** (**week/month/year**), **two nights** (**days/weeks/years**) **ago,** and **yesterday** frequently occur with simple past verbs; they clearly indicate that the period of time is cut off from the present.

- Notice that **for two hours** can occur with either the present perfect or the simple past. Expressions like **since seven o'clock** do not occur with the simple past, however. *Example:*

  He **has watched** TV **since seven o'clock.**
  (NOT: He watched TV since seven o'clock.)

  On the other hand, expressions like **two nights ago** do not occur with the present perfect. *Example:*

  He **saw** the program **two nights ago.**
  (NOT: He has seen the program two nights ago.)

7·11

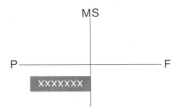

Toby **has watched TV every night this week.**

Toby **watched TV every night last week.**

■   Notice that in the sentences above both the simple past and the present perfect indicate repeated activity.

■   Time expressions like **every day, usually,** and **often** may occur with present, present perfect, and past verbs. *Example:*

Toby $\left\{ \begin{array}{l} \textbf{watches} \\ \textbf{has watched} \\ \textbf{watched} \end{array} \right\}$ TV **every night.**

Other time expressions are usually different, however. *Compare:*

He **watches** TV every night **now.**
(**now** = at the present time)

He **has watched** TV every night **this week.**
(**this week** = period of time up to the moment of speaking—so far this week)

He **watched** TV every night **last week.**
(**last week** = period of time definitely cut off from the moment of speaking)

7·12

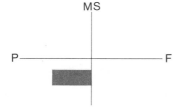

Recently Toby **has watched (has been watching)** the six o'clock news regularly.

He **used to watch** a children's program at that hour.

■   Notice that **has watched (has been watching)** indicates habitual or regular activity during a recent period that extends to the present. **Used to watch,** on the other hand, indicates habitual activity during an indefinite period of time in the past. Does Toby still watch a children's program at six o'clock? What has he been watching recently?

7·13

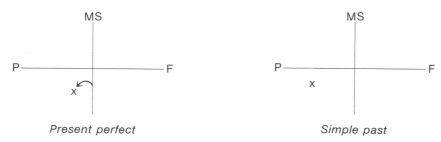

Present perfect   Simple past

Toby **has just turned off** the TV.   Toby **turned off** the TV **a little while ago.**

■ In the example on the left, **has just turned off** indicates a completed activity tied to the present in the mind of the speaker (see §7.8). We could also say "Toby just turned off the TV," but we wouldn't say "Toby has turned off the TV a little while ago," because the time expression, **a little while ago,** definitely cuts off the activity from the moment of speaking. In other words, **a little while ago** places the activity in the past.

IRREGULAR VERBS

The irregular verbs are arranged in alphabetical order for easy reference. It is sometimes useful, however, to group them according to vowel change (/iy/ to /e/, as in **meet-met-met**) or consonant change (**build-built-built**) or no change (**cost-cost-cost**), and so on. Arrange verbs from the list in these categories: (1) the three forms are the same; (2) the three forms are different; (3) the past form and past participle are the same; (4) the simple and past participle forms are the same. Also consider sound changes in grouping verbs in each category.

Simple form		Past form		Past participle	
arise	/ay/	arose	/ow/	arisen	/i/
be	/biy/	was	/wəz/	been	/bin/
bear	/er/	bore	/ɔr/	borne[1]	/ɔr/
beat	/iy/	beat	/iy/	beat[2]	/iy/
become	/ə/	became	/ey/	become	/ə/
begin	/i/	began	/æ/	begun	/ə/
bet	/e/	bet	/e/	bet	/e/
bite	/ay/	bit	/i/	bitten[3]	/i/
blow	/ow/	blew	/uw/	blown	/ow/
break	/ey/	broke	/ow/	broken	/ow/
bring	/i/	brought	/ɔ/	brought	/ɔ/
bróadcast	/ɔ/	bróadcast	/ɔ/	bróadcast	/ɔ/
build	/i/	built	/i/	built	/i/
burst	/ər/	burst	/ər/	burst	/ər/
buy	/ay/	bought	/ɔ/	bought	/ɔ/

[1] **Borne** is the active form; **born,** the passive. *Examples:* She **has borne** seven children. He **was born** in Hong Kong.

[2] ALSO: **béaten** /iy/.
[3] ALSO: **bit** /i/.

Which of the following sentences are possible? Why are the others not possible?

He has watched a program yesterday.
He watched a program last night.
He has just watched a program.
He just watched a program.
He has watched a program two nights ago.

7·14   The movie that Toby **saw** last night **began** at seven and **ended** at nine.
He **thought** it **was** very good.

- In the preceding examples, notice that the verbs express past actions (**began**/ **ended**) and states (**was**), sensory perceptions (**saw**), and mental perceptions (**thought**).

Simple form		Past form		Past participle	
catch	/æ/	caught	/ɔ/	caught	/ɔ/
choose	/uw/	chose	/ow/	chosen	/ow/
cost	/ɔ/	cost	/ɔ/	cost	/ɔ/
cut	/ə/	cut	/ə/	cut	/ə/
dig	/i/	dug	/ə/	dug	/ə/
do	/uw/	did	/i/	done	/ə/
draw	/ɔ/	drew	/uw/	drawn	/ɔ/
drink	/i/	drank	/æ/	drunk	/ə/
drive	/ay/	drove	/ow/	driven	/i/
eat	/iy/	ate	/ey/	eaten	/iy/
fall	/ɔ/	fell	/e/	fallen	/ɔ/
feed	/iy/	fed	/e/	fed	/e/
feel	/iy/	felt	/e/	felt	/e/
fight	/ay/	fought	/ɔ/	fought	/ɔ/
find	/ay/	found	/aw/	found	/aw/
fly	/ay/	flew	/uw/	flown	/ow/
forget	/e/	forgot	/a/	forgotten	/a/
forsake	/ey/	forsook	/u/	forsaken	/ey/
freeze	/iy/	froze	/ow/	frozen	/ow/
get	/e/	got[1]	/a/	got	/a/
give	/i/	gave	/ey/	given	/i/
go	/ow/	went	/e/	gone	/ɔ/

[1] ALSO: **gótten** /a/.

7·15   DRILL

1. Tell where the following people used to live, when they moved, where they are living now, and how long they have lived at the new address. (Assume that it is now early December.)

Name	Old address	Date moved	New address
John Smith	200 Page Street	September 5	101 Page Street
Tom Smith	350 Church Street	October 5	101 Page Street
Ellen Rich	98 Fir Street	August 10	230 Elm Drive
Sue Rich	48 Bell Street	about 6 weeks	230 Elm Drive
Lana Thompson	550 Spruce Avenue	about 2 weeks	890 Mason Road
Sharon Forsmark	89 Walnut Circle	about a week	513 Cherry Drive

Example: Tom Smith used to live at 350 Church Street. He moved on October 5 and is now living at 101 Page Street. He has lived there for about two months.

Simple form		Past form		Past participle	
grow	/ow/	grew	/uw/	grown	/ow/
hang	/æ/	hung	/ə/	hung	/ə/
have	/æ/	had	/æ/	had	/æ/
hear	/ir/	heard	/ər/	heard	/ər/
hide	/ay/	hid	/i/	hidden[5]	/i/
hit	/i/	hit	/i/	hit	/i/
hold	/ow/	held	/e/	held	/e/
hurt	/ər/	hurt	/ər/	hurt	/ər/
keep	/iy/	kept	/e/	kept	/e/
know	/ow/	knew	/uw/	known	/ow/
lay	/ey/	laid	/ey/	laid	/ey/
let	/e/	let	/e/	let	/e/
lead	/iy/	led	/e/	led	/e/
leave	/iy/	left	/e/	left	/e/
lend	/e/	lent	/e/	lent	/e/
lie[6]	/ay/	lay	/ey/	lain	/ey/
lose	/uw/	lost	/ɔ/	lost	/ɔ/
make	/ey/	made	/ey/	made	/ey/
meet	/iy/	met	/e/	met	/e/
pay	/ey/	paid	/ey/	paid	/ey/
put	/u/	put	/u/	put	/u/
quit	/i/	quit	/i/	quit	/i/
read	/iy/	read	/e/	read	/e/
ride	/ay/	rode	/ow/	ridden	/i/
ring	/i/	rang	/æ/	rung	/ə/
rise	/ay/	rose	/ow/	risen	/i/
run	/ə/	ran	/æ/	run	/ə/
say	/ey/	said	/e/	said	/e/
see	/iy/	saw	/ɔ/	seen	/iy/

[5] ALSO: **hid** /i/.   [6] Meaning "recline."

2. When did you move to your present address? How long have you lived there?

3. Which of the following movies have you seen and when and where did you see them?

Ben Hur	*Doctor Zhivago*	*Love Story*
My Fair Lady	*Gone with the Wind*	*Easy Rider*
City Lights	*La Dolce Vita*	*Wuthering Heights*
Grand Illusion	*War and Peace*	*Rashomon*

If you haven't seen any of these, what movies or plays have you seen recently? When and where did you see them?

Simple form		Past form		Past participle	
sell	/e/	sold	/ow/	sold	/ow/
send	/e/	sent	/e/	sent	/e/
set	/e/	set	/e/	set	/e/
shake	/ey/	shook	/u/	shaken	/ey/
shoot	/uw/	shot	/a/	shot	/a/
show	/ow/	showed	/ow/	shown[7]	/ow/
shut	/ə/	shut	/ə/	shut	/ə/
sing	/i/	sang	/æ/	sung	/ə/
sink	/i/	sank	/æ/	sunk	/ə/
sit	/i/	sat	/æ/	sat	/æ/
sleep	/iy/	slept	/e/	slept	/e/
speak	/iy/	spoke	/ow/	spoken	/ow/
spend	/e/	spent	/e/	spent	/e/
stand	/æ/	stood	/u/	stood	/u/
steal	/iy/	stole	/ow/	stolen	/ow/
strive	/ay/	strove	/ow/	striven	/i/
swear	/er/	swore	/ɔr/	sworn	/ɔr/
swim	/i/	swam	/æ/	swum	/ə/
take	/ey/	took	/u/	taken	/ey/
teach	/iy/	taught	/ɔ/	taught	/ɔ/
tear	/er/	tore	/ɔr/	torn	/ɔr/
tell	/e/	told	/ow/	told	/ow/
think	/i/	thought	/ɔ/	thought	/ɔ/
throw	/ow/	threw	/uw/	thrown	/ow/
understand	/æ/	understood	/u/	understood	/u/
wear	/er/	wore	/ɔr/	worn	/ɔr/
weave	/iy/	wove	/ow/	woven[8]	/ow/
win	/i/	won	/ə/	won	/ə/
write	/ay/	wrote	/ow/	written	/i/

[7] ALSO: **showed** /ow/.   [8] ALSO: **weaved** /iy/

4. Which of the following cities have you visited? (Add other cities to the list, if you wish.)

New York	Montreal	London	Istanbul	Bombay
Miami	Vancouver	Rome	Beirut	Bangkok
Chicago	Mexico City	Stockholm	Baghdad	Singapore
St. Louis	Bogotá	Berlin	Jerusalem	Djakarta
New Orleans	Caracas	Geneva	Teheran	Sydney
Denver	Lima	Amsterdam	Nairobi	Manila
Seattle	Santiago	Vienna	Monrovia	Hong Kong
San Francisco	Buenos Aires	Lisbon	Timbuktu	Peking
Los Angeles	Montevideo	Madrid	Addis Ababa	Seoul
Honolulu	Rio de Janeiro	Athens	Brazzaville	Tokyo

When were you there and how long did you stay? Have you been in any of these cities more than once? If so, about how many times have you been there?

Simple Past versus Continuous Past

7·16

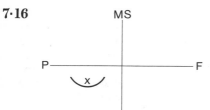

We **arrived** while Toby **was watching** his favorite TV Program.

■ In the example, **arrived** corresponds to x and **was watching** corresponds to ⌣⟋ . Both activities occur in past time, but one is in progress (**was watching**) when the other occurs (**arrived**).

■ The past continuous often occurs with reference to a point of time in the past.

Was Toby **watching** TV **at ten o'clock last night?**

7·17 DRILL

1. On his way home from school yesterday, Toby saw the following people and animals. Tell what they were doing when he saw them.

Name	Activity
Mr. Peters	washing his car
Mrs. Peters	working in the garden
Billy Peters	mowing the lawn
Rover, the Peters' dog	chasing a car
Four, the Peters' cat	sleeping in the sun
Nick Bradley	talking to a beautiful blonde
Mrs. Bottomly	gossiping with her neighbors

Example: When Toby saw Mr. Peters yesterday, he was washing his car.

2. What were you doing at this time yesterday? What were you doing a year ago? Five years ago?

Simple Past versus Past Perfect

7·18

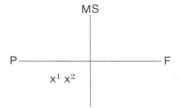

Toby **had seen** the movie a week ago, but he **watched** it on TV again last night.

- In the example, **had seen** corresponds to x^1 and **watched** corresponds to x^2. Both activities occur in past time, but x^1 occurs *before* x^2.

- Just as the present perfect indicates an activity in a period BEFORE NOW (the moment of speaking), the past perfect indicates an activity BEFORE THEN. *Compare:*

He **has seen** the movie **before.**
(BEFORE NOW—the moment of speaking)

He **had seen** the movie before he saw it again **last night.**
(BEFORE THEN—before last night)

Unless the idea BEFORE THEN is clearly indicated, both verbs may be simple past even though one activity obviously occurred before the other. *Compare:*

When he **finished** supper, he **watched** TV.

When the first commercial **came** on, he **ate** his dessert.

When he **finished** supper he **watched** the movie, even though he **had seen** it before.

He **hadn't eaten** his dessert yet.

- The past perfect continuous has almost the same meaning as past perfect. The continuous, of course, emphasizes the continuous nature of the activity. *Example:*

He **had watched** (**had been watching**) the program for ten minutes before he **realized** that he **had seen** it **before.**

7·19 DRILL   Answer the questions below, using the past perfect.

1. Tell where you went on your last vacation. Had you been there before? *Example:*
   I went hiking in Nepal on my last vacation. I had been there once before in the 1960s.

2. Yesterday Jim told Bob he would meet him for lunch at noon. Jim arrived at 1:15. How long had Bob been waiting? What had probably happened to Jim?

3. Two women suddenly stopped talking when another woman came into the room. What had the two women probably been talking about?

4. Henry and Emily met in 1966 and were married in 1970. How long had they known each other before they married?

5. Although Nancy Perkins' parents were British, she spoke Mandarin Chinese with no trace of a British accent. Where had she probably learned Chinese?

Future/Future Continuous/Future Perfect

7·20

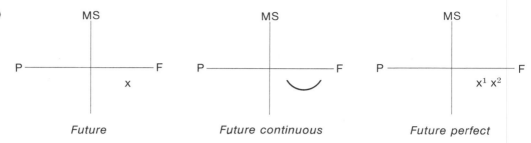

Future	Future continuous	Future perfect
Toby **is going to watch** TV tonight. He **will watch** the news at five o'clock.	He **will be watching** a sportscast from seven to eight.	Surely Toby **will have seen** enough TV by the time we **get**° there at eight-thirty.

- In the examples above, the future and future continuous mean about the same thing. **Will be watching** emphasizes the continuous nature of the activity, however, and would be required in a sentence of this kind:

    Toby **will** probably **be watching** TV when you get here.

- In the sentence under the right diagram, **will have seen** corresponds to x^1 and **get** corresponds to x^2. Both activities occur in future time, but x^1 occurs before x^2.

- The future perfect is much like other perfect tenses. *Compare:*

BEFORE THEN (Past)	BEFORE NOW (Moment of speaking)	BEFORE THEN (Future)
Last night he saw a film he **hadn't seen** before.	He **is watching** a movie **now** that he **has seen** before.	If he **watches**† the movie tomorrow night, he **will have seen** it three times.

The future perfect is not very common, however, unless the completion of the activity BEFORE THEN (point of time in the future) is clearly indicated. *Compare:*

He **will eat** dinner before he **watches** TV.
(statement of future activity)

Surely he **will have finished** dinner before seven o'clock.
(emphasis on completion of activity before another point in future time)

Toby **will have seen** his program and (will have) **gone** to bed by the time his father **gets** home.
(emphasis on completion of activities before another future activity)

° The verb in the time clause is present when the verb in the main clause is future (see §13.3).
† The verb in a conditional clause is present when the verb in the main clause is future perfect.

7·21   Toby **goes** to bed early tonight whether he likes it or not.

He **is going to** the airport tomorrow morning.

His father **is leaving** for New York.

■   Future time is commonly expressed by the present of many verbs + a future time expression.

7·22   DRILL   Answer the questions below, using the future or the future perfect, as appropriate.

1. What is the automobile going to be like by the year 2000? *Example:*
   For one thing, automobiles will be smaller.
2. What will have been accomplished in space travel by the year 2000? *Example:*
   Many things will have been accomplished by the year 2000. First, ... Second, ...
3. Which cities will be the largest in the world by the year 2000?
4. What kinds of houses will people live in by the year 2000? What kind of food will they eat? What kind of work will they do?
5. How will young people dress in the year 2000? What will they be interested in?
6. What progress will have been made in medicine by the year 2000?
7. What steps will have been taken to rid our cities, rivers, lakes, and oceans of pollution by the year 2000?
8. What will have happened to secure peace by the year 2000?

1   Read the following paragraph. Notice that it is *present narration;* that is, someone is describing the situation from a present point of view.

   It is noon. Farhad and Ali have been sightseeing all morning. They have been on a cruise around San Francisco Bay. They have visited Fisherman's Wharf, and they have climbed to the top of Telegraph Hill to see the view and to take pictures. They haven't seen San Francisco's famous Chinatown yet, but they are planning to go there after lunch.

   Now change the paragraph to *past narration.* Notice that the point from which the narrator views the scene is past. You might begin: *It was noon. Farhad and Ali had been sightseeing all morning.*

2   Read the following paragraph. Notice that it is *present narration.*

   It is now one o'clock. Farhad and Ali have just finished lunch. Before lunch they took a cruise around San Francisco Bay, visited Fisherman's Wharf, and climbed to the top of Telegraph Hill to see the view and to take pictures. At the present moment, they are sitting on a bench in Washington Square enjoying the view of the city from there. They haven't been to Chinatown yet, but they are going to go there next.

   Now change the paragraph to *past narration;* in sentence 4, change "at the present moment" to "at that moment." You might use this framework:

   It was one o'clock. Farhad and Ali had just finished .... Before lunch they had .... At that moment, they were ....

3   Assume that Farhad and Ali went sightseeing on Saturday and that it is now Sunday. Tell what they did in a brief *summary of past activity.* (Assume that they did everything mentioned in the two preceding paragraphs.) If you wish, use the following framework as a guide: *Yesterday Farhad and Ali went sightseeing. Before lunch they .... After lunch they ....*

4   Write a paragraph similar to that in Ex. 2 in which you describe some kind of activity.

   1. Set a present point of time: *It is noon (one o'clock,* etc.). Tell what someone has done up to that time and, if appropriate, what he hasn't done. Then tell what the person is planning to do later.

   2. Change to *past narration.* Make the point of time past, and then tell what the person had done, etc. You might begin: *It was noon (one o'clock,* etc.).

   3. Assume that the activity you have described in 1 and 2 took place three days ago (a week ago, etc.). Summarize the activity in a *past account.* You might begin: *Three days ago ....*

5   A sportscaster is reporting the events taking place at the Rolling Hills Tennis Club as they *are actually taking place.* This account is *present narrative:*

   It is a beautiful sunny afternoon at the Rolling Hills Tennis Club. The men's singles final of the Rolling Hills Tennis Tournament is about to begin. A few latecomers are trying to find seats in the stands, which appear to be almost full. Sam Klotz, who is defending his title, and his opponent, Nicky Lemmon, who recently won the men's singles title in the Fall City Tennis Tournament, have been rallying for about ten minutes. Both players look in top form. Nicky doesn't seem to be bothered a bit by his left leg, which he injured in a fall a week ago. The umpire is climbing into his box. The linesmen are taking their places. In a few minutes, the match will be underway.

Change to past narration. Assume that sportscaster is retelling the events *after* they have taken place. You might begin: *It was a beautiful sunny afternoon . . . .*

6   Assume that the tennis match took place on Saturday afternoon and that it is now Sunday and that Nicky Lemmon defeated Sam Klotz. The score was 7–5, 6–2, 7–5. Using this information and information from the narrative in Ex. 5, summarize what took place. You might begin: *Nicky Lemmon defeated defending champion . . . .*

7   Assume the role of narrator.

1. Report a sports event or some activity as it is actually taking place (or as though it were actually taking place—*present narration*).

2. Report the same event as though you were recalling what actually took place (*past narration*).

3. Give a brief account of what took place (*past summary*).

8   Complete the following paragraph by filling in the verbs in the blank spaces. The paragraph is *present narration.*

I am sitting at a corner table in a restaurant. A middle-aged man and woman

_____ at a table next to me. The woman, who _____ dyed blond hair
        (sit)   (have)

and who _____ about fifty, _____ coffee and _____ to the
            (look)   (drink)   (talk)

man. The man, who _____ gray-haired and distinguished looking, _____
                        (be)   (not pay)

any attention to what she _____. He _____ to catch the eye of the
                               (say)   (try)

waitress, who _____ successfully avoiding him. The man _____ some-
                   (be)   (say)

thing to the woman. She _____ displeased but _____ her head. Now
                            (look)   (nod)

they _____. They _____ toward the door. The waitress, who appar-
         (get up)   (walk)

ently _____ eyes in the back of her head, _____ after them and
          (have)   (run)

_____ "Oh, sir, sir, here _____ your check."
    (say)   (be)

9 Change the paragraph in Ex. 8 to *past narration*. You might begin: *I was sitting* . . . .

10 Assume that the incident in Ex. 8 happened on Friday night and it is now Sunday. Give a summary of what happened in the past. You might begin: *Friday night a middle-aged couple were sitting at a corner table next to me in a restaurant.*

11 Assume the role of narrator.

1. Describe an incident similar to the one in Ex. 8 as it is (or as though it were) actually taking place (*present narration*).

2. Describe the same incident as though you were recalling what actually took place (*past narration*).

3. Give a brief, straightforward account of what took place (*past summary*).

AUXILIARIES

Possibility and Probability

8·1   *Mr. Bell:* I think it **might rain** today, but I **could be** wrong.

Mr. Lee: You are often wrong about the weather, but this time you **may be** right. The weatherman says there is a storm on the way.

Mr. Bell: The farmers **must be** happy to hear that. I read in the newspaper recently that the crops really need rain.

Mr. Lee: I've heard a lot about that too. I'm sure it **must be** true from all that I've heard.

- **Might rain, could be, may be,** and **must be** all express probability; but there is often a difference in meaning, depending on the situation. For example, **will probably rain** seems to be a good substitute for **might rain,** but **am possibly wrong** seems to be a better substitute for **could be.** After saying that he thinks it will probably rain, Mr. Bell grants that he is possibly wrong. With the prediction of the weatherman to back him up, Mr. Lee grants that Mr. Bell is probably right. **May, might,** and **could,** then, can mean anything from slight possibility to fairly high probability. Mr. Bell has read that the crops need rain. He concludes, therefore, that the farmers are undoubtedly happy about the prospect of rain; and Mr. Lee indicates that all that he has heard leads him to the same conclusion.

- **Possibly** often occurs with **may, might,** and **could.** *Compare:*

  He **may (might/could) possibly be** wrong.
  He **is possibly** wrong.

- Notice that **may, might,** and **could** are followed by the simple form of the verb.

  It might **rain.** (NOT: It might to rain.)

8·2   DRILL   Complete the following sentences, using *may, might, could,* and *must* as you think appropriate. In some cases, there may be more than one possibility.

1. Take your raincoat. It _____*might*_____ rain today.

2. My raincoat isn't here. I wonder if it _____ be at the office.

3. It _____ be at the office, but I don't think you left it there. Look in the front closet. You _____ find it there.

4. The street looks wet. It _____ be raining now.

5. You're right. It _____ be. There are raindrops on the window.

8·3   — It **may have rained** a little last night.
       — It **must have rained** quite a bit. There are still puddles on the ground.

   ■ **May have rained** and **must have rained** indicate past probability. **Must have rained** is a statement, however, of strong probability. The speaker comes to the conclusion that it has rained quite a bit during the night because there are still puddles in the street.

   ■ Compare **must have rained** and **may have rained** with the forms expressing present probability. How do they differ?

8·4   DRILL   Complete the sentences.

1. Mr. McKee works five days a week. In his work he talks to people and handles money. Most of the time, he stands behind a counter. What is his occupation?

   1. He could _____   3. He may _____

   2. He might _____   4. He must _____

2. When Mrs. Scatterbrain came home from a shopping trip, she looked under the flowerpot for her house key, but it wasn't there. What had she probably done with the key?

   1. She could have _____   3. She may have _____

   2. She might have _____   4. She must have _____

Necessity

8·5   **Must** you leave so soon?
       Yes, we really **must**. We **have to be** home by seven.
       What a pity! Last time you **had to leave** early, too.

   ■ For present necessity we have **must** and **have to;** for past necessity, however, we have only one choice—**had to.** Remember that **must have** + *past participle* expresses probability, not necessity (see §8.3). **Have to** seems more common than **must** for expressing necessity.

   ■ Native speakers usually pronounce **have to** as [hæftə] and **has to** as [hæstə].

8·6   DRILL

1. Name three things that you absolutely *must* or *have to* do today (tomorrow/ next week, etc.).

2. Name several things that you *had to* do yesterday (the day before yesterday/ last week, etc.).

Permission

8·7   — Should I say "**May** I leave now," "**Could** I leave now," or "**Can** I leave now"?

— It all depends on the situation. They are all recognized ways of asking for permission to do something. If you are talking to an older person or a person of great importance and want to be especially polite, say "**May** I leave now?" **Could** is good middle ground; you won't offend anyone by using it. **Can** is also common, especially among friends or family members. There is nothing really wrong with it, but some people still think it is a bit rude or impolite.

8·8   DRILL   You have lost or forgotten your pen and need one to sign a paper or a form of some kind. Decide whether you would say *"May (could or can) I borrow your pen"* if you were asking the people listed below. Give reasons for your choice.

1. your roommate
2. your teacher
3. a young girl
4. a librarian
5. a prospective employer
6. an elderly, distinguished-looking stranger

Ability and Capability

8·9   — **Can** he **speak** Arabic?

— Yes, he **is able to carry on** a conversation without difficulty.

— **Could** they **speak** Arabic when they first went to Lebanon?

— No, they **weren't able to say** anything in Arabic.

■   As the sentences above show, **can-could**/ **are able-was able** correspond to ability in present or past time.

8·10   DRILL   Answer the questions.

1. How many languages can you speak?

2. Are you able to read and write these languages as well as speak them?

3. Could you speak English when you were a child?

4. How old were you before you were able to read?

5. How long have you been able to write letters in English?

Obligation

8·11   — We **ought to contribute** more to the Art Foundation this year.

   — Yes, we **should.** We **should have given** more last year, too.

- **Should** and **ought to** mean approximately the same thing. **Should** seems more common, however, in questions, short answers, and expressions of past obligations.

8·12   DRILL

1. Name three things you feel you *should* or *ought to do* today (tomorrow, next week, etc.).

2. Name several things you feel you *should have done* or *ought to have done* yesterday (last week, etc.) but did not do.

Suggestion

8·13   — Please tell me which courses to take next semester.

   — Well, you **could take** a history course. You **might** also **take** an art course, and you **should** certainly **take** a science course. Oh, you'**d better ask** your adviser. **Let's go see** him now.

- Notice that the suggestions are for the present or future even though the form of the auxiliaries are past (**could/might/should**).

- "You **could have taken** a science course last semester, but you didn't" is an example of suggestion or possibility in past time that was not realized or carried out.

- Suggestions are often very similar to statements of obligation, particularly with **should** or **ought to** as the auxiliary. *Examples:*

Tell me what I **should do. Should** I **help** her?
Of course. You **ought to do** everything for her that you can.

- **Had better** is used for both present and past. *Examples:*

You'**d better** see him **now. Yesterday** I **told** you you'**d better** see him right away.

Had better is sometimes used as to a warning. *Examples:*

You'**d better** be careful.
You'**d better** watch your language.

- **Let's go see** is a type of suggestion that includes the speaker. It is always a present or future suggestion. Notice that two simple verbs often follow **Let's.** The meaning is this: "Let us **go** to **see** him now." We could also say: "Let's **see** him now."

8·14   DRILL   A very thin person you know wants to gain weight and a very fat person you know wants to lose weight. They have both asked you for advice. Complete the list of suggestions—first for the thin person and then for the fat person.

1. You could   2. You might   3. You ought to   4. You should   5. You'd better

Preference

8·15 — **Would** you **rather go** to a movie tonight or watch TV?

— **I'd rather watch** TV.

— What's the matter? Don't you like to go to the movies any more?

— No, I don't. The last one I saw was terrible. **I would rather have stayed** home and **watched** TV.

- **Would rather** means "prefer"; and **I'd rather** means "I would rather."
- **Would rather have stayed home** in the last sentence indicates a past preference that was not realized.

8·16 DRILL   Answer the questions; use *would rather . . .* or *would rather have . . . .*

1. Would you rather go to a symphony or an opera?
2. Would you rather see a baseball game or a soccer game?
3. Would you rather be lucky or rich? Why?
4. Would you rather be a host or a guest? Why?
5. Would you rather have known Beethoven or Michelangelo? Why?
6. Would you rather have been Gandhi or Genghis Khan? Why?

Repeated or Habitual Past Activity

8·17 Professor Lopez **used to give** his students a quiz every Friday. He **would assign** a composition every week, also.

- When the meaning is customary, repeated, or habitual activity in the past, **used to** and **would** are interchangeable. For example, **used to** and **would** can be exchanged in the preceding sentences. In other situations, however, the two are not interchangeable. *Compare:*

  Professor Lopez **used to teach** beginning Spanish, but he doesn't any more.
  (The meaning is "no longer teaches beginning Spanish." In this sentence, **used to** does not express habitual activity; therefore, **would** cannot be substituted.)

  Professor Lopez **would teach** beginning Spanish now if he could.
  (The meaning is conditional; **used to** cannot be substituted.)

8·18 DRILL   Answer the questions; use *would . . .* or *used to . . . .*

1. When you were nine or ten years old, what did you *used to do* on Saturday afternoon?
2. What *would* you usually *do* on Sunday?
3. Where did you *used to go* for your vacation?
4. What *would* you *do* during the summer?

1 *Situation:* Mr. Sellers comes home at six o'clock. He is surprised to find the front door is open. When he gets into the living room, he notices that the television set is missing and that a lamp has been knocked over. Tell what *must have happened* or *could have happened* to the television set and what *should* or *might* Mr. Sellers *do* about it.

2 What are some things someone *must* or *has to do* before he *can travel* to a foreign country?

3 What *can* people *do* or *have* today that they *couldn't do* or *have* a hundred years ago? What *could* they *do* or *have* a hundred years ago that they *can't do* or *have* today?

4 In the twentieth century, women have steadily gained rights and freedom to do as they wish. What are they *able to do* socially, economically, and politically today that they *were not able to do* in the early 1900s?

5 State several things that you think people have a *moral obligation* to do (that is, they *should* or *ought to do*).

6 State several things that you think someone had a moral obligation to do in the past but did not do.

7 *Situation:* Mrs. Silva was called to the hospital suddenly one afternoon to see a friend who had been in an automobile accident. Mr. Silva, who prided himself on the fact that he had never lifted a finger in the kitchen and couldn't boil water if his life depended on it, came home after work and found a note from his wife telling him that she wouldn't be home until nine or ten o'clock. It happened that he was very hungry, but he just sat in the living room feeling sorry for himself and waiting impatiently for his wife to come home to get his dinner. What *could* (*might* or *should* or *ought*) he *have done* instead of sitting there doing nothing?

8 When you were in high school, did your teachers *used to give* you a lot of homework? Who *used to help* you with your homework? How often *would* your teachers *assign* a composition? *Would* your teachers always *correct* your compositions and return them to you?

9 Read the paragraph below:

Almost everyone complains about pollution, but few are doing anything about it. The average person shrugs his shoulders and says the problem is too big for him; but there are, surprisingly, many things that he can do. In fact, the problem will not be solved without the cooperation of millions of people like him. An individual's contribution will involve sacrifice, but surely the price is not too high to pay for clean land, air, and water.

1. Make a list of things that people (businessmen, students, etc.) can do. For example, housewives can stop using so many disposable items. They can buy items that are in reclaimable containers. They can use a basket for grocery shopping and cut down on the number of plastic bags and paper bags they bring home. They can also use cloth towels and napkins instead of disposable paper ones.

2. Using the paragraph above as an introduction, develop a composition. You might make each item on your list into a paragraph by including details and examples. You might also use signals like *first, second, also, in addition, moreover,* and *furthermore* to introduce each point.

10 Write a composition in which you discuss what your government (and/or private industry) *has done* in the last decade to fight pollution (to improve education, to promote peace, to raise the standard of living), what it *is doing now,* and what it *is planning to do* in the future. You might also include things that you think should be done but are not being done.

ADVERBIALS

9

Position of Adverbials*

9·1 San Francisco is **usually** cool **in the summer.** The skies are **almost always** overcast **in the morning,** and **often** the fog rolls in off San Francisco Bay, to cover the city **completely. Sometimes,** however, the weather turns warm and sunny. The temperature **even** reaches 85 or 90 degrees **occasionally.** When this happens, San Franciscans **immediately** head for the parks and the beaches **with joyful expectations.** There isn't a minute to be wasted **then,** for the fog may come in **soon.**

In the city proper, there are many small parks and squares and, of course, the vast, world-famous Golden Gate Park. **On warm days,** you will see San Franciscans **happily** sunning themselves **in the parks** and **at the beaches. In Marin County,** which lies **just across San Francisco Bay,** there are also many recreation areas, parks, and beaches where San Franciscans can **fully** enjoy the fine summer weather. Not all San Franciscans like warm weather, but those who do try to spend as much time as possible **outdoors.**

- Most adverbials can occur in more than one position in a sentence, as the boldfaced adverbials in the passage above show.

- Single-word adverbials of frequency (**usually, always, often,** etc.), of manner (**happily, fully,** etc.), of time and sequence (**immediately, then, just,** etc.) commonly occur in the middle of the sentence.

  See the first two sentences in the passage for examples. Find other examples in the passage.

- For *emphasis* or *variety*, speakers sometimes place adverbials at the beginning or end of a sentence, although they would normally occur in the middle of the sentence. They may also place them at the beginning to serve as *sequence signals* (that is, to relate the sentence to what has gone before).

---

*The term *adverbial*, as used in this book, includes all simple words and phrases that tell *where* (place), *when* (time), *how often* (frequency), in *what way* (manner). The term also includes words like **almost, just, nearly, barely, scarcely, only, even,** and **practically,** which limit or restrict elements in the sentence.

See the third and fourth sentences in the passage for examples. Find other one-word adverbials placed at the beginning or end of the sentence. Decide whether the adverbial was placed there for emphasis or as a sequence signal.

- Adverbial phrases like **with joyful expectations** (manner), **on warm days** (time), and **at the beaches** (place) commonly occur at the end of the sentence but can occur at the beginning for emphasis or variety or as sequence signals.

    Find examples of phrases at the beginning of sentences in the passage; decide whether they add variety or emphasis or act as sequence signals.

9·2   Outside, the building was shabby.
After lunch, time seemed to go more slowly than ever.

- There is no general agreement on punctuation for adverbials at the beginning of the sentence. Some writers use a comma after an adverbial; others punctuate by ear or by sense, sometimes using a comma and sometimes not. It is a general practice, however, for all writers to use a comma wherever the absence of one might result in a misreading of the sentence, as in the examples above.

9·3   DRILL   Go over the passage about San Francisco weather, changing the position of the boldfaced adverbials whenever possible. Decide which changes would be entirely satisfactory (that is, the result would be as good as, or better than, the original). Decide which changes would not be satisfactory and tell why.

9·4   Last Sunday was a beautiful day, so we decided to drive to Marin County for a picnic. **First,** we found a park with tables and barbecue pits, and we unpacked the car. **Next,** we gathered wood and made a fire. **After that,** we set the table and waited for the fire to settle down so we could cook our hamburgers.
    After lunch, we rested awhile. **Then,** some of us took a short hike through a redwood grove. When we returned, we all watched the sunset. **Finally,** we packed the car and drove home.

- Sequence signals are more obvious at the beginning of the sentence; however, many of them can occur in other parts of the sentence. *Compare:*

    Then some of us took . . . .
    Some of us **then** took . . . .

9·5   DRILL   Fill in the blanks with possible sequence signals (*first, then, next, later, finally*). Add punctuation as appropriate.

When Mr. Sass reaches the office in the morning, he _____ reads the financial pages of several newspapers. _____ he reads his mail. He _____ calls in his secretary and dictates letters. His secretary _____ types the letters. _____ she brings them to him for his signature.

9·6   Miss Wesson is an excellent secretary—for several reasons. **First of all,** she has all the necessary secretarial skills. **In addition,** she is intelligent and experienced enough to answer routine correspondence by herself. **Furthermore,** she is experienced and competent enough to run Mr. Sass's office while he is away on short business trips.

■   The boldfaced adverbials are listing or additive signals. The reader or listener knows that additional points of information will follow. **Also, too, besides, second** (third, fourth, etc.), **moreover,** or **furthermore** could be used in place of **in addition.**

Besides being additive signals, **furthermore** and **moreover** often suggest expansion or intensification of something mentioned previously.

Mr. Sass said that he was more than satisfied with Miss Wesson's work. **Moreover,** he gave her a $50 raise.

9·7   Bryce is not entirely satisfactory as a mail boy. **First,** he is often late to work. He also takes long lunch hours and morning and afternoon coffee breaks. **Furthermore,** he wastes a lot of time on the job. **To be sure,** he sometimes does not leave the office until after five, but this time hardly compensates for his inefficiency during working hours.

■   **To be sure** operates here as another type of additive signal; it introduces a sentence that qualifies what has been said previously. Other signals of this type are **of course, admittedly, even so, granted,** and **in practice.**

9·8   DRILL   Fill in with the appropriate additive signals: *first (second,* etc.)*, in addition, besides, furthermore, moreover, even so, in practice, to be sure.* (There is more than one possibility for each blank.)

Mr. King, the office manager, has drawn up procedures for the ABC Company.

In practice, however, they leave much to be desired. _____ the procedures are

not stated in sufficient detail to be particularly helpful. _____, one can seek clarifi-

cation from Mr. King, but he does not always have time to talk to employees. _____,

most employees are hesitant to ask him questions. _____, they are not certain that

his explanations would make the procedures workable.

9·9   Someone sent flowers **to the hospital faithfully every day last week.**
                         PLACE   MANNER   FREQUENCY   TIME

■   When more than one adverbial occurs at the *end* of a sentence, a usual order is *Place – Manner – Frequency – Time.* Here are some additional details on adverbial word order:

1) *Manner* can also precede *place.*

Someone sent flowers $\begin{cases} \text{to the hospital } \textbf{faithfully.} \\ \textbf{faithfully} \text{ to the hospital.} \end{cases}$

2) *Frequency* normally precedes *time.*

Someone sent flowers **every day** last week.
(NOT: Someone sent flowers last week every day.)

3) *Place* normally precedes *time.*

Someone sent flowers **to the hospital** last week.
(NOT: Someone sent flowers last week to the hospital.)

4) Adverbials do not normally separate the verb and object.

Someone **sent flowers** to the hospital every day last week.
(NOT: Someone sent to the hospital flowers every day last week.)

5) One-word adverbials of manner may come before the verb, but they do *not* separate the verb and object. *Compare:*

He sent flowers to the hospital **faithfully.**
He **faithfully** sent flowers to the hospital.
(NOT: He sent faithfully flowers to the hospital.)

Also, adverbials should not separate a noun object and its modifiers.

Someone closed the door to the office **quietly.**
OR: Someone **quietly** closed the door to the office.
(NOT: Someone closed the door quietly to the office.)

6) Adverbials indicating *agent*—such as **by someone,** or *instrument,* such as **with a pen,** or *accompaniment,* such as **with a friend**—occur in essentially the same positions as adverbials of manner (**hurriedly, in a Rolls-Royce**). *Examples:*

The letter was written $\begin{cases} \textbf{hurriedly} \\ \textbf{by someone} \\ \textbf{in ink} \\ \textbf{with a pencil} \end{cases}$ on a piece of notepaper.

He went to a reception $\begin{cases} \textbf{in a Rolls-Royce} \\ \textbf{with a friend} \\ \textbf{by himself} \text{ (alone)} \end{cases}$ last Saturday night.

9·10 DRILL   Read the sentences. Change adverbials that are not in usual positions.

1. The prime minister visited three times last week the United Nations.
2. He answered cleverly the questions the newsmen asked him.
3. He had lunch with friends twice last week at Chez Pierre.
4. The chauffeur took him through the city streets at breakneck speed.
5. He got out of the limousine in front of the restaurant with a sigh of relief.
6. He thanked hurriedly the driver and quickly walked into the restaurant.

9·11   Mr. Prasad's office is **on the fourth floor.**
Across the hall is his son's office.

A large advertising agency is **on the first floor.**
On the floor above (there) is an import-export firm.

- What is the word order when the adverbial occurs at the beginning of the sentence? Notice that the use of **there** is optional in the last sentence (that is, **there** may or may not be used).

- Would the sentence "Across the hall is his son's office" be a good beginning sentence for a conversation or composition? Why or why not?

9·12   **Seldom** is the symphony over before ten-thirty.
Only once this season has it ended before ten o'clock.
Rarely do we hear works by modern composers.

- Notice the word order when **seldom, only once,** or **rarely** occur at the beginning of the sentence. Is a form of **be** or an auxiliary placed before or after the subject?

- Other adverbials that require a change in word order when they occur at the beginning of the sentence include **never, hardly ever, scarcely,** and **barely.**

9·13   DRILL   Place the *italicized* adverbs in the beginning position. Some will require reversing the order of subject and verb and some will not.

1. We go to the symphony *every Friday night.* →
Every Friday night we go to the symphony.

2. The Campbells are *in the row in front of us.* →
In the row in front of us are the Campbells.

3. Wilson and Lois Graham are *across the aisle.*

4. The orchestra has played only well-known classics *at the last three concerts.*

5. They have presented a modern program *only once this season.*

6. We *rarely* have the opportunity to hear first-rank soloists.

7. The conductor's son-in-law is *almost always* the violin soloist.

8. The concerts are *surprisingly* well attended.

9·14   San Francisco is **usually** cool in summer.   New York **rarely** is.
We **seldom** suffer from the heat in   In New York, we **frequently** do.
the summer.

- Adverbials of frequency like **often, usually, never, seldom, always, occasionally,** and **frequently** normally occur after a form of **be** or an auxiliary in an affirmative statement. They occur before a form of **be** or an auxiliary, however, in a short statement or rejoinder.

9·15 Chicago **occasionally doesn't** have any snow until December.
In fact, it **sometimes doesn't** have any snow until January.
One **just can't** predict the weather.

- Most one-word adverbials can occur either before or after the contraction. *Examples:*

There **isn't often** snow in December.   There **often isn't** snow in December.

Always and **ever** occur after the contraction, however. *Examples:*

There **isn't always** snow in December.   There **isn't ever** any rain in July.
(NOT: There always isn't snow . . . .)   (NOT: There ever isn't any rain . . . .)

Adverbials like **occasionally, sometimes, just, almost,** and **still** occur before the contraction. *Example:*

One **just can't** tell what the weather will be like.
(NOT: One can't just tell . . . .)

9·16 **DRILL** Place the adverbial on the left before or after the *italicized* verb or auxiliary, as appropriate.

frequently	1. We *have* lunch in the cafeteria. →
	We frequently have lunch in the cafeteria.
occasionally	2. We never have lunch before noon, but Don *does.*
hardly ever	3. Steve *has* lunch with us.
seldom	4. Bruce *is* free at noon.
ever	5. We often call Vicky. She *doesn't* call us.
always	6. We invite Joan to our parties, but she *doesn't* invite us.
often	7. We usually invite Don, too, but he *doesn't* invite us.
usually	8. We almost always give large parties, but Joan and Bob *don't.*
sometimes	9. Corinna likes to receive letters, but she *doesn't* get around to answering them.
just	10. She *isn't* a good correspondent.

Special Usage

EVER/ NEVER/ SELDOM/ RARELY/ SCARCELY/ HARDLY/ BARELY

9·17 *Patient:* Is it **ever** possible to see the doctor without an appointment?
Receptionist: No. No one **ever** sees him without an appointment.
Patient: Doesn't he **ever** see anyone on Saturday?
Receptionist: No, he doesn't **ever** take appointments on Saturday.

- Does **ever** occur in both affirmative and negative *yes/no* questions? Does it occur in both affirmative and negative statements?

9·18   *Patient:* Is the doctor **never** in on Saturday?

Receptionist: No. He **never** takes appointments on Saturday.

- **Never, seldom, rarely, scarcely,** and **barely** make a sentence negative. It is not necessary to add **not.** *Compare:*

The doctor isn't **ever** in on Saturday.   The doctor is **never** in on Saturday.

(NOT: The doctor isn't never in on Saturday.)

9·19   DRILL   Restate the sentences using the adverbials on the left.

never	1. He *doesn't ever* talk to strangers. → *He never talks to strangers.*
often	2. He *seldom* talks to anyone without being introduced.
rarely	3. He *doesn't often* go to parties.
ever	4. He *never* misses a baseball game, though.
seldom	5. We *don't often* see him anymore.
hardly ever	6. We *don't often* go to baseball games.

ALREADY/ YET/ STILL/ ANYMORE

9·20   — The passengers have **already** boarded the plane, but the loading ramp hasn't been removed **yet.**

— Have you checked your baggage **already?**

- **Already** occurs in affirmative statements; **yet** (meaning "so far") occurs in negative statements. **Already** normally occurs in the middle of the sentence but can appear at the end; **yet** normally occurs at the end of the sentence, but is sometimes shifted forward when there is a long predicate. *Example:*

He hasn't **yet** checked the baggage that will go straight through to Rome.

- **Yet** and **already** both occur in *yes/no* questions. **Already** in a question indicates surprise or disbelief that something has been accomplished so soon. *Compare:*

Have you checked your baggage **already?**   Have you checked your baggage **yet?**
(How clever you are to get it done so soon.)   (Have you done it so far?)

With **yet** the question can be either affirmative or negative. *Example:*

Has (Hasn't) the plane taken off **yet?**

9·21   DRILL   Give appropriate responses, using the adverbials at the left.

already	1. Let's go to the movie at the Roxie. → *I've already seen it.*
yet	2. Have you seen the movie at the Palace?
yet	3. Has Katy seen the movie?
already	4. Let's ask Katy to go with us.
already	5. Why don't you call the theater to find out when the main feature goes on?

9·22   His uncle **still** lives in Rome, but his cousin doesn't live there **anymore.**

He **still** hasn't written to his cousin, but I'm not going to worry about it **anymore.**

- ■ **Anymore** (meaning "no longer") occurs only in negative statements; **still** occurs in negative as well as affirmative statements.

  In negative statements, **still** occurs before the contraction. *Compare:*

  He is **still** here.   He **still isn't** here.

- ■ Both **still** and **anymore** occur in *yes/no* questions. **Anymore** occurs in negative questions; **still** occurs in both affirmative and negative questions. *Compare:*

  Is (Isn't) he **still** in Rome?   **Isn't** he in Rome **anymore?**

9·23   DRILL   Give appropriate responses, using the adverbials on the left.

still	1. Do you still hear from Dolly? → *Yes, we still hear from her.*
anymore	2. Do you still hear from Vicki?
still	3. Don't the Prestons live in London anymore?
anymore	4. Don't the Bauers still live in Munich?
still	5. Do you ever see them?

9·24   DRILL   Substitute *still* for *yet,* and *yet* for *still.*

1. We have a long way to go *yet.* → *We still have a long way to go.*
2. The bus *still* hasn't arrived.
3. We *still* have quite a while to wait.
4. She hasn't bought her ticket *yet.*
5. She has plenty of time *yet.*

DURING/ FOR/ SINCE/ AGO

9·25   — When did they arrive?
— They arrived **during lunch.**

— How long ago did they arrive?
— They arrived **one hour ago.**

— How long have they been here?
— They've been here **for over an hour.**

- ■ **During** and **for** both indicate periods of time. Notice the types of time expressions used with each. *Compare:*

He arrived **during** { 1973. / May. / the summer. / the lunch hour.   He was here **(for)** { a day. / two weeks. / three months. / a long time.

■ **For** is optional in the preceding examples. However, **for** cannot always be omitted. For instance, it cannot be omitted in time phrases after the verbs **leave, go,** and **return.** *Examples:*

He stayed here (for) a week.	He **left for** a week.
He traveled (for) five days.	He **went** to Mombasa **for** five days.
He didn't remain in Europe (for) two months.	He didn't **return for** two months.

■ **For** is frequently used in answering "how long" questions.

9·26   — **When** will you give some thought to it?
— I'll give some thought to it **during the weeks to come.**

— **When** did he write to her?
— He wrote to her **during the years he was in India.**

■ **During** is used in the answer to a "when" (*not* a "how long") question; it is, therefore, not followed by expressions like **a day, two weeks, several months. During** can be followed by noun phrases like **the weeks that followed** and **the days ahead** when these prepositional phrases are answers to "when" questions.

9·27   — It is now ten o'clock. He left at nine.
— How long **ago** did he leave?
— He left an hour **ago.**

■ *Time expression* + (**a week/month/year**) **ago** measures a period of time from the present to a point of time in the past. **Ago** occurs with the simple past tense.

9·28   — How long has he been here?
— He has been here **since** May 1971.

— How long had he been there?
— He had been there **since** Tuesday.

■ **Since** is followed by time expressions like **June, winter, Tuesday, last week, 1971,** and **one o'clock** that establish a point of time; it cannot be followed by time expressions like **two days** or **a year.** *Example:*

He has been here **since last spring.**
(NOT: He has been here since five days.)

Since occurs with the perfect tenses; it does not usually occur with simple present and past tenses. *Example:*

I **have been** here **since one o'clock.**
(NOT: I am here since one o'clock. OR NOT: I was here since one o'clock.)

CONTRAST OF SINCE/ FOR/ AGO:

9·29   *1966   1967   1968   1969   1970   1971   1972   (Now)*

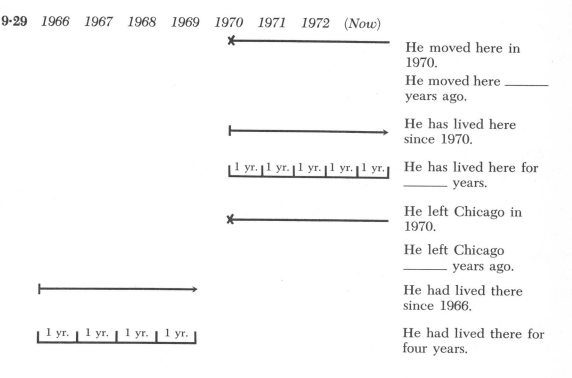

He moved here in 1970.

He moved here _____ years ago.

He has lived here since 1970.

He has lived here for _____ years.

He left Chicago in 1970.

He left Chicago _____ years ago.

He had lived there since 1966.

He had lived there for four years.

■ Extend the time to the present by adding years after 1972. Then fill in the blanks in the second, fourth, and sixth sentences.

9·30   DRILL   Read the paragraph and then answer the questions, using *during, since, for,* or *ago.*

It began to rain at eight o'clock this morning and didn't stop until noon. By one o'clock the sun was out, but it was too wet for grandfather to go out for his customary afternoon walk until four-thirty. When he left, he said he would be back by six o'clock. It's almost six o'clock now, so he should be back any minute.

1. When did it rain? → *It rained during the morning.*
2. When did the sun come out?
3. How long did it rain?
4. Since when has the sun probably been out?
5. How long ago did grandfather leave the house?
6. When does grandfather usually take a walk?

IN/ ON/ AT

9·31   — Where does he live?
　　　　　　　　　　　⎧ **in** North America (Canada, Ontario, Toronto).
　　　— He lives ⎨ **on** Carl Street.
　　　　　　　　　　　⎩ **at** 123 Carl Street.

- **In** is followed by the name of a continent, country, state, city, district; **on** is followed by a street name; **at** is followed by house number + street name.

9·32　　　　Mrs. Robb bought some roses **at** a flower stand **in** the Farmers' Market. When she got home, she took the roses **into** the kitchen and put them **in** a vase. She put the vase **on** the chest **in** the hall.

- The adverbials of place **in, on, at** + *noun phrase* have roughly these meanings in the preceding examples.

　　in = inside a place or within an area

　　in(to) = movement inside a place or area

　　on = on the surface rather than inside or within

　　at = general location without reference to position inside or on the surface

9·33   DRILL   Answer in full sentences for practice in using **in, on, at.**

1. Where is he staying? (Ritz Hotel) → *He's staying at the Ritz Hotel.*
2. What floor is his room on? (sixth)
3. Where are we going to meet him? (lobby of the Ritz Hotel)
4. Where will he be? (information desk)
5. Where shall we leave the car? (hotel parking lot)
6. Where shall I put this parking ticket? (the windshield)
7. Where's my overcoat? (back seat)
8. Where do you want to put your camera? (overcoat pocket)

9·34   The No. 10 bus goes by the Palace Hotel every twenty minutes, and it is usually **on time.** If you hurry, Larry, you should get there **in time** to catch the next bus.

- **On time** means on or at the scheduled or appointed time. If the No. 10 bus is scheduled to arrive at the Palace Hotel at 4:20 and it gets there at 4:20, it is **on time.** If it gets there at 4:25, it isn't **on time.**

- **In time** means in sufficient time to carry out or accomplish a purpose. If Larry hurries, he will probably get to the Palace Hotel **in time** to catch the next bus at 4:20. If he gets there after 4:20, he probably won't be there **in time** to catch the bus. If the bus is late, however, he may still be **in time** to catch it.

■ In some situations, either **on time** or **in time** might be appropriate, depending on the emphasis. *Compare:*

Was Larry **on time** for his appointment?
(Was he there at the scheduled time?)

Was Larry **in time** for his appointment?
(Was he there early enough to keep his appointment?)

9·35 DRILL   Read the sentences; then restate the sentences, using *on time* or *in time*, as appropriate.

1. The play was supposed to begin at 8:30, but it began about ten minutes late. →
   The play was supposed to begin at 8:30, but it didn't begin on time.

2. We like to arrive at the theater early enough to look over the program before the play begins. →
   We like to arrive at the theater in time to look over the program before the play begins.

3. If the play had started at 8:30, quite a few people would have been late for the first act.

4. Some people are almost always late for performances. I wish people would get to the theater early enough to get settled in their seats before the performance begins.

WITH/ IN/ BY—AGENT/ ACCOMPANIMENT/ INSTRUMENT

9·36 — Please sign the paper **with a pen.** Only signatures **in ink** are acceptable.

■ Notice that it is **with a pen** when reference is to the instrument (pen, pencil, crayon, etc.) and **in ink** when the reference is to the substance (ink, pencil, crayon, etc.).

9·37 — Your signature must be witnessed **by two persons.** Did you bring anyone **with you?**
— No. I came **by myself.**

■ In the sentences above, **by** and **with** have these meanings:

by two persons = agent   **with you** = accompaniment
                                  by myself = alone, unaccompanied

9·38 — Did you come **by bus** or **on foot?**
— Neither. I came **in a taxi.**

■ **By bus (car/train/plane/taxi/ship)** and **on foot (horseback)** indicate the general means of transportation. When referring to private means of transportation, **in** as well as **by** can be used with **taxi** or **car.** *Compare:*

Shall we go **by taxi** or **by car?**
Shall we go **in a taxi** or **in a car?**

9·39   DRILL   Complete the answers, using *with, in,* or *by.*

1. How did he write it?   He wrote it *in ink.*
2. Did he go to the bank alone?   No, he went
3. Did anyone help him fill out the application?   No, he filled it out
4. Does Dave usually use a pen to take notes?   No, he usually takes notes
5. Would you prefer to use a pencil or a pen?   I prefer to write
6. Are you going to take a taxi to the station?   No, I'm going

THERE (PLACE) VERSUS THERE IS/ THERE ARE

9·40   — Did you go to the lecture last night?

— Yes, but I didn't see you **there.**

— I'm not surprised. **There** were so many people **there** that it was impossible to find anybody.

■   Adverbial of place **there** should not be confused with subject filler **there** (when it is used to fill the subject position in a sentence). Decide whether each **there** in the preceding sentences is an adverbial of place or a subject filler.

9·41   DRILL   The following sentences have two uses of *there:* (1) *there* as an adverbial of place; (2) *there* as a subject filler—"*there* is, *there* are," etc. Substitute another adverbial of place wherever possible.

— Did you see Steve *there?*

— No, he wasn't *there.* But *there* were a lot of people *there* who said they knew you.

— I can't think of anyone I know who might have been *there.*

— *There* were some interesting people *there.* You and Harry should have been *there.*

Expression of Purpose

9·42   — Why do you suppose they stopped at Centerville instead of Lake City as planned?

— They possibly stopped in Centerville because they wanted **to get some coffee.**

— Most likely they stopped there (**in order**) **to get some gas.**

■   The last two sentences express about the same meaning. They could be restated:

They possibly stopped in Centerville (**in order**) **to get some gas.**
(**In order** is optional in this sentence and in the last sentence in the examples above.)

Most likely they stopped there because they wanted **to get some gas.**

9·43   — Did they stop in Centerville **to get some coffee?**

— No, they stopped there **for gas.**

■ A **for**-phrase instead of a **to**-phrase can be used to express purpose. What kind of a word follows **to**? What kind of a word follows **for**?

■ Sometimes using **for** instead of **to** causes a change in meaning. *Compare:*

He went to the bank **to get some money.**   BUT: He went to the bank **to cash some checks.**
He went to the bank **for some money.**   He went to the bank **for some checks.**

9·44 DRILL Change *for*-phrases to *to* + verb phrases, and *to* + verb phrases to *for*-phrases, in these sentences.

1. Jerry went to his room *for a sweater.* → *Jerry went to his room to get a sweater.*
2. He had to run *to catch the bus.* → *He had to run for the bus.*
3. Did he stop at the Snack Shop *for lunch?*
4. Did he have to wait long *for a table?*
5. He went to Long's Drugstore *to buy some toothpaste.*
6. He had to get a large shopping bag *to carry all of his purchases.*

Modifiers of Adverbs and Adjectives

9·45 She is **very** talkative.
He is **rather** quiet.
She speaks French **extremely** well.
He speaks Spanish **pretty** well.

■ The boldfaced modifiers magnify or limit the quality or characteristic specified by the adverb or adjective. See the shaded area below for rough meanings of various modifiers.

MODIFIERS BY DEGREE

too	to an excessive degree (for a purpose)	**particularly** **especially**	to a good degree (for a purpose)
entirely **completely** **perfectly** **thoroughly** **extremely** **absolutely**	to a maximum degree (for a purpose)	**certainly** **surely** **very**	to a more satisfactory degree
almost **nearly** **practically** **just about**	to a degree nearing perfection or completion	**kind of** **sort of** **somewhat** **fairly** **rather** **pretty** **quite**	to some degree
barely **hardly** **scarcely**	to a mimimum degree (for a purpose)	**enough**	to a sufficient degree (for a purpose)

9·46   DRILL   Read the following sentences; then decide which of these adverbials of degree seems most appropriate for each blank space: *extremely, very, quite, rather, pretty.*

1. The audience applauded the singer for ten minutes. The audience was _____ enthusiastic. Everyone was _____ excited.

2. My art professor seldom praises my work highly. On the other hand, he is not overcritical. He usually says, "This painting is _____ good. You are improving."

3. My mother likes all of my paintings. She says to her friends, "My son is _____ talented. He paints _____ beautiful landscapes."

9·47   I usually cook a steak **too** long, but I didn't cook this steak long **enough**.
The steak is probably not well done **enough** for you, but it isn't **too** rare for my taste.
You poured the tea **too** soon. It isn't strong **enough**.
On the contrary, I didn't pour it soon **enough**. It's **too** strong for me.

- Does **enough** occur before or after the adjective or adverb? Where does **too** occur?

- **Too** indicates an excessive or more than desirable degree; **enough** indicates a sufficient or satisfactory degree.

- **Too** and **enough** are often followed by **for** + (pro)noun or **to** + simple form of the verb.
   The tea is **too weak for you,** but it isn't **weak enough for me.**
   The cake is **too warm to cut.**
   The cake isn't **cool enough to cut.**

9·48   DRILL   Fill in the blanks with *very, too,* or *enough,* as appropriate. Remember that *very* means to a high degree; *too,* to an excessive degree for a person or a purpose; *enough* means sufficient or satisfactory for a person or a purpose.

1. The coffee is _____ good. It's just right. It isn't _____ strong for me, and it is apparently strong _____ for you.

2. These apples are _____ ripe to eat, and those aren't ripe _____ . Those apples over there are ripe _____ , and they look _____ good.

3. It is _____ difficult to cook a roast for a large group of people. It is always _____ rare for some and not well done _____ for others.

4. Please read the directions _____ carefully. You often read the directions _____ hurriedly to grasp the correct sequence of operations. You don't follow the directions carefully _____ to get the best results.

1 Read the following sentences, adding the modifiers at the left.

today	1. The professor was late.
nearly	2. He always gets to class on time.
in his office	3. He held conferences this morning.
at noon	4. He went to the laboratory.
almost	5. He goes to the lab every afternoon.
very much	6. He likes research.
especially	7. He enjoys analyzing plant cells.
sometimes	8. He works too hard.
for relaxation	9. He likes gardening.
very much	10. He also likes tennis.
this term	11. Harold is taking calculus.
too	12. Isn't calculus difficult for him?
enough	13. No, it isn't. The course isn't difficult for him.
too	14. Does he find all his courses easy?
very	15. No, he doesn't. Physics is difficult for him.
often	16. He reviews the material early in the morning.
every week	17. He has to spend extra hours in the laboratory.
very	18. He takes the course seriously.
very much	19. He likes it.
next term	20. He will take another physics course.

2 Here is a chronology° of the life of Gandhi. Read it carefully. Then copy the following paragraphs; substitute adverbials for the question words in parentheses, using the information in the chronology below.

1869: October 2—Mohandas K. Gandhi born in Porbandar, near Bombay.

1887–1890: Gandhi studied law for three years at University College, London.

1891: Admitted to the bar; returned immediately to India; practiced law in Bombay.

1893–1915: Lived in South Africa; practiced law successfully; worked very hard for civil rights of Indians there.

1915–1947: Returned to India; gave up Western ways completely; opposed British policy with nonviolent resistance; gradually convinced that India must become an independent country; undoubtedly a major force in India's fight for freedom.

1947: India finally became an independent country.

1948: January 30—Gandhi fatally wounded by an assassin's bullet in New Delhi.

°**Chronology** = the arrangement of dates or events in the order of their occurrence.

Mohandas K. Gandhi, the great Indian leader, was born (*where? when?*). He studied law (*how long? where?*), and (*when?*) he was admitted to the bar. He then returned (*how soon?*) to India, where he practiced law (*where? how long?*). From (*when?*) to (*when?*) he lived (*where?*), where he practiced law (*how?*) and worked (*how hard?*) for the civil rights of Indians there.

(*When?*) Gandhi returned to India. There he gave up Western ways (*how much?*) and began opposing British policy (*how?*). He (*how soon?*) became convinced that India, in order to have real freedom, must achieve independence. Over the years, he was (*how sure?*) a major force in India's fight for independence. India (*how soon?*) gained independence (*when?*), but only a year later the great leader was (*how seriously?*) wounded by an assassin's bullet (*where? when?*).

3   A chronology, in five parts, of Charles Darwin's life is given here. (1) With long responses, answer the questions that follow each part of the chronology. (2) Then write a short paragraph based on the information in the chronology and your answers to the questions. Use *adverbials* wherever appropriate. The first two questions and the first two sentences of the first paragraph are given as examples. Notice that the sentences in the paragraph are not exactly like the sentences in the answers to the questions.

PART 1

1809: February 12—Charles Darwin, the eminent scientist, was born in Shrewsbury, England; showed unusual interest in natural sciences even at an early age; studied science as an undergraduate.

1831: In December, a few months after graduating from Cambridge University, sailed as a naturalist with a British expedition on the H.M.S. *Beagle.*°

1. Where and when was Charles Darwin born? →
    He was born in Shrewsbury, England, on February 12, 1809.

2. At what age did he show an interest in natural science? →
    He showed unusual interest in science even at an early age.

3. Did he study science as an undergraduate?

4. When did he graduate from Cambridge University?

5. What did he do a few months later?

Example:

   Charles Darwin, the eminent scientist, was born in Shrewsbury, England, on February 12, 1809. Even at an early age, he showed unusual interest in natural science. [Continue paragraph.]

PART 2

1831–1836: Explored the coasts of South America and the Galapagos Islands in the Pacific; searched for fossils and studied plants and animals ceaselessly; observations during the voyage led him eventually to examine evolution, a problem that would preoccupy him the rest of his life.

1836: At the end of the expedition, settled in London and began his writing career; from then on, concerned with the problem of evolution.

°Notice that names of ships are *italicized* in print; in handwriting or typing, they are <u>underlined</u>.

1. How long did the voyage last?

2. Where did the expedition take Darwin?

3. What did he study ceaselessly during that time?

4. What did his observations lead him to?

5. Where did he settle at the end of the voyage?

6. What did he begin to do?

7. What problem did he concern himself with from then on?

PART 3

1842: Moved from London to Down, Kent; published *The Structure and Distribution of Coral Reefs,*° which set forth a theory of reef formation that is still generally sound.

1846–1854: Chiefly engaged in writing monographs on fossils.

1856: Began his first major work, a lengthy volume of his views on evolution through natural selection.

1858: When about half-finished with his manuscript, he received a manuscript from Alfred Russel Wallace, another scientist; startled to discover that it contained a similar theory.

1. When did Darwin move to Down?

2. What else happened in that same year?

3. What did he do from 1846 to 1854?

4. When did he begin his first major work? What was it about?

5. What happened when the manuscript was about half-finished?

6. Why was Darwin startled?

PART 4

1858: July 1—at a historic meeting of the Linnean Society, both Darwin and Wallace presented papers setting forth their coincidentally but separately formulated theories of evolution through natural selection; immediately afterward, Darwin hastened to complete his first major work.

1859: November 24—published *Origin of Species,* which set forth facts on which he based his theory of evolution through natural selection; complete first printing of 1,250 copies sold out on the first day of publication.

1. When was the historic meeting of the Linnean Society held?

2. What happened at that meeting?

3. How soon after that meeting did Darwin proceed with the completion of his first major work?

4. When was *Origin of Species* published? What did it set forth?

5. When was the first printing sold out?

° Notice that titles of books are *italicized* in print; in handwriting or typing, they are underlined.

PART 5

1871: Published *The Descent of Man,* which proposed the theory that man descended from the same group of animals as did the apes. Violent debates raged for many years, but Darwin seldom took part in the controversy; evolution was publicly championed by such prominent scientists as Thomas Huxley in England, Asa Gray in the United States, and Ernst Haeckel in Germany.

1. When was *The Descent of Man* published?

2. What theory did it propose?

3. How long did debates rage about the theory?

4. Did Darwin take part in the controversy?

5. Who publicly championed the evolutionary theory in England? In the United States? In Germany?

PART 6

1882: April 19—died; buried in Westminster Abbey. Controversy still going on and would continue for many years; Darwin, however, destined for a permanent place among the great scientists of all time.

1. When did Darwin die and where is he buried?

2. At the time of his death, was the controversy over the theory of evolution still going on?

3. What was Darwin's destiny?

4   Summarize Charles Darwin's life in 150–200 words based on information in the paragraphs written for Ex. 3. Pay particular attention to adverbials, including sequence signals, as you write.

5   Prepare a short chronology of the life of a great man or woman of your country; then write a brief essay of 100–150 words based on the chronology. Pay particular attention to adverbials, including sequence signals, as you write.

The Indefinite Articles: A/ AN/ SOME

10·1 Would you like **a** ham sandwich or **an** egg salad sandwich?

- **Sandwich** and **egg** are count nouns; that is, they can be counted (**one sandwich, two eggs,** etc.). **An** occurs before singular count nouns beginning with a vowel sound (**an** egg, **an** apple); **a** occurs with other singular count nouns. The following examples show that it is clearly the vowel *sound,* not the letter, that determines the choices of **a** or **an.**

an uncle	**a** heart
an umbrella	**a** university
an hour	**a** union

10·2 Help yourself to **some** cookies and coffee. There's **some** sugar and cream on the coffee table. There's milk in the refrigerator, if you would rather have that.

- **Some** occurs before plural count nouns (**some** pickles, **some** eggs) and noncount nouns (**some** salad, **some** milk). When quantity is not emphasized, **some** is omitted ("There's milk in the refrigerator . . . .")

10·3 There are**n't any** cookies left, and there is**n't any** sugar in the bowl. There's **no** cream in the pitcher either.

- **Not any** and **no** indicate absence of quantity. Are they interchangeable?

- In a question, both **some** and **any** indicate indefinite quantity. *Compare:*

  There isn't **any** cream. Do you have $\begin{Bmatrix} \textbf{some} \\ \textbf{any} \end{Bmatrix}$ milk?

10·4 He ate **two** sandwiches and drank **three** cups of coffee.

- A count noun like **sandwich** can be counted (**two sandwiches,** etc.); however, a noncount noun like **coffee** cannot be counted without measure words like **a cup of** (coffee), **two pots of** (coffee), **three pounds of** (coffee).

- Measure words like **a carton of, a box of,** or **a basket of** can be used with noncount nouns to indicate larger units. *Example:*

Each **box of candy** contains fifty pieces.

These same phrases can also be used with plural count nouns to indicate larger units. *Compare:*

a cracker	**some** crackers	**a box of** crackers
an egg	**some** eggs	**a carton of** eggs

10·5   DRILL   The nouns listed below are all noncount. Use appropriate measure words in answering the question "What did she buy?"

1. gasoline → *She bought ten gallons of gasoline.*

2. oil → *She bought a quart of oil.*

3. wax	7. paste	11. cheese	15. sugar	19. cream	23. honey
4. soap	8. glue	12. bacon	16. salt	20. beer	24. cereal
5. ink	9. milk	13. bread	17. coffee	21. jam	25. lettuce
6. paper	10. butter	14. flour	18. tea	22. jelly	26. beef

10·6

Noncount—material (mass)	*Count—unit*
She likes **lemon** in her tea.	Here's **a lemon.**
It smells like **lime.**	Yes, I just cut **a lime.**
I taste **onion** in the salad.	There's **a large onion** in the salad.
Do you like **roast?**	If so, I'll buy **a roast** for dinner.
Do you like **steak?**	Why don't you order **a steak?**
Do you usually have **dessert?**	No, but I think I'll have **a dessert** now.
We usually have **salad** with dinner.	Did you order **a salad?**
Would you like **pie** or **cake?**	She made **a pie** and **a cake** today.

- Many nouns are *noncount* when they refer to material or substance (**lemon**) and *count* when they refer to units (**a lemon**).

10·7

Noncount—mass	*Count—kind, type, or variety*
Would you like (**some**) **tea?**	Would you like **a green tea** or **a black tea?**
	Would you rather have **a Chinese tea? Our Chinese teas** are especially good.
Would you like **cream** in your coffee?	This is **a rich, heavy cream.**
I smell **gas.**	Is it **a natural gas?** Is it **a gas** or **a liquid? Various gases** are escaping.

■ These examples contain nouns indicating mass of material (noncount) and kind or variety (count).

10·8   *Noncount—abstraction*   *Count—unit*
Beauty is **truth.**   She's **a beauty.**
                                                  A truth is often more painful than
                                                  a lie.

He has **courage.**   He has **a courage** equaled by few of
                                                  his contemporaries.

He has **pride.**   He has **a fierce pride.**

■ The preceding sentences show abstract nouns (noncount) and the same nouns as count units.

10·9   *Noncount—portion or part*   *Count—unit*
Would you like $\begin{cases} \textbf{some} \\ \textbf{a piece of} \end{cases}$ orange?   Sue brought me **an orange** from her tree.

■ These pairs contrast part with the whole unit. *Other examples:*

She made **a pie** and cut it in six pieces.
How many **pieces of pie** did she cut?
Did she ask you if you wanted **some pie?**

10·10   *Waitress:* Did you order **a beer** or **a coffee?**
Customer: Neither. I ordered **a Coke.**

■ Some nouns generally considered noncount are commonly used as units. *Other examples:*

He ordered $\begin{cases} \textbf{a tea.} \\ \textbf{a milk.} \\ \textbf{an ice cream.} \\ \textbf{a whiskey.} \\ \textbf{an orange juice.} \end{cases}$

10·11   DRILL   Make up sentences using the pairs of count and noncount nouns.

1. steak – a steak → *If you like steak so much, why don't you order a steak?*
2. cake – a cake → *She likes cake, so I'll buy a cake for dessert.*

3. dessert – a dessert   9. oil – an oil
4. roast – a roast   10. coffee – a coffee
5. fish – a fish   11. fire – a fire
6. cereal – a cereal   12. courage – a courage
7. ice cream – an ice cream   13. liberty – a liberty
8. gas – a gas   14. beer – a beer

10·12   DRILL   Read the first two examples and follow the same pattern with the others.

1. I'm peeling *an orange.* →

    Would you like some (orange)?
    Would you like a piece of orange?

2. She baked *a cake* today. →

    Would you like some (cake)?
    Would you like a piece of cake?

3. There's *a pie* in the kitchen.

4. Here's *an apple.*

5. I'm slicing *a lemon* for our tea.

6. She baked *a ham.*

7. That looks like *a delicious salad.*

8. There's *a chocolate pudding* in the refrigerator.

PLURAL NOUNS

Regular Plurals: Add the plural suffix—s or es

Group A	Final sound	Plural spelling	Pronunciation
purse	/s/	purses	
rose	/z/	roses	
dish	/š/	dishes	/əz/
lunch	/č/	lunches	
judge	/ǰ/	judges	
garage	/ž/ or /ǰ/	garages	

Notice that after the final sibilant sounds /s, z, š, č, ǰ, ž/, the plural suffix is spelled s or es and pronounced /əz/. Words ending in the letter x, like **box** and **fox,** are spelled **boxes** and **foxes** and pronounced /əz/ because the letter x is pronounced as a consonant cluster /ks/.

Group B	Final sound	Plural spelling	Pronunciation
plate	/t/	plates	
cup	/p/	cups	
cook	/k/	cooks	/s/
chef	/f/	chefs	
breath	/th/	breaths	

In Group B, notice that the plural suffix is spelled s and pronounced /s/. With the following nouns, f changes to v in the plural; the pronunciation is /vz/.

calf-calves	knife-knives	life-lives	thief-thieves
elf-elves	leaf-leaves	sheaf-sheaves	wife-wives
half-halves	loaf-loaves	shelf-shelves	wolf-wolves

The plural of **scarf** and **hoof** can be either scarfs /fs/—hoofs /fs/ or scarves /vz/—hooves /vz/.

The plural of **house (houses)** can be pronounced either /hawsəz/ or /hawzəz/.

Oaths, sheaths, breaths, baths, paths, months, mouths, and **truths** can be pronounced either /ths/ or /thz/.

10·13
Here is **some** { information.
advice.
homework.
news.

- **Information, advice,** and **homework** are noncount nouns and are always singular. **News,** though it looks plural, is also singular.

10·14
Here are **some** { groceries (food).
scissors.
pliers.
tweezers.
trousers.
slacks.
glasses (spectacles).

Here is **a box of** groceries.
Here is **a pair of** scissors.
Here are **two pairs of** pants.

- The nouns in the preceding examples have no singular form; measure words are used to count them.

Group C	Final sound	Plural spelling	Pronunciation
drum	/m/	drums	
bag	/g/	bags	
song	/ng/	songs	
shoe	/uw/	shoes	/z/
play	/ey/	plays	
lady	/iy/ (unstressed)	ladies	

The plural suffix of all words ending in vowel sounds, and of all voiced consonants (see the list of voiced consonants on page 266) except those included in Group A, is spelled **s** or **es** and pronounced /z/. The spelling is **es** when final **y** is changed to the letter **i,** as in **ladies.** The letter **y** is changed to the letter **i** only if it is preceded by a consonant. *Compare:*

lady	ladies		BUT: key	keys
family	families		monkey	monkeys

The spelling of the plural varies for nouns that end in the letter **o.** For the nouns on the left, the spelling is **es;** for those on the right, the spelling is **s.** However, the pronunciation is the same /z/.

hero – heroes	piano – pianos
tomato – tomatoes	solo – solos
potato – potatoes	concerto – concertos
echo – echoes	soprano – sopranos
tornado – tornadoes or tornados	ditto – dittos (sometimes dittoes)

How are the plurals of these nouns pronounced and spelled?

church	vote	monkey	baby	shelf
street	tenor	wish	occupation	wife
son	building	veto	wolf	age
height	address	hero	desire	cat
dog	daughter	lobby	opera	fox
hope	weight	husband	echo	bill

10·15   There were **some people** in front of the store. Four or five **people** were buying newspapers.

- **People** is a plural count noun; **a person** is sometimes used when a singular form is required.

10·16   DRILL   Fill in the blanks with the correct form of the verb.

1. There _____ some people here who want some advice.
   (be)

2. Advice _____ usually free, but information usually _____ money.
   (be)   (cost)

3. There _____ some groceries in that bag. There _____ also a box of groceries on the back porch.
   (be)   (be)

4. There _____ some scissors on the table. There _____ also a pair of scissors in the desk drawer.
   (be)   (be)

5. Homework _____ often boring.
   (be)

6. Here _____ some good news.
   (be)

Plurals of Compound Nouns

Group A	Final sound	Plural spelling	Pronunciation
roómmate	/t/	roómmates	/s/
bóokshelf	/f/	bóokshelves	/z/
lándlady	/iy/ (unstressed)	lándladies	/z/
drúgstore	/ɔr/	drúgstores	/z/
bútter dish	/š/	bútter dishes	/əz/
téaspoon	/n/	téaspoons	/z/
téaspoonful	/l/	téaspoonfuls	/z/

Spelling and pronunciation are determined by the second word in the compound.

Group B	Final sound	Plural spelling	Pronunciation
móther-in-law	/ər/	móthers-in-law[1]	/z/
són-in-law	/n/	sóns-in-law	/z/
córt-martial	/t/	córts-martial	/z/
lady-in-wáiting	/iy/ (unstressed)	ladies-in-wáiting	/z/

Spelling and pronunciation are determined by the first word in hyphenated compounds. Generally the first word receives the heavier or heaviest stress; however, in compounds like **lady-in-wáiting** and **artist-in-résidence** the final word is stressed.

How are these plural compounds pronounced and spelled?

cupful	streetcar	bystander	hanger-on
passer-by	dream wife	maid-of-honor	matron-of-honor
crybaby	sister-in-law	bridesmaid	poet-in-residence

[1] The possessive forms are **mother-in-law's, sons-in-law's,** etc.

The Definite Article: THE

10·17   Here's **a** pen, **some** paper, and **some** envelopes.
Please return **the** pen, but you can keep **the** paper and **the** envelopes.

- **The** occurs with both count and noncount nouns: **the** pen, **the** paper, **the** envelopes.

- A speaker or writer presumably uses **the** instead of **a, an,** or **some** when the identity of the person or thing he is talking about is clear to him and the person he is addressing. *Identity* can be established in several ways.

  1) The identity is clear because the person or thing has just been mentioned.

  Here's **a** pen. Please return **the pen** when you are through with it.

  2) The identity is established by a phrase or clause in the same sentence.

  The pen **that you gave me** doesn't write.   The pen **on the desk** doesn't write.

  Presence of a clause or phrase, however, does not necessarily establish identity. *Compare:*

  I met **a man** who said he knew you.   I met **the man** you told me about.

  3) The situation establishes identity.

  Please close **the door.** (Presumably there is only one door.)
  Did you find **the cat?** (Presumably there is only one cat.)
  Where did you park **the car?**
  Where's **the post office?**

Collective Nouns

	Plural spelling	Pronunciation
committee	committees	/z/
team	teams	/z/
family	families	/z/

Collective nouns like **team, committee, group,** and **family** have plural forms. They differ from other nouns in that both the singular and plural forms can occur with a plural verb. *Compare:*

The committee usually **disagrees** with the mayor on financial matters.
(The committee as a whole disagrees.)

The committee usually **disagree** on financial matters.
(The various members of the committee disagree.)

The committees usually **disagree** on financial matters.
(Two or more committees disagree.)

Nouns with One Form for Singular and Plural

one fish⎫
two fish⎭ (trout, deer, fowl, sheep, species, series)

one Swiss⎫
two Swiss⎭ (Chinese, Japanese)

The plurals **fishes** and **fowls** are used in fields such as marine biology and poultry husbandry, where they have special meanings, but these words have one form in most situations. (See also the proceding section on collective nouns.)

4) The identity is clear because of the uniqueness of the person or thing.

Man has realized his dream of traveling to **the moon.**

The sun and **the planets** remain a mystery.

That wind is coming from **the north.**

5) The identity is clear because of the established use of **the** before cardinal numbers and superlatives. *Examples:*

The first speaker was excellent, but **the second** was dull.

The best speech came first. **The worst** came last.

Although **the** ordinarily occurs before cardinal numbers and superlatives, **a/an** can be used in certain contexts. *Examples:*

The speaker asked for questions. **A man** got up and asked what the speaker thought about the population problem. Before the speaker could answer, **a second man** got up and said he thought the question was improper.

10·18   DRILL   Fill in the blanks with articles (*a/ an/ the/ some*).

1. There were ＿＿＿＿＿＿＿ professional basketball players on Flight 727 from Chicago. ＿＿＿＿＿＿＿ players were all young, lean, and tall. ＿＿＿＿＿＿＿ tallest must have been nearly 7′ tall; ＿＿＿＿＿＿＿ shortest must have been at least 6′2″.

2. Mrs. Neal bought ＿＿＿＿＿＿＿ small chicken and ＿＿＿＿＿＿＿ vegetables for dinner. ＿＿＿＿＿＿＿ first thing she did when she got home was to prepare ＿＿＿＿＿＿＿

Irregular Plurals

Singular

Singular		Plural	
child	/čayld/	children	/číldrən/
foot	/fut/	feet	/fiyt/
gentleman	/jéntəlmən/	gentlemen	/jéntəlmən/
goose	/guws/	geese	/giys/
louse	/laws/	lice	/lays/
man	/mæn/	men	/men/
mouse	/maws/	mice	/mays/
ox	/aks/	oxen	/aksən/
tooth	/tuwth/	teeth	/tiyth/
woman	/wémən/	women	/wímən/

Foreign Plurals

Singular		Plural	
crisis	/əz/	crises	/iyz/
basis	/əz/	bases	/iyz/

Other nouns that follow this pattern are thesis/ theses; hypothesis/ hypotheses; analysis/ analyses.

chicken. She wiped _____ chicken with _____ damp cloth. Then she put _____ oil, wine, vinegar, and seasonings in _____ large bowl. Then she let _____ chicken marinate in _____ mixture for _____ hour before she broiled it. She prepared and cooked _____ vegetables at _____ last possible moment because she didn't want them to be overcooked.

10·19 DRILL   Give additional information about the *italicized* nouns. Notice that these nouns are preceded by *a*; when they are mentioned again, use *the*.

1. *A man* and *a woman* were sitting on *a park bench.* →
   The man was about forty years old. The woman looked somewhat younger. The bench they were sitting on had recently been painted.
2. The man was wearing *a blue suit.*
3. The woman was wearing *a red coat.*
4. The man was looking at *a newspaper.*
5. There was *a picture* on the front page of the newspaper.
6. It was *a picture* of *a large black dog.*
7. The dog was looking into *a telescope.*
8. There was *a caption* below the picture.

Singular		Plural	
alumnus	/əs/	alumni	/ay/
locus	/kəs/	loci	/say/
nebula	/ə/	nebulae	/iy/
alumna	/ə/	alumnae	/iy/
datum	/əm/	data	/ə/
criterion	/ən/	criteria	/ə/

Other nouns in the /əm/–/ən/ category are **agendum/ agenda; stratum/ strata; phenomenon/ phenomena.**

Nouns with Foreign and Regular Plurals

		Foreign plural		Regular plural	
currículum	/ləm/	currícula	/ə/	currículums	/z/
memorándum	/dəm/	memoránda	/ə/	memorándums	/z/
fórmula	/ə/	fórmulae	/iy/	fórmulas	/z/
índex	/deks/	índices	/dəsiyz/	índexes	/əz/
platéau	/tow/	platéaux	/tow/	platéaus	/z/
sýllabus	/bəs/	sýllabi	/bay/	sýllabuses	/əz/

Foreign plurals are preferred in some academic or formal situations, but the regular forms are widely used.

A/ AN/ THE before Nouns Referring to a Group

10·20

The company hired {
a tax expert.
some tax experts.
the tax expert you met.
}   **A tax expert** is
Tax experts are
The tax expert is
} in demand today.

The company bought {
a car.
some cars.
the car you like.
}   **A car** is
Cars are
The car is
} no longer a luxury.

- In the first group of sentences on the left, we are talking about individual persons:

  a tax expert—an unidentified person, someone who is a tax expert

  some tax experts—unidentified persons who are tax experts

  the tax expert you met—the person is identified as "the tax expert you met"

- In the first group of sentences on the right, we are talking about the whole or total group or class of persons:

  a tax expert—a member representing the total group or class

  tax experts—members representing the total group or class

  the tax expert—(**the** + singular noun) represents the total group of tax experts as distinguished from **the tax expert you met.**

POSSESSIVES OR GENITIVES

Possessives of Singular Nouns with Regular Plurals

Singular		Singular + 's		Plural		Plural + '	
prince	/s/	prince's	/əz/	princes	/əz/	princes'	/əz/
judge	/ǰ/	judge's	/əz/	judges	/əz/	judges'	/əz/
cat	/t/	cat's	/s/	cats	/s/	cats'	/s/
clerk	/k/	clerk's	/s/	clerks	/s/	clerks'	/s/
lady	/iy/	lady's	/z/	ladies	/z/	ladies'	/z/

The singular possessive, the plural, and the plural possessive of most nouns are pronounced exactly alike, as illustrated in the preceding examples. Where there is a sound change from singular to plural, as in **wife**, the change will be reflected in the plural possessive.

wife	/f/	wife's	/fs/	wives	/vs/	wives'	/vz/

Possessives of Irregular Nouns

Singular		Singular + 's		Plural		Plural + 's	
man	/æ/	man's	/z/	men	/e/	men's	/z/
ox	/ks/	ox's	/əz/	oxen	/ən/	oxen's	/z/
mouse	/s/	mouse's	/əz/	mice	/s/	mice's	/əz/
child	/d/	child's	/z/	children	/rən/	children's	/z/

The pronunciation of possessives of singular nouns with irregular plurals is determined by the last sound, as shown in the preceding examples. The spelling is 's in both cases.

How are the singular and plural possessives of these nouns spelled and pronounced?

gentleman	mouse	child	thief
woman	goose	alumnus	monkey

- The sentences in the second group (**a car, some cars, the car you like**) are parallel in meaning to those in the first group except that we are talking about *things* instead of *persons.*

- The definite article before a noun is sometimes ambiguous. For example, in the sentence "He likes **the piano,**" it is not clear without knowing the context whether he likes the particular piano under discussion or the class of musical instruments known as **the piano.**

10·21   DRILL   Tell whether the *italicized* nouns refer to an individual or to the whole group.

1. Jack's uncle gave him *a dog.* (one dog, not described here)
2. *Dogs* make good pets. (the whole group of animals classified as dogs)
3. *The dog* is man's best friend.
4. Ben is an excellent *tennis player.*
5. *Tennis players* should display good sportsmanship.
6. A good *tennis player* is highly competitive.
7. There is *the tennis player* who won *the tournament.*
8. He has received *a scholarship* to Yale.

Possessives of Proper Nouns

Singular		Singular + 's		Plural		Plural + '	
Mr. Rich	/č/	Mr. Rich's	/əz/	the Riches	/əz/	the Riches'	/əz/
Mrs. Lake	/k/	Mrs. Lake's	/s/	the Lakes	/s/	the Lakes'	/s/
Dr. Brown	/n/	Dr. Brown's	/z/	the Browns	/z/	the Browns'	/z/
Rose	/z/	Rose's	/əz/				

Proper nouns that end in a consonant + /z/ present a special problem in both pronunciation and writing. Some people write **Charles'** and **Dr. Jones'**; others write **Charles's** and **Dr. Jones's**. Some people say /čarlz/; others say /čarlzəz/. You will not go wrong, however, if you follow the general rules. *Examples:*

the boss	/s/	the boss's	
Alice	/s/	Alice's	} /əz/
Jess	/s/	Jess's	

How are the possessives of these proper nouns spelled and pronounced?

John	Mrs. Smith	Dr. Tadish	Aristotle
Mike	Miss Cox	Senator Church	Euripides

Summary of Plural and Possessive Suffixes

1 Singular noun + possessive suffix: **the lady – the lady's; the woman – the woman's**
2 Singular noun + plural suffix: **the lady – the ladies; the woman – the women**
3 Plural noun + possessive suffix: **the ladies – the ladies'; the women – the women's**

10·22   We need **some money.**   **Money** is the root of all evil.

The money you give can save **a life.**   **Life** can be beautiful.

- Nouns that refer to the whole mass (**all money**) and abstract nouns (**life**) are *not* preceded by articles. *Example:*

   Honesty is a virtue. (NOT: The honesty is a virtue.)

10·23   DRILL   Tell whether the indefinite article *some* or the definite article *the* could be inserted before the *italicized* nouns.

1. Do you like *milk?* (The meaning is "all milk"; reference is to the total mass or class. *Some* cannot be inserted. "Do you like the milk?" is possible, but the meaning would be "the milk in the glass" or "the milk you are drinking.")

2. *Life* is but a dream.

3. Patrick Henry said, "Give me *Liberty* or give me *Death.*"

4. *Absence* makes the heart grow fonder.

5. Put *water* in the bowl.

6. *Water* is essential to *life.*

7. *Time* and *tide* wait for no man.

8. He was willing to put *time* and *effort* into the project.

Prearticles

10·24   **Several of the**
A few of the } boys are members of the club.
Many of the

- Prearticles are phrases like **several of (the)**, **a few of (the)**, and **many of (the)**. Some prearticles change from definite to indefinite when **the** or **of the** is omitted. *Compare:*

several of the people	**several** people
a lot of the people	**a lot of** people
some of the people	**some** people

   Some prearticles, however, remain definite even after **of the** is omitted. *Examples:*

both of the boys	**both** boys
each of the boys	**each** boy

10·25   DRILL   Make up a sentence in which you use a definite prearticle.

1. Joe meets *a lot of* people. → *A lot of the people he meets are tourists.*

2. He introduced us to *several* people. → *We had met several of the people before.*

3. He talked to *some* people.

4. Someone asked him to sing *a few* songs.

5. He doesn't know *many* new songs.

6. I don't know *any* new songs.

7. He listens to *a great deal of* music.

8. I don't listen to *much* music.

10·26 **All** (**of the**) box lunches are in those cartons.

The box lunches are **all** in those cartons.

Each of the children **is** given a box lunch.

The children **are each** given a box lunch.

There is **enough** (**of the**) potato salad for an army.

There is potato salad **enough** for an army.

Both (**of the**) baskets contain fruit.

The baskets **both** contain fruit.

- The sentences with the prearticles on the left can be restated, as shown in the sentences on the right. Sentences with **half** (**of the**) can be stated like this:

  Half (**of the**) sandwiches are chicken.

  Of the sandwiches, **half** are chicken.

  The sandwiches are **half** chicken (and half ham).

10·27 **Any**(**one**) **of the boys** should be able to ride a bicycle.

Any boy should be able to ride a bicycle.

None of the small children will sit still for more than a few minutes.

No small child will sit still for more than a few minutes

- **Any boy** in the first sentence on the right means "all boys"; **no small child** in the second sentence on the right means "not any small children at all."

10·28 DRILL   Give the alternate form.

1. There is enough food for everyone. → *There is food enough for everyone.*

2. All of the box lunches contain two sandwiches. →
   The box lunches all contain two sandwiches.

3. Each of the sandwiches is wrapped separately.

4. All the beverages are in that large box.

5. There are enough oranges for everyone.

6. Both of the boxes contain oranges.

7. Half of the apples are red and half are yellow.

8. Half of the cake is chocolate and half is lemon.

10·29   **Each of the boys** is given a key.   **Each boy** is given a key.

Every one of the boys has a locker.   **Every boy** has a locker.

Neither of the boys is here.   **Neither boy** is here.

Either of the boys is capable of that. **Either boy** is capable of that.

- When **of the** is omitted after **each, every, neither, either,** and **any** in this example, the noun changes to the singular form. Notice, however, that the verb is singular in both cases. You may hear native speakers use a plural verb after "either (neither) of the boys," but in careful writing the singular verb is customary.

10·30   DRILL   Omit *of the* and restate the sentences.

1. Each of the men contributes a dollar a week to the recreation fund. →
   Each man contributes a dollar a week to the recreation fund.
2. Every one of the men has a membership card. → *Every man has a membership card.*
3. Any of the members can propose you for membership.
4. Neither of the members is a friend of mine.
5. Either of the vice-presidents can help you.

Insert *of the* and restate the sentence.

6. Each member is entitled to membership privileges for his dependents. →
   Each of the members is entitled to membership privileges for his dependents.
7. Any dependent of a member is authorized to use the club facilities.
8. Neither swimming pool is very large.
9. Either pool could be enlarged at a minimum cost.
10. Every tennis court is taken by ten o'clock.

10·31   — Has **either of the secretaries** taken the key?

— No. Either **the janitor** or **the security guards have** taken the key.

— Neither **the security guards** nor **the janitor has** the key.

- The verb is singular with **either of the** + *plural noun.* Notice, however, that the verb in the **either . . . or/neither . . . nor** sentences agrees with the second noun. Some native speakers have a tendency to use a plural verb even when the second noun is singular. In careful writing, however, it is customary to make the verb agree with the second noun. (See also §4.8, as well as §14.8.)

10·32   DRILL   Complete the sentences. Use present tenses.

1. — Do any of the children speak Tagalog?

   — No. Neither the older boys nor the little girl _speaks Tagalog_ .

2. — Who erases the chalkboard after class?

   — Either the children or the teacher _____ .

3. — Who turns out the lights and locks the classroom door?

   — Either the teacher or the janitors _____ .

4. — Have you heard anything about next Monday being a holiday?

   — No. Neither the teachers nor the principal _____ .

5. — Are some of the people interested in learning Swahili?

   — No. Neither the men nor the women _____ .

10·33   — Did the guitarist play **much** folk music?

— No, he didn't play **much** folk music, but he played **a lot of** popular music.

— Did he sing **many** French songs?

— No, he didn't sing **many** French songs, but he did sing **a lot of** Brazilian songs.

- **Much** occurs before noncount nouns; **many** occurs before plural count nouns; **a lot of** occurs before both plural and noncount nouns.

10·34

Does he have $\begin{Bmatrix} \textbf{much} \\ \textbf{a lot of} \end{Bmatrix}$ time?   No, but he has $\begin{Bmatrix} \textbf{a lot of} \\ \textbf{lots of} \\ \textbf{plenty of} \end{Bmatrix}$ money.

He doesn't have $\begin{Bmatrix} \textbf{many} \\ \textbf{a lot of} \end{Bmatrix}$ close friends, but he has $\begin{Bmatrix} \textbf{a lot of} \\ \textbf{lots of} \\ \textbf{plenty of} \end{Bmatrix}$ acquaintances.

$\begin{Bmatrix} \textbf{Much} \\ \textbf{A lot of} \end{Bmatrix}$ time was wasted.   We wasted $\begin{Bmatrix} \textbf{a lot of} \\ \textbf{lots of} \\ \textbf{plenty of} \end{Bmatrix}$ money, too.

- **Much** and **many** are interchangeable with **a lot of** in questions, in the predicate of negative sentences, and in subject position in sentences. **A lot of, lots of,** and **plenty of** usually occur in the predicate of short affirmative sentences. In long predicates, however, **much** and **many** are fairly common. *Compare:*

  We wasted **a lot of time**.   We wasted **much time** trying to locate an inexpensive hotel.

- **A lot of, lots of,** and **plenty of** are quite informal in tone. In situations where formality seems in order, **much, a great deal of, many,** and **a large number of** are more appropriate.

10·35   DRILL   Answer these questions, using *a lot of, lots of, plenty of, a great deal of, a large number of, much,* or *many,* as appropriate.

1. Do you spend lots of time in the library? → *Yes, I spent a lot of time there.*
2. Do you get plenty of sleep?
3. Do you have a lot of outside reading to do?
4. Do you have many assignments to complete?
5. Do you spend much time with your friends?
6. Does your country spend a great deal of money on education?
7. Are there many technical schools in your country?
8. Is there much need for teacher-training institutions?

10·36   **Quite a few** of the students who study at the conservatory become music teachers. **A few** students become professional musicians, but very **few** of them become first-rate artists.

The string quartet played **quite a little** eighteenth-century music, **a little** nineteenth-century music, but very **little** twentieth-century music.

- **Few/a few/quite a few** occur before plural count nouns; **little/a little/quite a little** occur before noncount nouns.

- **A little bit of** is used in much the same way as **a little.** *Example:*

    He drank $\begin{Bmatrix} \textbf{a little bit of} \\ \textbf{a little} \end{Bmatrix}$ coffee.

- **Few (a few/little/a little/a little bit of)** + *noun* indicates an unspecified small quantity. **A few, a little,** and **a little bit of** have positive emphasis; **few** and **little** (especially **very few** and **very little**) have a negative emphasis. *Compare:*

    She goes to **a few** operas but **very few** concerts.
    He has **a little** talent but **very little** formal training.

- **Quite a few, quite a little,** and **quite a little bit of** indicate a rather large quantity. *Compare:*

    He has **few** enemies, **a few** very close friends, and **quite a few** business friends.

- **Only** before **a few, a little,** and **a little bit of** has a negative effect. *Compare:*

    He wants **a little** time off, but he has $\begin{Bmatrix} \textbf{only a few} \\ \textbf{very few} \end{Bmatrix}$ vacation days left.

10·37   DRILL   Restate the sentences, using *few/ little/ a few/ a little/ quite a few/ quite a little/ very few,* etc., as appropriate.

1. Mr. and Mrs. Jones have *a lot of friends* in London. →
    Mr. and Mrs. Jones have quite a few friends in London.
2. They have *two or three friends* in Paris.
3. Mr. Jones has *some relatives* in Scotland.
4. Mrs. Jones has *dozens of relatives* in Dublin.

5. Mrs. Jones has *some knowledge* of Irish history.

6. Mr. Jones has *a minimum of interest* in sightseeing.

7. They always spend *two or three days* in London.

8. *Only two or three of their friends* live in central London.

10·38 We need **more money** and **more volunteers** to expand the Summer Camp Program for city children.

So far we have **less money** and **fewer volunteers** than we had last year.

Two years ago we had **the most money** and **the most volunteers** we have ever had in the history of the program.

- **More** and **most** can precede either a noncount or a plural count noun. In formal English, you are likely to see or hear **less** before a noncount noun and **fewer** before a plural count noun. In more informal situations, you will also hear "less volunteers," "less people," and so on.

- **More, most, fewer,** and **less** can be followed by **of the.** *Examples:*

Most of the volunteers are women.   **More of the volunteers** should be men.

10·39 DRILL Fill in the blanks with *more, less, fewer,* or *most,* as appropriate.

1. There is _____ of a need than ever for community projects.

2. However, people seem to have _____ time than ever to devote to these projects.

3. _____ men are too busy with their jobs to volunteer their services.

4. _____ women can afford to stay home today than, say, a decade ago.

5. Today_____ family income goes for food and rent, and parents need_____

   money than one salary allows to provide for the education of their children.

10·40 There **are a number of experienced salesmen** in the shoe department. **A couple of the salesmen have been** with the company for more than thirty years.

The number of men who leave the department **is** surprisingly small.

- With **a couple of** or **a number of** + *plural noun,* the verb is plural; with **the number of** + *plural noun,* the verb is singular.

10·41 DRILL Fill in the blanks with appropriate forms of *be.*

1. There _____ a number of customers in the store.

2. A couple of them _____ very impatient.

3. The number of salesclerks in comparison to the customers _____ very small.

4. A number of people _____ complaining about the service.

5. The number of complaints _____ indicative of customer dissatisfaction.

10·42   I'll take **two** pencils, and you keep **the rest.**
I'll take this **much** paper, and you keep **the rest.**

- **The rest** can be used to indicate the remainder of count units (**pencils, envelopes**) or noncount material (**paper, glue**).

10·43   Here are **five** pencils. I'll take **two**, and you take $\begin{cases} \textbf{the rest.} \\ \textbf{the others.} \end{cases}$

Here are **two pens.** You take **one**, and I'll take **the other.**
I have **three notebooks.** I need **two**, but you can have **the other.**

- **The others** is used when the remainder is more than one; with **the other**, the remainder is always one.

10·44   DRILL   Complete the sentences with *the others* or *the other*, as appropriate. In which sentences is *the rest* also a possibility?

1. Bill used to have two tennis rackets, but he sold one to me and _____ to his cousin.

2. Bill received two red shirts for his birthday. He gave one to his brother and kept _____ for himself.

3. Bill also received five popular records for his birthday. He liked one very much, but he didn't care for _____ .

4. Bill bought six tickets to the Youth Fair. He kept one ticket and gave _____ to his friends.

10·45   *Situation:* I have two pens.

I want $\begin{cases} \textbf{the red one} \\ \textbf{this one} \\ \textbf{that one} \end{cases}$, but you can have $\begin{cases} \textbf{the other one.} \\ \textbf{the other.} \end{cases}$

Situation: I have a lot of pencils.

I need $\begin{cases} \textbf{the red ones} \\ \textbf{these} \\ \textbf{those} \end{cases}$, but you can have $\begin{cases} \textbf{the other ones.} \\ \textbf{the others.} \\ \textbf{the rest.} \end{cases}$

- **The other ones**, like **the others**, means that the remainder is more than one; **the other one**, like **the other**, means the remainder is one. What can we use in place of **the other ones**? Can we use **the rest** in place of **the other one**?

- Notice that **ones** does not follow **these** or **those.** *Example:*

I need **these.**   (NOT: I need these ones.)

10·46 DRILL Complete the sentences, using *the other one* or *the other ones*, as appropriate. What could you use in place of *the other one?* What could you use in place of *the other ones?*

1. I have two dictionaries. You can use this one, and I'll use _____ .

2. — Do you like these shirts?

   — I rather like the yellow one, but I don't like _____ at all.

3. Joe took two pictures of Peggy. He gave the better one to her and put _____

   in his wallet.

4. — You have a lot to carry. Let me help you.

   — Thank you. If you carry this large package, I can manage _____ .

5. Joe had three $10 bills. He spent two and put _____ away for a rainy day.

10·47

I've had **two cups of coffee**, but I'd like $\begin{cases} \textbf{another.} \\ \textbf{another one.} \\ \textbf{another cup of coffee.} \end{cases}$

- **Another** means "one more." It is used with singular count nouns; however, because some nouns generally considered noncount are used as units, you will hear: "I'd like **another coffee** (orange juice/tea, etc.)." (See also §10.10.)

   We would ordinarily say, "I'd like **some more cream**" (NOT: "I'd like another cream") unless the cream is served in individual containers.

- To avoid confusing **another** with **the other** (**one**) remember that **another** means "one more" and **the other** (**one**) means "the one remaining." *Compare:*

   — I've had two cups of coffee, but I'd like **another.**
   — Have you tried both cakes?
   — No, I've had a piece of the chocolate, but I haven't tried **the other.**

10·48 DRILL Complete the dialog, using *another* or *the other* (*one*), as appropriate. *Situation:* One of the hostesses at a meeting notices that a guest has finished eating a piece of chocolate cake.

Hostess: Would you like _____ piece of chocolate cake?

Guest: No, thank you. I couldn't possibly eat _____ piece. It's very delicious, but it *is* rich.

Hostess: We have two kinds of cake. Would you like to try a piece of _____ ?

Guest: What kind of cake is _____ ?

Hostess: I believe _____ is a sponge cake. At any rate it is not as rich as the chocolate cake.

Guest: Thank you. I'm tempted, but I couldn't eat _____ thing. I'd like _____ cup of coffee, though.

10·49   — Would you say **Americans** are friendly?

— I'd say **some Americans** are friendly.

— I agree. **Some of the Americans** we've met have been very friendly.

■ In the question above, the person is asking whether the total group of Americans is friendly. The reply is that various members of the total group are friendly. The third person agrees and adds that certain ones of those he has met have been friendly.

■ **Some** as a prearticle receives more stress than **some** as an indefinite article. *Compare:*

We met **sŏme** English people.
(individuals who were English)

Sóme of the English people we met were very friendly.
(a portion of the particular English people we met)

Sóme English people are very reserved.
(part of the total group known as Englishmen)

10·50   **Sóme Americans** are very friendly, and **others** are quite unfriendly.

■ Notice that **others** does not necessarily include the remainder of the total group. Compare **others** with **the others** in these sentences:

Some people are foolish; **others** are wise.
(still others might be somewhere in between)

She gave me four magazines. I want to keep this one, but you can have **the others**.
(the remainder—the three that are left—the rest)

10·51   DRILL   The statements below are about the *total* class of persons or things. Make sentences about *part* of the total class; use *sóme* and *óthers*.

1. Americans are aggressive. →
   Sóme Americans are aggressive, and óthers are quite timid.

2. Swedes are blond.

3. Italian men are very romantic.

4. Canadians speak both French and English.

5. Chinese students are very serious.

6. Russians have no sense of humor.

7. Mexicans are very industrious.

8. Arabs are born public speakers.

1 Fill in the blanks with *a/ an/ some/ the*. If an article is not needed, leave the space blank.

1. I have saved _____ money, and I am now planning to buy _____ new car. _____ car must meet the following qualifications: (a) it must be _____ compact model; (b) it must get at least twenty miles to _____ gallon of _____ gas; (c) it must have _____ automatic shift. _____ color isn't so important, but I would prefer _____ blue or beige to other colors.

2. Bangkok, _____ capital of Thailand, is _____ city of more than _____ million inhabitants. It is _____ headquarters of many international business firms and _____ popular city for _____ conventions. It is also one of _____ favorite stopover points in _____ airline travel in Southeast Asia.

    Although Bangkok keeps pace with _____ modern world, _____ tourists, enchanted by _____ splendor of its temples and palaces and _____ colorful life along its canals, usually come away with _____ impression that they have visited _____ fairy-tale city.

3. In his youth, Samuel Langhorne Clemens worked as apprentice to _____ pilot on _____ steamboat that traveled up and down the Mississippi River. In measuring _____ depth of _____ river, it was customary to use _____ phrase "mark twain," meaning "two fathoms deep." This is _____ origin of _____ celebrated name Mark Twain, which Clemens assumed when he began his remarkable literary career.

4. Yesterday I received _____ book from _____ friend. _____ title of _____ book is *Italian Villas and Palaces* by Georgina Masson. It is _____ very beautiful book, full of _____ photographs of _____ elegant buildings and gardens. I am sure I will spend many pleasant hours looking at _____ photographs and dreaming of _____ trips to Italy. I think my friends will also enjoy looking at it and choosing _____ favorite palace or villa.

    I have already selected _____ villa of my dreams, and I hope to make _____ trip to it some day. _____ villa, called Isola Bella, is located on _____ rocky island in Lake Maggiore in _____ province of Piedmont in northern Italy. _____

villa, according to _____ book, was named after the wife of the Italian count who began, in 1630, to convert _____ island into _____ pleasure garden. Even today _____ gardens there are perhaps _____ most famous in all Italy. Several terraces, rising like steps above _____ lake, are covered with statuary, green lawns, and exotic shrubs such as _____ giant camellias and magnolias.

5.   _____ poet Robert Frost once remarked that nature hints and hints until _____ man finally takes _____ hint. _____ point seems well taken, for _____ history provides _____ excellent examples of _____ men who profited from _____ lessons of nature. Consider this well-known story about _____ scientist Isaac Newton.

Newton was sitting in _____ garden drinking _____ tea when he saw _____ apple fall from _____ tree to _____ ground. No doubt he had seen _____ apples fall from trees before, but for _____ first time he was struck by _____ significance of what he had seen. He suddenly realized that the same force that pulled the apple to _____ ground kept _____ moon moving in _____ orbit around _____ earth and _____ planets moving in _____ orbits around _____ sun. _____ incident started him on _____ train of thought that eventually resulted in the formulation of _____ law of gravity.

6.   The solar system is so vast that it is difficult to comprehend _____ great distances between _____ various members of _____ system. _____ ray of _____ sunlight, traveling at _____ rate of 186,280 miles per second, takes _____ fraction over 8 minutes to reach _____ earth, almost $5\frac{1}{2}$ hours to reach Pluto, _____ outermost planet in _____ solar system, and about 4.3 years to reach _____ nearest star, Alpha Centauri. These distances are great, but they are insignificant in comparison with _____ vastness of _____ universe, which staggers _____ imagination.

7.   Pluto, _____ last planet in _____ solar system to be discovered, was first observed in 1930 when it appeared as _____ faint object on _____ photographs taken by Clyde Tombaugh, _____ young astronomer, at _____ Lowell Observa-

tory at Flagstaff, Arizona. Pluto has _____ average distance from _____ sun of 3,675,300,000 miles and travels at _____ rate of about three miles per second in its orbit. It takes nearly 248 years to go around _____ sun. Some astronomers believe that Pluto may have been _____ satellite of Neptune.

8.   Prehistoric man did not make the same demands on his eyes as modern man. His light was _____ sun and _____ moon; he didn't sit in _____ cave reading _____ newspapers and _____ books or watching television; and _____ air he breathed was free from smoke and smog. His distance vision, sharpened from birth by _____ precarious existence he led, was so extraordinary that on _____ clear night he could see ten stars in the Pleiades. (We know this from _____ drawing on _____ cave wall.) As _____ centuries went by and _____ demands on human eyes became highly diversified, it was believed that only six stars made up this famous cluster of stars. _____ invention of _____ telescope proved prehistoric man was on _____ right path, for it revealed not just ten major stars but hundreds of minor ones as well.

9.   According to evolutionary concepts, human speech was _____ last in a long line of _____ developments that led to the day when _____ man truly became _____ man—that is, when he learned to talk. First, _____ animals that crawled out of _____ sea to roam _____ earth developed _____ hearing in order to be prepared for approaching dangers. Next, perhaps over billions of years, _____ terrestial creatures learned to phonate; they gradually developed _____ crude sounds, which served as _____ communication signals. Eventually, _____ sounds were refined, as is evidenced in _____ singing of _____ birds. Finally, again after millions of years, man further refined phonation into _____ articulated language.

       We can witness this development with each newborn baby, who hears for about _____ year before he can intentionally produce _____ speech sounds. Too, _____ infants can babble _____ melodies before they can talk. Furthermore, _____ child takes at least _____ year to form his babbling into meaningful communication.

In short, _____ sequence in _____ development of _____ human speech is as follows: (1) _____ hearing, (2) _____ phonation, and musical use thereof, and (3) _____ refinement of articulated sounds into _____ language.

2 Fill in the blanks, as appropriate, with words like *several, many, more, another, the other, other, others, one, a few, all* (*of the*), *some* (*of the*), etc. There may be more than one possibility for some blanks. (Refer to §10.24–10.51.)

1.   There are _____ types of rocks, but they can be conveniently classed into three categories: _____ type is classed as igneous; _____ type is the sedimentary; and _____ type is the metamorphic.

Almost _____ igneous rocks are solid and crystalline, but _____ of them appear so dense that the crystals cannot be seen by the naked eye whereas _____ (of them) have large, easily seen crystals. Sedimentary rocks are often found in layered formations; _____ of them contain fossils, and _____ of them have markings from mud cracks or ripples from waves. _____ type, the metamorphic, is rock that has changed over time; for example, _____ marble results from the recrystallization of calcite in limestone. _____ metamorphic rocks are readily recognized by their band marks; _____ of them can also be split into slabs.

2.   Although expressions like "Actions speak louder than words" and "One picture is worth a thousand words" have been around a long time, only recently have social scientists turned their attention to nonverbal communication. In the last decade or so, however, they have made _____ startling discoveries. _____ of them, for example, is that we convey _____ meaning through nonverbal means than by the words we speak. _____ discovery is that, where there is _____ inconsistency between verbal and nonverbal messages (for instance, when we say *no* but our eyes and vocal inflections say *yes*), the nonverbal messages "win"; that is, _____ listeners give greater credibility to the nonverbal than to the verbal.

There are _____ kinds of nonverbal messages. _____ type includes bodily gestures, postures, and positions; for example, _____ gestures convey friendliness, while _____ convey anger. Handshakes are _____ means of expressing "hidden" meanings. Perhaps you can recall _____ hands that are warm and firm but _____ that are weak and limp. What do different handshakes say to you?

_____ nonverbal messages can be "spoken" by furniture arrangement in a room. Can you think of _____ rooms that convey _____ warmth and _____ rooms that suggest coldness? What is there about _____ of these rooms that makes you feel as you do?

Strangely enough, up to now there has been almost _____ consideration of nonverbal communication in education. _____ educators, now aware of this vital force, are considering _____ ways to include nonverbal training throughout the curriculum.

3 List the main points in passage 9 of Ex. 1. From this list, summarize the main points of the passage. Pay particular attention to the use of articles as you write your summary.

4 Look up information in an encyclopedia about one of the other planets—Neptune, Mercury, Uranus, Mars, Jupiter, Saturn, or Venus—and write a paragraph similar to the one about Pluto in passage 7 of Ex. 1. For example, you might tell (1) when and by whom the planet was discovered; (2) how far the planet is from the sun; (3) how fast the planet travels in orbit and how many years it takes to go around the sun; and (4) whether or not it has satellites. Pay particular attention to the use of articles as you write your paragraph.

5 List the main categories of a scientific classification (trees, birds, chemicals, etc.) or from an area of interest to social scientists (types of families, basic human needs, learning processes, etc.); if necessary, refer to an encyclopedia or a basic sociology or psychology book. Then write one or more paragraphs similar to those in Ex. 2. Pay particular attention to the use of prearticles as you write.

ARTICLES WITH

PROPER NOUNS

No Article versus THE before Place Names

11·1 **Chicago** is on **Lake Michigan.**
The Great Lakes are between **Canada** and **the United States.**

- Place names occur with and without **the.** Sometimes it is necessary to learn **the** as part of the name (**the White House, the Hague,** etc.). However, in many cases, we can associate **the** with types of place names.

11·2 **Australia** is the smallest of the six continents.
Chicago is in **Cook County, Illinois.**
Yellowstone National Park is a popular vacation spot.
Mr. Driggers' office is on **Davis Drive.**

- *Continents, countries, states, counties, cities, streets,* and *parks*—with few exceptions—occur without **the.** *Exceptions:*

  the Hague (a city in **the Netherlands**)
  the Avenue of the Americas (a street in New York City)
  the Champs Élysées (a street in Paris)
  the Ringstrasse (a series of connected streets in Vienna)
  the Alameda (a park in Mexico City; also a street in Berkeley, California)

11·3 **France** is noted for its great wines.
The Republic of France was among the original signers of the United Nations Charter.

- Most countries and states have two forms of proper names—one without an article (**France, Canada,** etc.) and one with **the** + *class name* + **of** (**the Republic of France, the Kingdom of Thailand, the State of Michigan,** etc.). Although the names **the United States, the Soviet Union, the Netherlands,** and **the United Kingdom** are widely used, for most countries the form with **the** is used primarily in formal contexts. *Compare:*

  Charunee lives in **Thailand.**
  The Kingdom of Thailand is also known as Siam.

11·4   DRILL   Cover the left-hand column and give the alternate names for the countries in the right-hand column. Then cover the right-hand column and see whether you can give the alternate names in the left-hand column.

the Union of Soviet Socialist Republics	the Soviet Union/Russia
the United States of America	the United States
the Republic of the Philippines	the Philippines
the United Arab Republic	Egypt
the Empire of Ethiopia	Ethiopia
the Kingdom of Afghanistan	Afghanistan

Add names of other countries; then practice these names, using the same procedure as above.

11·5   **Miami University** is in Oxford, Ohio.
The University of Miami is in Coral Gables, Florida.
Michigan State University is in East Lansing, Michigan.
The University of Michigan is in Ann Arbor, Michigan.
The State College of Washington is in Pullman, Washington.

■   When the name that identifies (**Miami, Michigan,** etc.) comes first, there is no article. *Compare:*

Miami University	BUT: **the** University of Miami
Michigan State University	**the** State College of Washington

11·6   DRILL   Tell where each college or university is located. Use *the* before the name where appropriate.

1. University of Oregon/Eugene, Oregon ⎫ →
   Oregon State University/Corvallis, Oregon ⎭
   The University of Oregon is in Eugene, Oregon. Oregon State University is in Corvallis, Oregon.

2. University of Washington/Seattle, Washington
   Washington University/St. Louis, Missouri

3. University of Texas/Austin, Texas
   Texas Christian University/Fort Worth, Texas

4. University of Virginia/Charlottesville, Virginia
   Virginia State College/Petersburg, Virginia

5. University of Florida/Gainesville, Florida
   Florida State University/Tallahassee, Florida

6. Harvard University/Cambridge, Massachusetts
   University of Massachusetts/Amherst, Massachusetts

7. University of Arizona/Tucson, Arizona
   Northern Arizona University/Flagstaff, Arizona

8. University of Montreal/Montreal, P.Q., Canada
   Huron College/London, Ontario, Canada

11·7   **The Panama Canal** connects **the Atlantic** and **the Pacific.**
The Nile flows into **the Mediterranean.**
The Painted Desert and **the Petrified Forest** are two of Arizona's attractions.

- **The** occurs before the proper names of *oceans, seas, gulfs, rivers, canals, deserts,* and *forests.* The word **ocean** is often omitted; the word **sea, river,** or **desert** is also often omitted, particularly when the place is well known. **Ocean** and **Sea** are not omitted in **the Indian Ocean** and **the China Sea,** however.

ARTICLE USAGE WITH PROPER NAMES

Type of name	Name (no THE)	THE + name	THE (class name) of + name
1. Continents	Africa/ Asia/ Europe/ South America		the continent of Africa/ the continent of Asia
2. Countries, states, provinces, counties, empires, kingdoms, dynasties, etc.	Austria/ Indonesia/ Canada/ Oklahoma/ Quebec/ Cook County	the Sudan/ the United States/ the Soviet Union/ the United Kingdom/ the Netherlands/ the United Arab Republic/ the Ottoman Empire/ the Ming Dynasty	the Republic of Austria/ the Kingdom of Norway/ the State of Oklahoma/ the Province of Quebec/ the United States of America (the USA)/ the Union of the Soviet Socialist Republics (the USSR)/ the British Commonwealth of Nations
3. Geographical areas	Eastern Europe/ North Africa/ Southern California	the North Pole/ the South Pole/ the Equator	
4. Cities	Boston/ Tokyo	the Hague	the city of Boston
5. Streets	Spruce Street/ Fifth Avenue/ Sunset Boulevard	the Champs Élysées/ the Ringstrasse	the Avenue of the Americas
6. Parks, plazas, squares, etc.	Central Park/ Hyde Park/ Yosemite (National Park)/ Plaza Liberdad/ Washington Square	the Alameda/ the Zócalo/ the Tuileries/ the Everglades	
7. Islands, lakes, and mountains	*Singular:* Wake Island/ Lake Geneva/ Mount Whitney[1]	*Plural:* the Canary Islands/ the Great Lakes/ the Andes Mountains	the Isle of Man
8. Oceans, seas, rivers, canals, deserts, and forests		the Atlantic Ocean/ the Red Sea/ the Tigris River/ the Suez Canal/ the Sahara Desert/ the Black Forest	

[1] For exceptions, see §11.9.

11·8 **DRILL** Use *the* where appropriate.

1. Tiber (river)/ Italy → *The Tiber (River) is in Italy.*
2. Gobi (desert)/ Asia
3. Mojave (desert)/ United States
4. Black Forest/ Germany
5. Panama Canal/ Central America
6. Grand Canal/ Venice
7. Volga (river)/ Soviet Union
8. Waal (river)/ Netherlands

(*continued on next page*)

Type of name	Name (no THE)	THE + name	THE (class name) of + name
9. Universities, colleges, schools, institutes	Oregon State University/ New York University		the University of Oregon/ the City College of New York/ the State College of Washington
10. Businesses (stores, companies, hotels, restaurants, etc.)	Penney's/ Sears/ Mary's Beauty Salon/ Joe's Cafe[2]	the J. C. Penney Company/ the All-Nite Grocery Store/ the Fox Theater/ the Ritz Hotel/ the Hotel Ambassador	
11. Libraries, museums		the Louvre/ the British Museum/ the Huntington Library	the Museum of Modern Art/ the Library of Congress
12. Buildings, monuments	Independence Hall/ Carnegie Hall/ Wheeler Auditorium	the Empire State Building/ the Civic Auditorium/ the Eiffel Tower/ the White House/ the Taj Mahal/ the Sphinx/ the Acropolis	the Tomb of the Unknown Soldier/ the Statue of Liberty
13. Holidays	Christmas/ Thanksgiving/ New Year's Day/ Washington's Birthday		the Fourth of July
14. Title of officials	Queen Elizabeth/ President Kennedy/ Prime Minister Nehru		the Queen of England/ the President of the United States/ the Prime Minister of India/ the Secretary of State[3]
15. Official bureaus, documents, etc.		the Magna Carta/ the Monroe Doctrine/ the U.N. Secretariat/ the U.S. Congress	the Department of State/ the Declaration of Independence

[2] A business title containing the possessive form of a proper noun does not usually require an article. When the noun would be common rather than proper if it were not in the title, **the** is usually required. *Compare:* **Penney's** is in the next block.   There's a sale at **the Youth Arcade.**
[3] Full titles are often shortened when the reference is obvious; for example, we may say "the President" when we know we are referring to "the President of the United States."

9. Nile (river)/ Mediterranean (sea) → *The Nile flows into the Mediterranean.*

10. Amazon (river)/ Atlantic (ocean)

11. Yukon (river)/ Pacific (ocean)

12. Yangtze (river)/ China Sea

13. Lena (river)/ Arctic (ocean)

14. Godavari (river)/ Indian Ocean

11·9   **Lake Ontario** is one of **the Great Lakes.**
Mont Blanc rises to 15,781 feet, the highest point of **the Alps.**
Luzon is the largest of **the Philippine islands.**

■   **The** occurs before *plural* islands, lakes, and mountains; however, *singular* islands, lakes, and mountains usually occur without **the.** *Exceptions:*

the Matterhorn	**the Great Salt Lake**
the Jungfrau	**the Gran Paradiso**
the Finsteraarhorn	**the Isle of Man**

11·10   DRILL   Use *the* where appropriate.

1. Lake Louise/ Canada → *Lake Louise is in Canada.*

2. Lake Geneva/ Switzerland

3. Great Lakes/ North America

4. Lake Victoria/ Africa

5. Blue Lakes/ California

6. Samoa/ South Pacific

7. Mindanao/ Philippines

8. Kauai/ Hawaii

9. Nassau/ Bahamas

10. Queen Elizabeth Islands/ Arctic Ocean

11. Mount Ararat/ Turkey

12. Mount Everest/ Himalayas

13. Matterhorn/ Switzerland

14. Andes/ South America

15. Pike's Peak/ Rocky Mountains

A/AN versus THE before Proper Nouns

11·11   — There's **an Alice Mills** on the phone.
— Is that **the Alice Mills** you told me about?

— There's **a Broadway** in almost every city.
— **The Broadway** I'm referring to is in New York City.

■   In the first pair of sentences, **an Alice Mills** is "a woman by the name of Alice Mills," and **the Alice Mills** is "the particular woman by that name that you told me about." Is there a shift from **a** to **the** in the second pair of sentences? What does **a Broadway** mean? What does **the Broadway** mean?

11·12   — Do **the Andersens** live on Elm Street?

— There's **an Andersen family** on Elm Street, but I don't think it's **the Andersen family** you mean.

■ **The Andersens** and **the Andersen family** mean about the same thing. **An Andersen family** means "a family by the name of Andersen."

11·13   DRILL   Shift from *a/an* to *the*.

1. Main Street in Los Angeles →

   I know there's a Main Street in Los Angeles, but it's not the Main Street I'm talking about.

2. Charles Jones on the list

3. Woolworth's on First Street

4. Post office in the next block

5. Hilton Hotel in Istanbul

6. Rotary Club in your city

7. Paris in Texas

8. Bank of America down the street

9. Foster's Restaurant in the Tower Building

10. Earle family across the street

1 Fill in the blanks with *the* where appropriate. (*Note:* This exercise serves as a review of articles before common nouns and proper names.)

Here is a geography quiz. How many of the questions can you answer?

Q: Name the world's three largest cities.

A: _____ three largest cities are _____ Tokyo, _____ New York City, and _____ London.

Q: What is Tasmania?

A: Tasmania is a large island, bounded by _____ Indian Ocean and _____ Tasman Sea. Politically, it was part of _____ New South Wales until 1825; and it became a state in _____ Commonwealth of _____ Australia in 1901.

Q: Describe the Great Lakes.

A: These five fresh-water lakes are located between _____ Canada and _____ United States. _____ largest is _____ Lake Superior and _____ smallest is _____ Lake Ontario. _____ lakes are linked to _____ Atlantic Ocean, by means of _____ Saint Lawrence Seaway, as well as to _____ Mississippi River and _____ Gulf of Mexico.

Q: What countries make up the United Kingdom?

A: _____ United Kingdom consists of _____ England, _____ Scotland, _____ Wales, and _____ Northern Ireland. _____ Channel Islands and _____ Isle of Man are also under the jurisdiction of _____ United Kingdom.

Q: Name the four largest oceans in the world.

A: The four largest oceans in _____ world are _____ Pacific Ocean, _____ Atlantic Ocean, _____ Indian Ocean, and _____ Arctic Ocean. _____ Pacific Ocean is _____ largest; _____ Arctic Ocean is _____ smallest of _____ four.

Q: What is the name of the mountain range that stands between the Caspian Sea and the Black Sea?

A: _____ Caspian Sea and _____ Black Sea are separated by _____ Caucasus.

Q: What is the largest inland body of water?

A: _____ Caspian Sea is _____ largest inland body of water.

Q: What is the smallest independent state in Europe and who is the ruler?

A: _____ smallest independent state in _____ Europe is _____ Vatican City, which consists of 108.7 acres, including _____ Vatican Palace and _____ Saint Peter's Cathedral. _____ Pope is the supreme ruler of _____ Vatican City and its some 1,000 inhabitants.

Q: What is the second smallest independent state in Europe?

A: The principality of Monaco is _____ second smallest independent state in _____ Europe. _____ Monaco covers an area of 370 acres. It is encircled by the French department of the Alpes-Maritimes and _____ Mediterranean Sea.

2 Fill in the blanks with *a/an* or *the* where appropriate. (*Note:* This exercise also serves as a review of articles before common nouns and proper nouns.)

1.   _____ Captain John Preston gave a speech in _____ Johnson Memorial Hall on _____ Wednesday evening, _____ seventh of _____ June. _____ captain talked about his experiences in _____ Merchant Marine. His ship carried cargo to every continent in _____ world, from _____ tip of Africa to _____ northernmost ports in _____ North America.

Among the ports of call were _____ Pago Pago in _____ Samoan Islands in _____ South Seas; _____ Cartagena in _____ Republic of _____ Colombia in _____ South America; and _____ Istanbul on _____ Bosporus, which he reached through _____ Mediterranean and _____ Aegean Sea. _____ captain had _____ side trips to many interesting places. He recalled, in particular, _____ camel ride across _____ Sahara Desert and _____ mountain-climbing expeditions in _____ Himalayas and up _____ Mont Blanc. He once spent two nights in _____ igloo with _____ Eskimo family; in contrast, five weeks later he stayed a week in _____ Raffles Hotel in _____ Singapore.

2.   Professor Doe was born in _____ State of _____ Tennessee. He lived on _____ Dogwood Road in _____ north part of _____ town in which he spent his childhood. He attended _____ Jackson Grammar School and _____ Robert E. Lee High School. He received _____ A.B. degree at _____ University of Tennessee, _____ M.A. at _____ Vanderbilt University, and _____ Ph.D. at _____ Teachers College, _____

Columbia University. He now teaches in _____ education department at _____ university in Texas. Recently he presented _____ paper at _____ National Science Educators convention, which was held at _____ Holiday Inn Hotel in _____ nation's capital.

3.   According to _____ Census Bureau survey made public in 1971, nearly 5 percent of _____ total population of _____ United States identify themselves as having _____ origins in _____ Spanish-speaking country. These some 9,230,000 Americans are _____ next largest minority group to _____ American Negroes, or Blacks, who comprise 11.1 percent of _____ total population, according to _____ census figures published in 1971.

Of the 9,230,000 Americans with _____ origins in _____ Spanish-speaking countries, 5,000,000, or 55 percent, are _____ Mexican Americans; 1,150,000, or 15.8 percent, are of _____ Puerto Rican origin; 565,000, or 6.1 percent, are of Cuban origin; 556,000, or 6 percent, have _____ origins in either _____ Central or _____ South American country; the remaining 1,582,000, or 17.1 percent, are listed as "other Spanish."

_____ census survey also revealed that three-fifths of _____ Americans with _____ origins in _____ Spanish-speaking countries live in _____ states of _____ Arizona, _____ California, _____ Colorado, _____ New Mexico, and _____ Texas; that _____ Spanish is currently spoken in the homes of about one-half of _____ population; and that 7,300,000, or 79 percent, were born in _____ continental United States, _____ Puerto Rico, or outlying areas of _____ United States.

4.   According to _____ preliminary count for _____ 1970 Census, _____ American Indian population of _____ United States was 791,839. This figure amounts to _____ increase of 268,248, or 50 percent, since 1960. _____ count also revealed that 53 percent of _____ Indians were living in _____ five states in 1970. _____ state with _____ largest number of Indians was _____ Oklahoma, with _____ Indian population of 97,731. _____ Arizona and _____ California were close behind, with populations of 95,812 and 91,018, respectively. _____ Indian population in _____ New Mexico was 72,788, and _____ North Carolina had _____ population of 43,387.

3 Write brief dialogs about some of the names below (or names which you add to the list), shifting from *a* to *the* or vice versa in referring to the proper name. *Example:*

A: There's *a* Christopher Columbus on the phone for you.

B: Is it *the* Christopher Columbus who discovered America?

A: Don't be silly. You know perfectly well that he died a long time ago. This is *a* Christopher Columbus from New York City.

B: Oh, then that must be *the* Christopher Columbus who's in stocks and bonds. My uncle has known *the* Columbus family for years.

1. Christopher Columbus	8. Jacqueline Onassis
2. Aristotle	9. Albert Einstein
3. Mahatma Gandhi	10. Simón Bolívar
4. William Shakespeare	11. Greta Garbo
5. Marco Polo	12. W. C. Fields
6. Benjamin Franklin	13. Enrico Caruso
7. Napoleon Bonaparte	14. Sigmund Freud

4 Develop one or more paragraphs from each of the lists. First, read the information in the lists. Second, decide how the material could be organized into a paragraph or several paragraphs. Finally, write the paragraph or paragraphs. List A has been worked out as an example. Your paragraphs, of course, might be quite different if you organized your material differently. (*Note:* Articles do not appear before names in the lists; you are to add them, where appropriate, as you compose the paragraphs.)

LIST A

Country: United States

Capital: Washington (many consider this one of the world's beautiful cities, filled with parks, wide streets, and impressive buildings)

Location: District of Columbia

Principal government building: Capitol (meeting place of Congress, where laws are made)

Location: Capitol Park, in the center of the city

Official residence of President: White House (a great attraction for visitors)

Address: 1600 Pennsylvania Avenue N.W.

Famous rooms (of more than 100): East Room (largest; scene of many state receptions, balls, and musical events); Green, Blue, and Red rooms (used for afternoon teas and for receptions before state dinners); Blue Room (most formal, an oval room connecting Green and Red rooms); Lincoln Room (on second floor on the same floor with family quarters and other guest rooms; President Lincoln used this room as an office—here he signed Emancipation Proclamation of 1863; now an honor guest room)

Other landmarks: memorials to three Presidents—Washington Memorial, Jefferson Memorial, and Lincoln Memorial; Library of Congress; National Gallery of Art; John F. Kennedy Center for the Performing Arts; and Smithsonian Institution

Example:

The city of Washington, the capital of the United States, is located in the District of Columbia. Many people consider Washington, D.C., to be one of the most beautiful cities in the world. It is filled with many parks, wide streets, and impressive buildings. In the center of the city, in Capitol Park, visitors' eyes focus on the Capitol, where Congress convenes to enact laws.

Perhaps equally high on a visitor's list is the White House, the official residence of the President, situated at 1600 Pennsylvania Avenue N.W. The largest room in this building of over a hundred rooms is the East Room, scene of many state receptions, balls, and musicales. Other famous rooms are the Green, Blue, and Red rooms, which are used for afternoon teas and for receptions held before state dinners; the Blue Room, the most formal of these "color" rooms, is an oval-shaped room connecting the Green and Red rooms. On the second floor, the floor with the family quarters and guest rooms, is the Lincoln Room, which once served as an office for President Lincoln but today serves as an honor guest room. In this room, Lincoln signed the Emancipation Proclamation of 1863.

Other landmarks in Washington, D.C., include memorials to three Presidents (the Washington Memorial, the Lincoln Memorial, and the Jefferson Memorial), the Library of Congress, the National Gallery of Art, the John F. Kennedy Center for the Performing Arts, and the Smithsonian Institution.

LIST B

National Park Service: bureau of U.S. Department of Interior

Established: 1916

Number of national parks today: over 30

Variety of parks: Everglades (in Florida; a maze of jungle islands and watercourses); *Carlsbad Caverns* (in New Mexico; awesome for their underground limestone "sculptures"); *Yellowstone* (in Wyoming, Montana, and Idaho; with magnificent mountains and valleys and famous Old Faithful Geyser, which sends a jet of steaming water 150 feet into the air every hour)

Also under care of the service: over 150 monuments (examples: Petrified Forest in Arizona; George Washington's Birthplace in Virginia; Statue of Liberty); also national cemeteries, parkways, and historic sites

Method of establishing national parks and monuments: national parks—established only by acts of Congress; national monuments—may be named by President

LIST C

City: Paris—famed for, among many other things, its shops and restaurants

Shops (examples): *Pierre Cardin* (one of the *haute couture* houses for women's fashions; also is noted for its ties for men); *Hermès* (home of beautiful silk scarves—dozens of styles to choose from; also elegant handbags and gloves); *Guerlain* (one of the many famous perfume shops at Place Vendôme); *Baccarat* (exquisite crystal); *Técla* (jewelry—specializes in pearls); *Au Main Bleu* (largest toy shop in Paris—a wonderful variety)

Restaurants: Maxim's (one of the most expensive gourmet restaurants in the world; clientèle includes many important and glamorous people); *Lapérouse* (famous for its chicken and soufflés; consists of a number of small, old-fashioned rooms that give the feeling of dining in a home); *Café de la Paix* (a famous sidewalk cafe near the Opera House—a good place to watch people go by); *Taillevent* (offers dishes from all the French provinces—a good place to sample all kinds of French food)

LIST D

Country: Switzerland

Location: high in European Alps

Two mountain ranges:

(1) *Alps*—famous mountains: *Mont Blanc* (15,781 feet)—highest mountain in Alps, often called "monarch of mountains," rises on border between France, Italy, and Switzerland; *Matterhorn*—about 40 miles east of Mont Blanc, famous peak in Pennine Alps, on border between Switzerland and Italy; *Jungfrau*—in Bernese Alps, about 12 miles south of Interlaken, a famous resort

(2) *Jura*—less imposing than Alps, always less than 6,000 feet; rise between Rhine and Rhone rivers; form part of boundary between Switzerland and France; an important industrial city, Basel, at northeast end of the range

Lakes: Lake Maggiore—shore, lowest point in Switzerland, northern part in Switzerland, southern part in Italy; *Lake Geneva*—in southwest Switzerland, largest, borders on France for about 50 miles; *Lake Constance*—in northeast Switzerland, borders on Germany and Austria

Rivers: Rhine—starts with two branches (Vorder Rhine and Hinter Rhine), which flow into Lake Constance, then join to flow westward to form part of boundary between Switzerland and Germany; *Rhone*—starts in Great Rhone Glacier, flows through Lake Geneva, finally empties into Mediterranean; *Ticino*—starts on the southern slopes of Saint Gotthard, flows through Lake Maggiore, joins Po River and empties into Adriatic Sea; *Inn*—starts in the east, flows into Austria, joins Danube, and empties into Black Sea

5 Compile lists of information (from atlases, travel guides, or encyclopedias) on other cities, countries, or geographical areas; then write short compositions (150–250 words) based on the information. *Examples:*

1. The capital of your country

2. Natural wonders in your country

3. The shops and restaurants of any city you have lived in or visited

4. The geographical highlights of your country or of an area you know something about (the Philippine islands, the African deserts, etc.)

TWO-WORD VERBS AND

12

OTHER COMBINATIONS

Two-Word Verbs: Structure and Meaning

12·1   Mrs. Lopez **looked over** the list of students in need of financial aid and decided to **look into** the possibility of raising some money for scholarships. After **thinking** the matter **over,** she made plans to **drop in on** Mrs. Carrillo, president of the Women's Auxiliary, that afternoon. Mrs. Lopez **looked up to** Mrs. Carrillo and frequently **called on** her for advice.

- In this book, two-word verbs are treated as fixed combinations of verbs and prepositions, such as **look over, look into, think over.**

- Some two-word verbs are separable; that is, the verb and preposition can be separated by a direct object. These separable combinations are described in some grammars as *verb + particle. Example:*

  She **looked over** the list.   She **looked** the list **over.**

- The meaning of a two-word verb is often idiomatic; that is, the meaning of the combination is somewhat different from the meanings of the separate parts. Consider the meanings of the boldfaced two-word verbs in the preceding examples.

  looked over the list = examined or scrutinized the list

  look into the possibility = investigate the possibility

  thinking the matter **over** = considering the matter

  drop in on Mrs. Carrillo = visit Mrs. Carrillo informally

  looked up to Mrs. Carrillo = admired Mrs. Carrillo

  called on her for advice = went to her for advice

- The second element receives heavier stress in most two-word verbs with idiomatic meanings. *Examples:*

  look it óver   think it óver   look ínto it   look úp to her

  Notable exceptions are "**cóunt on** her" (depend or rely on her), "**cáll on** her" (visit), or "**cáll on** her for advice" (go to her for advice).

- Some two-word verbs require another preposition before an object can follow. *Compare:*

  Please **drop in** sometime.   She decided to **drop in on** Mrs. Carrillo.

Some combinations like **look up to** (admire) and **look down on** (regard as inferior) never occur without the second preposition + object.

■ Two-word verbs followed by objects often look like verbs followed by prepositional phrases, especially of place, but they function differently and are, therefore, not easily confused. *Compare:*

Where did Mrs. Lopez **look** for the book?

She **looked** on the desk.

How did Mrs. Lopez **look on** (regard) Mrs. Carrillo?

She **looked on** her as a friend.

■ To summarize: Two-word verbs are of various types. Some are separable; some are not. Some require objects; some do not. Some of these differences are pointed out in the following sections.

Separable Two-Word Verbs

12·2   Tom **looked** {the paper / it} **over.**   Tom **looked over** the paper.

He **turned** {his assignments / them} **in.**   He **turned in** his assignments.

■ Some two-word verbs are separable; that is, the verb and preposition can be separated by a direct object. In fact, if the object is a pronoun, it always occurs between the verb and preposition, as shown in the preceding examples.

■ Prepositions in separable two-word verbs receive heavier stress than the verb. *Examples:*

He **called** her **úp.**   When did he **call úp?**

12·3   DRILL   Put the direct object between the verb and preposition.

1. The men took off their hats. → *The men took their hats óff.*
2. They hung up their coats.
3. They put out their cigarettes.
4. They picked up the menu.
5. They turned in their orders.

12·4   DRILL   Change the *italicized* direct object to a pronoun and put it between the verb and preposition.

1. Did you turn in *your report?* → *Did you turn it ín?*
2. Did you call up *Mrs. Lee* today?
3. Did you pay back *the money?*
4. Please put out *the lights.*
5. Did you turn off *the radio?*

12·5   DRILL   Restate the sentences, using the two-word verb at the left in place of the *italicized* verb. Remember that if the object is a pronoun, the two-word verb must be separated.

carry out   1. Were they able to *realize* their objectives? →
              Were they able to carry out their objectives?

drop off   2. Shall I *leave* it at the reception desk for you?

take back   3. Did you *return* the book?

pick out   4. Please *select* another book.

talk over   5. Let's *discuss* it now.

throw away   6. Don't *discard* the tax records.

call off   7. The manager *canceled* the meeting today.

call up   8. He *telephoned* them today.

keep up   9. They are trying to *continue* their good record.

try out   10. They *are testing* a new method.

LIST OF TWO-WORD VERBS AND BE/HAVE COMBINATIONS

This list is by no means complete. You may wish to add additional items or to add other meanings for some of the items.

The items are listed alphabetically; be/have combinations appear under **be** and **have** respectively.

Symbols used:

— A dash between the verb and preposition indicates that the combination is separable; that is, the object may occur between the verb and the preposition. *Example:*

Look—up   Look up the word.   **Look** the word **up.**

. . . Three dots indicate that an object almost always occurs between the verb and the preposition. *Example:*

blame . . . for   Don't **blame** him **for** the error.

* An asterisk indicates that a combination can occur with or without an object. *Example:*

*Cheer—up   Cheer her **up.   Cheer up!**

accuse . . . of · He **accused** her **of** breaking the mirror.

add . . . to (or **with**) · Now **add** 29 **to** 147.

agree on (or **upon**) · We all seem to **agree on** the definition of the terms.

agree with · We **agree with** you on that point.

approve of · She doesn't **approve of** smoking.

argue with · He **argued with** the taxi driver about the fare.

arrive at (a place), **arrive in** (a country, city) · He **arrived at** the airport in time to have dinner before the flight. · They **arrived in** Rangoon in January.[1]

ask for [request] · The salesman **asked for** a new car.

ask . . . for · Why don't you **ask** your father **for** some money?

be afraid of · He says he **is** not **afraid of** anything.

be an authority on · Professor Walker **is an authority on** sensory perception.

be aware of · We **are** well **aware of** the situation.

be certain of · Are you **certain of** the date?

be composed of · A molecule **is composed of** atoms.

be delighted with (or **by**) · I am **delighted with** the gift.

be different from · This car **is** very **different from** the one I usually drive.

be disappointed in (or **by**) · Are you **disappointed in** the results of the election?

be any (or **no**) **doubt about** · There **is no doubt about** the authenticity of the painting, is there?

be familiar with · I'm **familiar with** his work.

[1] **At** sometimes precedes the name of a city in referring to the arrival of a train, bus, etc. (See also §9.31.) *Compare:*
The train will **arrive at** Miami at 5:30 p.m.
We will **arrive in** Miami tomorrow.

turn down	11. Why did Mr. King *reject* the applicant?
take on	12. When does she *assume* her new responsibilities?
bring back	13. Will you *return* them early in the morning?
look up	14. You *should visit* them the next time you are in Toronto.
give up	15. Don't *abandon* your plan until you are absolutely sure it won't work.
get through	16. You may *get* your plan *accepted* if you persist.
put off	17. Why *are* you *postponing* the decision?
take over	18. Will they *assume control of* the company at the beginning of the year?

12·6   The president **called** the meeting **off.**
The president **called off** the meeting scheduled for four o'clock.

■ Direct objects with long clause or phrase modifiers usually occur after the preposition.

be famous for · This restaurant **is famous for** its charcoal broiled steaks.

be fed up with [tired or sick of] · Joe **is fed up with** his job. We **are fed up with** his complaining about it.

be fond of · They **are** especially **fond of** Mexican food.

be frightened by · The senator **is** not easily **frightened by** the threats of his opponents.

be happy with · The Russells **are** very **happy with** their new television set.

be hung up on (or **with**) [obsessed by something, often to the extent of its being a problem; very informal—generally regarded as slang] · He **is hung up on** his dislike of chemistry.

be interested in · Don **is interested in** skiing.

be in charge of · Mr. Parnes **is in charge of** sales.

be in favor of · Are you **in favor of** going to this movie?

*****be** (or **fall**) **in love** (**with**) · They **are** very much **in love** (**with** each other). · Anthony **fell in love with** Cleopatra.

be (or **get**) **in touch** (or **contact**) **with** · The governor **is** constantly **in touch with** his advisers. · He **got in touch with** his advisers right away.

be known for · This town **is known for** its pleasant climate.

be made of (or **out of, from**) · These shoes **are made of** the finest leather.

be an opportunity for · There **is** a great opportunity for creativity here.

be opposed to · The senator **is opposed to** the new bill.

be out of date · The information in this table **is** way **out of date.**

be out of order · The candy machine **is out of order.**

be (or **look**) **out of place** · That modern table **looks out of place** in this room full of antiques.

be relevant to · What he said today **is relevant to** the problem.

be run down [be in a weakened physical condition] · Henry **is** very **run down.** He needs a lot of rest.

be satisfied with · I **am satisfied with** my progress so far.

be sensitive to · He is quite **sensitive to** criticism.

be surprised by (or **at**) · I **am surprised at** your lack of enthusiasm.

be thankful for · We **are thankful for** our blessings.

be thrilled by (or **with**) · We **are thrilled with** your good news.

be tired of · We **are tired of** studying two-word verbs.

become of [befall or happen to] · What **became of** Mary's boyfriend?

12·7   DRILL   Substitute the direct object and modifiers in parentheses for the *italicized* direct object.

1. Did you do *the assignment* over? (the assignment that Professor Jones gave us last week) →

   Did you do over the assignment that Professor Jones gave us last week?

2. Can you figure *the problem* out? (the problem concerning the relationship of mass to density)

3. You had better look *the words* up. (the words that you do not understand)

4. We are supposed to turn *the books* in tomorrow. (the books we borrowed from the biology library)

5. Is Jack going to take *the girl* out again? (the girl who rooms with Margaret)

---

believe in · The Rogers certainly **believe in** having a good time.

belong to · That golf club **belongs to** Mr. Nishiyama.

blame . . . for · The policeman **blamed** Mrs. Read **for** the accident.

bring—back [return] · You may borrow my car if you will **bring** it **back** by five o'clock. Can you **bring back** the car by five? · [recall] · Your story **brings back** a lot of memories.

bring—on (or **about**) [cause] · She **brought** the trouble **on** herself. What **brought on** the argument?

bring—out [reveal, show] · The artist **brought out** the beauty in the woman's face.

bring—up [rear (children)] · They **brought up** their children in the country. · [introduce or mention (a subject)] · Why don't you **bring up** your proposal at the next meeting?

*** brush up (on)** [review] · Have you **brushed up** yet? · Don't you need to **brush up on** your chemistry formulas?

*** call—back** [telephone again] · Why don't you **call** him **back** in an hour? · Why don't you **call back** at five o'clock?

call—down [scold] · The teacher **called** them **down** because they were so noisy.

call for [go to get] · I always **call for** my mail on Saturday.

call—in [ask (someone) to come in (for a purpose)] · We **called** him **in** to ask his advice.

call—off [cancel] · The president **called off** the meeting scheduled for this afternoon.

call on [pay a visit] · We **called on** the Lowrys the last time we were in Detroit. · [ask someone to answer or speak] · The teacher **called on** Jim and asked him to explain the problem.

*** call—up** [telephone] · Why don't you **call** her **up** now? When did they **call up**?

care for [like; usually **don't care for**] · I don't **care for** cream in my coffee, thank you.

carry—off [do a good job] · She was nervous about being hostess, but she **carried** it **off** beautifully.

*** carry on (with)** [continue] · Can you **carry on** now? He **carried on with** the discussion to the bitter end.

carry—out [complete, accomplish (a plan, a task, etc.)] · I have already **carried out** the details of the assignment.

*** carry—through** [complete, accomplish (a plan, a task, etc.)] · He **carried** it **through** to completion. Can you **carry through** now?

*** catch up (with)** [be up to date] · Are you **caught up (with** everything) now? · [overtake] · If we hurry, we can **catch up with** them.

check—off [mark (an item on a list) for identification or verification] As each person arrives, **check** his name **off** the list. · **Check off** my name. OR: **Check** my name **off.**

*** check out (of)** [pay the bill and leave] · When do we have to **check out (of** the hotel)?

check—out [remove officially from a library or take equipment from an office] · When did you **check out** these books from the library? · [verify or investigate] · You'd better **check** the report **out.**

12·8   He **turned** his assignments **in** on time.
His assignments **were turned in** on time.

■   Sentences with separable two-word verbs can usually be stated in the passive. (See §6.4 and 6.6.)

12·9   DRILL   Restate in the passive.

1. Why did Mr. King turn down the applicant? → *Why was the applicant turned down?*
2. He put off the decision until next week.
3. The Zeno Company will take over Barr's Department Store in June.
4. The Zeno Company will try out a new merchandizing procedure.
5. They must keep up their good record at all costs.

---

check up (on) [investigate] · Have you **checked up on** them recently?

* **cheer—up** [put (someone) in good spirits or in a good mood] · Try to **cheer** her **up**; she hasn't been feeling well lately. · **Cheer up!**

come across [find by chance] · I **came across** a new restaurant yesterday. · [communicate] · Are you **coming across** in English?

* **come along (with)** [succeed] · How are you **coming along (with** your work)? · [accompany] · Why don't you **come along (with** us)?

come out [end (in terms of results); see also **turn out**] · How did your interview **come out**? (What was the result of your interview?)

* **come to** [amount to or equal] · These groceries **come to** five dollars. · [appear suddenly] · The idea **came to** me while I was driving to work. · [regain consciousness] · The patient **came to** suddenly.

come up [present or produce] · We knew he would **come up with** some good ideas.

compare . . . with (or **to**) · **Compare** this product **with** the one you have been using.

comment on · She always **comments on** the weather.

complain about (or **of**) · The students are always **complaining about** the assignments.

congratulate . . . on (or **for**) · We **congratulate** you **on** your promotion.

consent to · The management has **consented to** the wage increase demanded by the union.

consist of · Water **consists of** two parts hydrogen and one part oxygen.

count on [depend on; rely on] · We can always **count on** him to help us in time of need.

cross—off [remove (an item from a list)] · **Cross off** my name. OR: **Cross** my name **off**. BUT: **Cross** my name **off** the list.

cross—out [delete or remove by drawing a line through] · When you misspell a word, **cross** it **out** and write it correctly.

decide on · Have you **decided on** the candidate?

depend on · Are you sure we can **depend on** her?

do—over [do again] · Your composition was poorly organized; you must **do** it **over**. · [redecorate] · We are planning to **do over** our living room soon.

* **do with** (or **without**) [exist or get along with or without] · Can't you **do without** for a while? · He **does with** very little sleep.

dream about (or **of**) · I **dreamed about** being in Nepal last night.

* **drop by** or **drop in (on)** [visit informally or without a definite invitation] · **Drop by** any time. · **Drop in** any time. · We hope you will **drop in on** us often.

drop off [fall asleep] · They had **dropped off** by nine o'clock. · [die] · His friends **dropped off** one after the other. · [decrease] · The sales **dropped off** in September.

drop—off [leave (someone or something at a place)] · I'll **drop** you **off** at the post office.

* **drop out (of)** [discontinue attendance or participation (in a class, club, etc.)] · George has **dropped out of** school for a year. Why did he **drop out**?

excuse . . . for · Please **excuse** me **for** being late.

explain . . . to · Please **explain** this problem **to** me.

12·10   Cheer her **up**!   Cheer **up**!
Did he **call** her **back**?   Did he **call back**?
The team won't **give** the championship   The team won't **give up** without a
up without a fight.   fight.

■   Some combinations like **cheer up, call back,** and **give up** can occur with or without
an object.

12·11   DRILL   Add the object in parentheses.

1. Why don't you cheer up?   (them) → *Why don't you cheer them up?*

2. He had difficulty placing the call, but he finally got through.   (it)

3. Don't give up.   (an opportunity like that)

4. He called up last night.   (Jim)

5. Jim took over.   (the sales department)

---

figure—out [solve or reason out] · The problem is very difficult. I just can't **figure** it **out.**

***get along (with)** [progress (with something); see also **come along**] · How is Laura **getting along** (**with** her volunteer work)? · [cooperate or have harmonious relations] · How are they **getting along?** Laura **gets along with** her mother-in-law very well.

***get back (from)** [return] · When did you **get back?** · When did you **get back from** your trip to Guatemala?

get—back [receive money, an object, or an answer from someone] · We **got** the reply **back** this morning. We **got** twenty-five cents **back** in change.

***get behind (in)** [lag or fall behind] · Why did you **get** so far **behind?** Once you **get behind in** your work, you are in trouble.

***get in (at, on, in)** [arrive] · When did you **get in** last night? The plane **got in at** nine o'clock. · He will **get in in** May. He **gets in on** Friday.

***get in (to), get out (of)** [get inside, leave (a car, a taxi, etc.)] · **Get in** the car, please. · **Get** him **into** the car. · We **got into** a taxi at the station and **got out** at the Ritz Hotel.

***get on, get off** [board, leave (a train, a bus, etc.)] · **Get on** the bus at Third Street and **get off** at Broadway. · Where did you **get off** (the bus)?

get over [recover from] · It took Mrs. Wilson a long time to **get over** the flu.

get . . . over (with [finish] · Let's **get** the meeting **over (with)** in a hurry.

***get through (with)** [manage to finish] · We **got through** early. · We hope to **get through (with)** the experiment by next week.

get . . . through [succeed in accomplishing something] · We **got** the telephone call **through** at six o'clock.

***get—up** [arise from sleeping] · **Get** them **up.** It's time to **get up.**

***give—up** [surrender, lose hope] · Don't **give** (the plan) **up** yet. OR: Don't **give up** (the plan) yet. BUT: Don't **give up** hope. (NOT: Don't give hope up.)

***go along (with)** [accompany] · Are they **going along?** · They will **go along with** us on the picnic.

go over [review] · Have you **gone over** the lesson?

***go over (with)** [succeed with] · How did the comedian **go over with** the audience? He didn't **go over** very well.

go through [search or look through] · I have **gone through** my files three times, but I can't find that letter.

hand—in [submit or turn in] · Bill forgot to **hand in** his homework today.

hang—up [place (a coat, etc.) on a hook or hanger] · Shall I **hang** it **up** for you?

happen to [befall or become of] · What **happened to** your plans for a trip to Japan?

have ability in (or **as**) · Ludwig **has** outstanding **ability as** a psychologist. · He **has** outstanding **ability in** psychology.

12·12 She **accused** him **of** deliberately wasting time.

You can't **blame** him **for** getting angry.

He perhaps **spends** too much time **on** unimportant things.

- Combinations like **accuse . . . of, blame . . . for,** and **spend . . . on** almost always have an object between the verb and the preposition.

12·13 DRILL Supply a preposition and then add the item in parentheses. (Consult the shaded list, if necessary.)

1. He subtracted five. (eight) → *He subtracted five from eight.*
2. They have *spent* a lot of money. (car repairs)
3. Why do you *prefer* this chair? (that one)
4. Didn't Carol *remind* you? (the meeting)
5. Please *compare* this suggestion. (the others)
6. *Add* 4951. (6098)
7. *Subtract* 40. (10149)
8. He *blamed* his assistant. (the error)

---

have access to · The accountant **has access to** all of the company's books.

have charge of · Heidi **has charge of** a nursery school.

have confidence in · We **have** a great deal of **confidence in** your judgment.

have faith in [trust] · First of all, you must **have faith in** yourself.

have influence over (or **on**) · They have never **had** much **influence over** him.

have a knack for [knack = a special ability] · Thurston **has a knack for** finding a good place to camp.

have an opportunity for (or **to**) · You should **have** every **opportunity for** achieving what you want to do here. · We hope he now **has an opportunity to do** what he has always wanted to do.

have patience with · He doesn't **have** any **patience with** details.

have a reason for · Do you **have** a good **reason for** taking that trip?

have a talent for · You **have** a great **talent for** saying the right thing at the right time.

hear about · Let me **hear about** your vacation.

hear from · I haven't **heard from** him for a long time.

introduce . . . to · I **introduced** him **to** my sister.

keep . . . for · Would you **keep** this money **for** me?

***keep—off** [stay off] · **Keep off** the grass. · The sign says "**Keep off!**" · **Keep** him **off** the grass.

***keep on** [continue] · How long can he **keep on** (making excuses)? · He **kept on** working for over ten hours.

***keep—out** [prevent from entering] · **Keep** them **out** of the office. ALSO: **Keep out!**

keep—up [continue or maintain a standard or level] · How long can you **keep** that pace **up?**

***keep up (with)** [stay abreast of] · How long can you **keep up (with** your changing field)?

laugh at · She always **laughs at** his jokes.

listen to · Do you like to **listen to** jazz music?

look after [watch or attend to] · Who is **looking after** the children today?

look at · Let's **look at** this map.

look down on [scorn or regard as inferior] · It doesn't pay to **look down on** anyone.

look for [search for or try to find] · Several students are **looking for** summer jobs.

look forward to [anticipate with pleasure] · We are **looking forward to** meeting your cousin at the party.

***look in (on)** [pay a brief informal visit to] · Can you **look in** again soon? · They **look in on** their old aunt every Sunday.

***look into** [investigate] · Is that worth **looking into?** · It would be a good idea to **look into** the matter again.

Nonseparable Two-Word Verbs

12·14   One day last week Henry **came across** a picture of an old college classmate on the financial page of the newspaper.
Last night he **ran into** him in a store on Market Street.

- Many combinations like **came across** and **ran into** are idiomatic but not separable; that is, the direct object cannot occur between the verb and preposition. *Compare:*

Last night Henry **ran into** him.   Last night Henry **called** him **up.**

- Like the separable group, the stress is heavier on the preposition than on the verb in most combinations. *Examples:*

When did he **come acróss** it?   BUT: Can we **cóunt on** you?
When did he **run ínto** him?   Did you **cáll on** her?

---

* look out (for) [watch out or be careful of] · **Look out!** You have to **look out for** other cars when you drive.

look—over [review] · You'd better **look over** this lesson again. · [examine] · We'd like to **look over** the coats on sale.

look to [rely or depend on] · She **looks to** her friend for advice on investing her money.

look—up [search for (in a reference book, etc.)] · You can **look up** population figures in an almanac. · [pay a visit to] · **Look** me **up** whenever you're in town.

look up to [admire] · Mrs. Watson **looks up to** him.

* make up (with) [end a quarrel] · Have you **made up (with** them)?

make—up [decide] · Have you **made up** your mind? · [construct] · Have you **made up** the list yet? · [apply cosmetics] · Has she **made up** her face? · [compensate for] · Did you **make up** the test you missed?

* move in (to or with) · Have they **moved in** yet? · Have they **moved into** their new house? · Has she **moved in with** you yet?

object to · Why do you **object to** this color?

pay—back [repay] · We promised to **pay** him **back** on Friday.

pay for · I can't **pay for** the tickets now.

pay . . . for · I can't **pay** him **for** the tickets now.

pick—out [select] · Please help me **pick out** a hat.

pick—up [collect an object or a person, as on a date] · Can you **pick** me **up** about 4:30? · [learn by chance] · We **picked up** some new ideas at the conference.

point—out [call attention to] · I want to **point out** several important facts to you.

praise . . . for · The president **praised** the committee **for** its outstanding report.

prefer . . . to · I **prefer** this painting **to** that one.

put—across [cause to be understood] · Professor Hendrix can **put across** the most difficult concepts so that everyone can understand them.

put—away [store, set aside] · We usually **put away** our winter clothes from May until November.

put—off [delay, postpone] · We are **putting off** our trip to New York until next month.

put—on [wear (as clothing)] · You should **put on** a raincoat because it has started to rain. · [start (coffee, radio, etc.)] · Should I **put on** the coffee now?

put—out [extinguish (cigarette, lights, etc.)] · Wait until I **put out** the fire in the fireplace.

put up with [tolerate] · Some people can't **put up with** noise.

rely on · May I **rely on** you to drive us to the station?

remind . . . of · Libby **reminds** me **of** my cousin. · Please **remind** me **of** my appointment.

run across [find by chance or **come across**] · We **ran across** some interesting data in this journal article.

* run away (from) [escape] · Did he **run away** again? · When did he **run away from** home?

run down [unwind, as with a clock; see also **be run-down**] · The clock has **run down** again.

run—down [locate] · They **ran down** the embezzler in Mexico.

12·15 Why don't you **come along?**   Why don't you **come along with** us?
Why don't you **drop in?**   Why don't you **drop in on** them?
Why did you **get behind?**   Why did you **get behind in** your work?
He **got through** early.   He **got through with** his work early.

- Some combinations require an additional preposition before an object can follow. Combinations of this type are not separable.

- The first preposition receives a heavier stress than the verb or second preposition. *Examples:*

drop ín	get behínd	come alóng
drop ín on	get behínd in	come alóng with

run into [meet a person by chance] · We **ran into** Henry in front of the theater. · [crash into] · The car **ran into** the building.

*** run out (of)** [exhaust a supply] · Have you **run out** yet? Some people never **run out of** things to say.

run—over [review] · Let's **run over** the lesson once more.

run up [increase a debt] · Maurine bought a lot of things and **ran up** an enormous bill.

save—up [collect or put aside (money, etc.) for a purpose] · He finally **saved up** enough money for a trip to Europe.

see about [investigate or find out about] · John wants to **see about** a scholarship.

see . . . about [discuss] · John wants to **see** the dean **about** a scholarship.

send for · Shall we **send for** more information?

send . . . for · Shall we **send** him **for** more information?

*** show up (at)** [appear] · Did they **show up (at** the reception)?

show—up [do better than or outshine] · We **showed** the other team **up** this time.

spend money (time, effort, energy) **on** · I have **spent** a great deal of time, money, and energy **on** my garden.

subtract . . . from · **Subtract** this figure **from** the total.

succeed in · Has your brother **succeeded in** getting a date with Martha?

take after [resemble] · Mark **takes after** his father in looks and character.

take—back [return] · Did you **take back** the chair? · [regain possession] · The store **took back** the damaged chair. · [retract a statement] · I **take** it **back,** and I'm sorry I said it.

take care of [watch over or look after] · Will you please **take care of** my dog this weekend?

take charge of [assume responsibility for] · Mr. Sass will **take charge of** the office after the first of the year.

take . . . into consideration · You should **take** all expenses **into** consideration before building a house. ALSO: **Take into** consideration all the expenses.

*** take off (for or from)** [leave (usually by plane)] · When do you **take off?** · When do you **take off from** London?

take—off [remove (clothing)] · Why don't you **take off** your coat and stay awhile?

take—on [assume responsibility or undertake] · She has **taken on** chairmanship of the scholarship committee.

take—out [escort] · John **took** Mary **out** last Saturday; they had dinner together and then went to see the play at the Star Theater. · [extract] · The dentist **took out** two of my wisdom teeth last week.

*** take—over** [assume control of] · Company A has recently **taken over** Company B. When did they **take over?**

take—up [become interested in (a subject, a hobby, etc.)] · Walter has **taken up** flying. · [discuss] · We'll **take** that subject **up** again tomorrow. · [introduce, begin, or discuss a topic] · Mr. Martin **took up** a new subject in class today.

talk about · I'd like to **talk about** the poets of my country.

12·16   DRILL   Substitute the item in parentheses for the *italicized* part of the sentence.

1. Jim has *tolerated* an incompetent assistant for a year.   (put up with) →
   Jim has put up with an incompetent assistant for a year.

2. She does not *cooperate* very well *with* others.   (get along with)

3. She *is* never *up to date in* her work.   (catch up with)

4. She sometimes *answers* people *rudely*.   (talk back to)

5. She *admires* Jim, nonetheless.   (looks up to)

6. She is trying hard not to *lag in* her work.   (get behind in)

7. How is Maury *progressing with* his book?   (come along with)

8. He is *reviewing* statistics.   (brush up on)

9. He is *continuing* his research.   (carry on)

10. Have the Blakes *returned from* their trip around the world?   (get back from)

11. When will they *leave* the Honolulu airport?   (take off from)

12. When will they *arrive* here?   (turn up)

13. Anne *resembles* her Aunt Catherine.   (take after)

14. She doesn't *consider* others *inferior*.   (look down on)

15. She is *investigating* a new job.   (look into)

16. She has been *trying to find* a job for weeks.   (look for)

---

* talk back (to) [answer rudely] · Don't you dare **talk back**! · Polite children never **talk back to** their parents.

talk—over [discuss] · Let's **talk** it **over** and see if we can't get to the root of the problem. BUT: They **talked over** the news. (NOT: They talked the news over.)

talk to · May I **talk to** you for a few minutes?

thank . . . for · **Thank** you **for** telling me about your plans.

think about (or of) · May I **think about** it before deciding? · I have **thought of** you a lot lately.

think—over [give thought to or (re)consider] · **Think** it **over** a little longer.

think—through [consider thoroughly to arrive at a conclusion] · I haven't had a chance to **think** it **through**.

think—up [invent] · The accountant **thought up** a new way to cut costs.

throw—away [discard] · Let's **throw away** these old papers.

throw—back [regress, cause a delay] · That has **thrown** us **back** two weeks.

throw—off [mislead] · Try not to **throw** them **off** the track.

throw—out [suggest] · We **threw out** a few ideas for the committee to discuss. · [discard or remove] · Let's **throw out** these old papers. (See also **throw—away**.) · The guards **threw** the demonstrators **out** (of the meeting).

* throw—up [vomit] · He **threw** his dinner **up**. Did you **throw up** too?

try—on [test the fit or appearance] · I'd like to **try on** these two suits, please.

* try out (for) [compete for a role in a play or for a position] · Marian **tried out for** the star role. · Why don't you **try out**?

try—out [test or experiment] · They are **trying out** a new method of taking reservations.

* turn away (or back) (from or at) [go in a reverse direction] · They **turned away (from** the crowd). · Why did you **turn back (at** the border)?

turn—away [dismiss or not accept] · The box office had to **turn** many people **away**. · [repulse or reject] · The police **turned** the crowd **away**.

turn in [go to bed] · Why don't we **turn in** now?

17. She hasn't *exhausted her supply of* money.   (run out of)

18. She *found* a new apartment *by chance*.   (come across)

19. She will *accompany* her aunt to Europe.   (go along with)

20. She *has finished reading* the home section of the newspaper.   (be through with)

12·17   DRILL   Add the correct preposition followed by the item in parentheses. (If you are not sure of the preposition to use, check the shaded list.)

1. Have you checked out?   (the hotel) → *Have you checked out of the hotel?*

2. Can you look in tomorrow?   (your sick uncle)

3. You'd better look out!   (falling rocks)

4. Are you about caught up?   (your reading)

5. Can you come along?   (us)

6. How are you getting along?   (your boss)

7. George didn't drop out, did he?   (the club)

8. Why didn't he keep up?   (us)

9. Why were they thrown out?   (the café)

10. They got behind.   (their rent)

turn—in [submit or hand in] · I have already **turned in** my composition.

turn—off [stop or shut off (a radio, water, lights, etc.)] · Please **turn off** the television by ten o'clock.

* **turn . . . off** [kill interest; informal, personal usage] · His lecture **turned** everybody **off**. I was **turned off**.

turn—on [start or put on (a radio, lights, etc.)] · Shall I **turn on** the radio for the six o'clock news? · [stimulate or make interesting] · The speaker really **turned** the audience **on**. FREQUENTLY PASSIVE: They were really **turned on** by the speaker.

* **turn out (for)** · [appear] · Did they **turn out (for** the game)? · [end or end up] · We expected the meeting to be a dismal failure, but it **turned out** rather well.

turn—out [extinguish (lights, etc.)] · Please **turn out** the lights in the living room.

* **turn—over** [change position] · The mother **turned** the baby **over**. · [transfer (goods, responsibility, etc.)] · She **turned** the problem **over** to her attorney.

* **turn up (at or in)** [appear, usually unexpectedly] · Bill **turned up (at** the meeting). · The lost manuscript **turned up in** the Folger Library.

turn—up [increase the intensity] · **Turn up** the heat, please.

vote for · Be sure to **vote for** your candidates on Tuesday.

wait for · How long have you **waited for** us?

wait on [serve] · Ask for Gaston to **wait on** you at that restaurant.

* **wake—up** [awake from sleep] · **Wake** them **up** now. · It's time to **wake up!**

waste money (time, energy, effort) **on** · We are **wasting** too much time **on** this problem.

wish for · What do you **wish for** your birthday?

work for · How long have you **worked for** your company?

work out [exercise] · He **works out** in the gymnasium every Saturday.

* **work—out** [solve or find solutions] · It's a problem, but we can **work** it **out**. · It took a long time, but we **worked out** the answers to the problem. · It's funny how things **work out** (work themselves out).

write—down [make notes] · You'd better **write** these items **down**.

12·18   Check-out time at the hotel was one o'clock, but we **checked out** at noon.

The information does not seem accurate. **Check** it **out.**

It was a terribly busy week. I don't know how we **got through** it.

The bill passed the House of Representatives. Now the problem is to **get** it **through** the Senate.

- There are a few separable combinations that have nonseparable counterparts. The meanings, however, are generally quite different, as illustrated by the combinations in the preceding examples.

  check it **out** = investigate or examine it carefully

  check out = pay the bill and leave the hotel

  get it (the bill) **through** = get it passed by the Senate

  get through it (the week) = manage to survive

  Note: **get** ... **through** meaning "get something accepted or passed (as a bill)" is always separated by an object (Senator Dellen **got** the bill **through**).

12·19   DRILL   Substitute the item in parentheses for the *italicized* part of the sentence. Separable combinations are indicated by a dash (*check—out*).

1. He *left* her at the bus station.   (drop—off) →
   He dropped her off at the bus station.

2. He *went* to sleep.   (drop off)

3. The telephone calls *decreased* in the afternoon.   (drop off)

4. The Martins *ended their quarrel* with the McCoys.   (make up)

5. That story about them isn't true. Someone *invented* it.   (make—up)

6. She *put cosmetics on* her face.   (make—up)

7. Have you *submitted* your term paper?   (turn—in)

8. They always *go to bed* early.   (turn in)

12·20   Roberta **believes in** having a good time.
She **objects to** working overtime.

- Combinations of this type are very much like the nonseparable ones in §12.14. With this type, however, the heavier stress is on the verb rather than the preposition. *Compare:*

  She **objécts to** it.   She **came acróss** it.

  The combinations in this group have about the same meaning as the verb alone. *Example:*

  He **approved.**   He **approved of** the plan.

- Notice that the verb-**ing** form follows **object to** (see also §18.18). *Example:*

  She **objects to** { **working** overtime.
                        overtime work.

  (NOT: . . . objects to work overtime.)

12·21 DRILL Fill in the blanks with an appropriate preposition. (If you are in doubt, check the shaded list.)

1. Do you agree _____*with*_____ us?

2. Did you decide _____*on*_____ a plan?

3. Does your uncle approve _____ an actress in the family?

4. Do you object _____ getting here a little early?

5. I don't care _____ mayonnaise.

6. Did anything happen _____ your plans?

7. Let me hear more _____ your trip to Peru.

8. Are you looking _____ a new apartment?

9. Do you listen _____ the six o'clock news regularly?

10. Why are you laughing _____ me?

12·22 DRILL Supply the correct preposition and then add the item in parentheses. (Consult the shaded list, if necessary.)

1. Would you like to *comment?* (this proposal) →
   Would you like to comment on this proposal?

2. They *called* in the morning. (the Lewises)

3. He decided to *ask.* (more money)

4. How long did it take him to *decide.* (the plan)

5. Have you *heard* recently? (Kevin)

6. How long did Frances *wait?* (him)

7. They *looked* five years. (the right location)

8. The bill *came.* (over a hundred dollars)

9. Don't *argue* any more. (your brother)

10. Are you going to *vote* on Tuesday? (Joe)

BE and HAVE Combinations

12·23 Luther Dow **is in charge of** the research project.
He **is an authority on** Black English.
We **have** the utmost **confidence in** him.
We **are looking forward to** meeting him.

■ There are many combinations that begin with **be** or **have**. In many instances, verb-**ing** forms as well as nouns and pronouns follow the prepositions. *Examples:*

He is looking forward to **meeting** him.
(NOT: He is looking forward to meet him.)

He is used to **working** hard.
(NOT: He is used to work hard.)

He is opposed to **hiring** untrained people.
(NOT: He is opposed to hire untrained people.)

12·24   DRILL   Supply the correct preposition and then add the item in parentheses. (Consult the *be* and *have* combinations on the shaded list, if necessary.)

1. Who's *afraid?* (Virginia Woolf) → *Who's afraid of Virginia Woolf?*

2. We're completely *delighted.* (the good news)

3. Who has *access?* (the confidential papers)

4. Margaret says she is *in love.* (Giovanni)

5. There isn't *any doubt,* is there? (the truth of the report)

6. Is everyone *in favor?* (adjournment)

7. Why were you so *surprised?* (the announcement)

8. This store is *well known.* (its quality merchandise)

9. Is there *a good opportunity?* (advancement)

10. We don't have *any influence* anymore. (them)

11. We are *opposed.* (expanding the company)

12. We are not *interested.* (incurring more debts)

12·25   DRILL   Add the verb-*ing* form before the *italicized* object.

1. Are they opposed to *the policy?* (adopt) →
   Are they opposed to adopting the policy?

2. We are looking forward to *the meeting.* (attend)

3. Are they interested in *the meeting?* (attend)

4. They aren't used to *debts.* (incur)

5. They are definitely opposed to *further indebtedness.* (incur)

1 Match the *italicized* part of the sentences with the two-word verbs in the column on the right. Indicate your choices by writing the letter (*a*, *b*, *c*, etc.) in the spaces provided on the left.

GROUP A

____ 1. Some patients *recover from* an operation quickly.

____ 2. Why did you *raise* that question during the discussion?

____ 3. I seldom *meet* anyone famous.

____ 4. Did John *telephone* Mary last night?

____ 5. The highway patrol is going to *experiment with* a new method of traffic control.

____ 6. Scholars *search for* truth.

____ 7. When did you *finish* your term paper?

____ 8. Did you *find out about* rooms at the housing office?

____ 9. We have to *review* the first five lessons before the quiz.

____10. Won't you please *reconsider* the offer our firm has made to you?

a) bring up
b) call up
c) call for
d) get in
e) get through with
f) get over
g) look over
h) look for
i) look up
j) run across
k) see about
l) think over
m) think of
n) try out
o) try on

GROUP B

____ 1. They will *board* the ship in Genoa.

____ 2. I want to *call* your *attention to* the painting on this wall.

____ 3. We had to *postpone* our trip to Miami.

____ 4. Please *remove* your hats, gentlemen.

____ 5. He will *continue* working here until June.

____ 6. Can't we *overtake* him in the car?

____ 7. When will the bus *arrive?*

____ 8. *Be careful of* that rock in the middle of the road.

____ 9. Have you *tested* the new computer?

____10. The children *respect* their teacher.

a) catch up with
b) get in
c) get on
d) keep off
e) keep on
f) look out for
g) look up to
h) point out
i) put across
j) put off
k) run across
l) take off
m) talk back to
n) try out
o) wait on

GROUP C

_____ 1. Teachers *scold* their pupils for being late.

_____ 2. I suggest that you *delete* that paragraph.

_____ 3. Can you *solve* the problem?

_____ 4. They refused to *surrender*.

_____ 5. When will you *put aside* enough money?

_____ 6. He is always trying to *invent* new ways.

_____ 7. Please *accompany* me to the bus.

_____ 8. You can *overtake* them if you hurry.

_____ 9. Nations must *cooperate* with each other.

_____10. Did you *request* an interview?

a) ask for
b) become of
c) call down
d) catch up with
e) check off
f) come along with
g) cross out
h) figure out
i) get along with
j) give up
k) hang up
l) think up
m) save up
n) take after
o) turn away

GROUP D

_____ 1. When do we have to *submit* our applications?

_____ 2. Please *extinguish* all lights when you leave.

_____ 3. Mothers-in-law often *scorn* their sons-in-law.

_____ 4. Sometimes scientists must *continue* experimenting for years without results.

_____ 5. The committee has been able to *accomplish* its plans.

_____ 6. Will you *investigate* these possibilities?

_____ 7. We are planning to *redecorate* our offices.

_____ 8. Will the gentlemen please *remove* their hats?

_____ 9. Let's *review* the past three lessons tomorrow.

_____10. I'm going to *request* a new desk.

a) ask for
b) carry out
c) do over
d) go over
e) go through
f) hang up
g) keep on
h) look down on
i) look forward to
j) put away
k) put out
l) see about
m) take back
n) take off
o) turn in

2 Restate these sentences, substituting a two-word verb (or other combination) for the *italicized* verb in each sentence.

1. Mrs. Anderson *left* her husband at the station. →
   Mrs. Anderson dropped her husband off at the station.
2. Mr. Anderson *boarded* the 8:15 train.
3. He *reviewed* some papers on the way.
4. He also *searched* the papers for the latest sales report.
5. The train *reached* the city at exactly 8:50.
6. Mr. Anderson *left* the train in a hurry.
7. He then *entered* a taxi and went directly to his office.
8. Right away he asked his secretary to *telephone* Mr. Oliver in Seattle.
9. Mr. Oliver was out, but she *telephoned* him again in an hour.
10. Mr. Anderson asked Mr. Oliver if he had *decided* to accept their offer.

3 Fill in the blanks with an appropriate preposition.

1.   When my brother and I were children, our grandmother had a great deal of influence _____ us. She looked _____ us during the day while our parents were at work. Although she was not in favor _____ sparing the rod and spoiling the child, we were never really frightened _____ her threats of punishment. She knew that my brother was sensitive _____ criticism, and she was especially lenient with him because she was afraid _____ hurting his feelings.

    All of the children in the neighborhood were very fond _____ her. She was famous _____ her chocolate cake and known _____ her generosity in cutting extra large slices. My parents didn't approve _____ our eating so many sweets. They said they didn't want to spend all their money _____ our teeth, but they never had the heart to complain _____ it to Grandmother. She wouldn't have listened to them anyway. She belonged _____ another generation and didn't believe _____ all this nonsense about everything that tastes good being bad _____ the teeth. I must say that I now agree wholeheartedly _____ my parents _____ that point, but you can hardly blame me _____ not heeding their advice at that time.

    We used to confide _____ Grandmother and talk our problems _____ with her. We could always count _____ her to help us or to cheer us _____ . She had a great deal of faith _____ us and used to tell us that we should have more confidence _____ ourselves. She also used to say that we should be interested _____ getting ahead in the world but that at the same time we should be thankful _____ what we had.

2. Last Wednesday right after lunch I walked into my boss's office and asked him _____ a raise. He didn't say anything for fully thirty seconds. I could see that my bringing _____ the matter of a raise had upset him. When he had regained his composure, he said that he would have to take the matter _____ with Mr. Smith, his partner. He said he was sure Mr. Smith would want to go _____ my record before making a decision and that it might be a day or two before he could give me an answer.

The next day he called me into his office and told me that he had talked the matter _____ with Mr. Smith and found that he was opposed _____ giving me a raise. He pointed _____ that I had been with the firm only six months and that it was company policy to give only annual raises. I was not about to be put _____ and reminded him _____ his promise when he hired me to look _____ the matter of a raise after I had been with the company six months. When I said this, he looked at me sharply.

"If you are not satisfied _____ your job here, I think you'd better look _____ another," he snapped.

This made me angry. "I've been thinking _____ doing just that," I countered.

Then he became really angry. "I don't like employees who talk _____ to me," he shouted. "I won't put _____ your insolence a day longer. Pick _____ your check at the cashier's office and get out. You're fired."

There wasn't much of anything I could say to that but "I quit." I said it, and then I walked back to my desk and started to go _____ the drawers looking _____ my personal belongings. Ed, the office boy, sensed that something was wrong and came over to talk to me. "What happened _____ you?" he asked, not unkindly. "You look like a man who has problems."

When I told him that Mr. Jones had just fired me, he grinned and said, "Oh, is that all? Is this the first time the boss has fired you? He's fired me at least six times, and I'm still here. Cheer _____. He'll get _____ it."

4 Some two-word verbs and other combinations that might be used in certain situations are listed below:

Going on a trip	*Looking at TV*
check out (of)	approve of
come across	don't care for
do without	happen to
drop in (on) or drop by	be interested in
get back	be out of order
get in	be thrilled by
go along with (accompany)	laugh at
keep on (with)	listen to
look forward to	look at
move in	turn on
take off (leave)	turn off
turn out (result in some way)	turn up (raise the volume)
turn up (appear)	wish for

Discussing a subject	*Getting a job or going into business*
agree on (something)	apply for
agree with (someone)	ask for
approve of	be aware of
argue with	be considered for
be an authority on	be eager to
be aware of	be sensitive to
be disappointed in	believe in
be opposed to	call back
be sensitive to	call up
come to (reach)	carry out
comment on	check up (on)
count on	come across
decide on	come up with
disagree with	count on
figure out	drop off (decrease)
go over	have confidence in
have access to	have an opportunity for
have no doubt about	hear from
keep on	take into consideration
look over	try out
look up	turn out (result in some way)
object to	turn up (appear or occur)
pick out	wait for
point out	work out
succeed in	write down

1. You may go through the shaded lists and add additional items. You may also make lists for other situations such as studying at the library, going shopping, renting and decorating an apartment.

2. Write dialogs, narratives, and letters using items from the preceding lists. Here are some examples:

DIALOG:

Joe: I hear you are *looking for* a job. Have you had any luck?

Bob: Not so far. Several firms have *asked* me *for* a résumé, but I haven't *heard* anything more *from* them. This morning I *ran across* an interesting ad for a salesman, and I'm going to *look into* it right away.

Joe: Well, don't get discouraged if it doesn't *work out.* Something is bound to *turn up.*

Bob: Sure. I'll just *keep on* looking until I *come up with* something.

NARRATIVE:

Last night about eight o'clock I decided to *look at* a TV program. I *turned on* the set and started to *look at* a mystery drama. I am not usually *interested in* mysteries, but I was completely *delighted with* this one. I was enjoying it thoroughly when something *happened to* the picture. I tried to adjust the set because I wanted to see who *turned out* to be the murderer, but the set was obviously *out of order.* The picture was so bad that I finally had to *give up* and *turn off* the set.

LETTER

1298 River View Road
Brookhill, CA 98000

Dear Mrs. Garcia,

Marie and I are coming into town next Thursday morning to do some shopping. In the early afternoon we are planning to *call on* Mrs. Rubio, who is just *getting over* a bad case of the flu. When we called the other day, her daughter told us that she was *getting along* all right but that she was in rather low spirits. We thought we would *drop by* and try to *cheer* her *up.*

Would you like to *come along* with us? We could *pick* you *up* about two o'clock. We are *planning on* getting an early start, so we should be in San Francisco by nine o'clock. We'll call you as soon as we *get in.* We are *looking forward* to seeing you, so we hope you don't have other plans for Thursday afternoon.

Sincerely,

Carmen Castillo

Position and Function of Adverbial Clauses

13·1   **When Wilton left for Europe,** we all went to the airport to see him off.
He was very excited **when he got on the plane.**
In fact, he was **so** excited **that he forgot his topcoat.**

- Adverbial clauses not closely tied to the predicate can occur at either the beginning or the end of the sentence. In writing, a comma usually follows an adverbial clause at the beginning of the sentence.

- Clauses that are closely tied to the predicate, however, can occur only at the end of the sentence, as shown in the last example above.

13·2   **When Wilton got on the plane,** the stewardess told him he could sit **wherever he wanted to since the plane was not crowded.**

- Adverbial clauses, like adverbials, tell *when* (time), *where* (place), *how* (manner), *how often* (frequency), and *for what purpose* (reason); they also show us such relationships as cause–effect, event–result, affirmation–concession. They are introduced by words like **when, while, before, after, because,** and **although;** these words are sometimes called *subordinators.* Look at the three boldfaced clauses in the preceding example and decide what these clauses indicate.

Clauses of Time

13·3   **As soon as Wilton arrived in Paris,** he called his friend François.
He usually stays with François and his wife, Earlene, **when he is in Paris.**
They have been friends **since they were university students.**
Wilton is going to go to London **after he leaves Paris.**
He plans to look up the Prestons **while he is in London.**
He sees as many plays as possible **whenever he is in London.**

■ As the preceding sentences indicate, verb tenses in adverbial clauses and main clauses occur in various combinations. There are restrictions, however. The following are important points to keep in mind in using time clauses.

1) When a future verb form occurs in the main clause, a present verb form usually occurs in the time clause.

He **is going to go** to London after he **leaves** Paris.
He probably **won't write** to us again until he **arrives** in London.

2) When a time clause is introduced by **since,** a present or past perfect verb form generally occurs in the main clause.

They **have been** friends since they were in college.
He **hadn't seen** them since they visited him in New York last year.

13·4   DRILL   Combine the following sentences. Be sure to change *will* in the time clause.

1. Wilton will leave for Paris. He will go to London. →
   When Wilton leaves Paris, he will go to London.

2. He will stay with the Prestons. He will be in London.

3. He will visit with the Prestons for a week. He will then go to Oxford.

4. He will see the Prestons again. He will leave England.

5. He will return to London on December 23. He and the Prestons will go to Scotland for the Christmas holidays.

13·5   DRILL   Complete the sentences with appropriate verb forms. Remember that with *since* time clauses, the verb in the main clause is generally present or past perfect.

1. Wilton __*has known*__ François since they were juniors in college.
   (known)

2. François _____ in Paris since he graduated from college.
   (live)

3. Wilton _____ in New York and Washington, D.C., since he graduated from college.
   (live)

4. The two friends _____ each other since François came to New York last year.
   (not see)

5. Before that, they _____ each other since Wilton was in Paris in 1970.
   (not see)

13·6   Wilton stayed with François and his wife, Earlene, **when (while) he was in Paris.** He called them **when he arrived in Paris.**

■ **When** can mean either "at a particular point of time" or "during a period of time." **While** can be used only when the meaning is "during a period of time." For example, in the first sentence, **during the time (that)** could replace either **when** or **while.** In the second sentence, replacements for **when** could be **as soon as, once,** or **the moment.**

13·7   He will go **when he has time.**
He will go **whenever he has time.**

■ **Whenever** indicates "any time"; **when** indicates "a particular period of time."

13·8   DRILL   Make one of the sentences into a time clause using the subordinator (the *italicized* word) to introduce the clause. In most cases, the clause can go at the beginning or the end of the sentence. (If this exercise is written, use a comma after the time clause *only* when it occurs at the beginning of the sentence.)

1. Wilton was in Paris last month. (*when*)   He stayed with friends.
   When Wilton was in Paris last month, he stayed with friends.
   OR: *Wilton stayed with friends when he was in Paris last month.*
2. He was in France. (*while*)   He had the opportunity to practice his French.
3. His French had greatly improved. He left for London. (*by the time that*)
4. He won't have much opportunity to speak French. He has left Paris. (*now that*)
5. He is going to stay in London. His friends who live in Oxford will return from Berlin. (*until*)
6. He will drive to Oxford. His friends have returned from Berlin. (*after*)
7. He is planning to drive through England. The weather will improve. (*if*)
8. He takes long walks in the country. The weather is good. (*whenever*)

Clauses of Place

13·9   Steve meets interesting people **wherever he goes.**
Everywhere he goes, he makes new friends.
He is going to open an art gallery **where the Pickwick Bookshop used to be.**

■ **Wherever** or **everywhere** introduces adverbial clauses when the meaning is "anyplace" or "everyplace." **Where** introduces adverbial clauses when the meaning is "a definite place."

13·10   DRILL   Make adverbial clauses of place using the information in the right-hand column; substitute the clauses for the *italicized* adverbials in the left-hand column.

1. We stopped the car *over there*.   the road starts downhill →
   We stopped the car where the road starts downhill.
2. There were tire marks *there*.   we put on the brakes
3. There were yellow flowers *everyplace*.   we looked
4. There were cars parked *along   the river was close to the road
   the river.*
5. We stopped to admire the view *here   it was possible
   and there.*

Clauses of Distance, Manner, and Frequency

13·11   Kathy drove down the country road **as far as she could.**
She drove **as fast as she felt was safe.**
She put the car in low gear **as often as she felt it was necessary.**

- **As . . . as** clauses generally contain only the subject and an auxiliary when the verbs in the two clauses are the same. *Examples:*

    She walked **as far as she could** (walk).
    She visits her aunt **as often as she can** (visit her).

- Clauses, but not phrases, indicating distance can also be introduced by **until; as far as** is used with phrases. *Compare:*

    She walked **until she came to the river.**
    (NOT: She walked until the river.)

    She walked **as far as the river.**

- **As** can also introduce clauses indicating manner. *Example:*

    She put the car in low gear on the steep grade **as her brother had taught her to do.**

13·12   DRILL   Answer the questions, using sentences containing *as . . . as* clauses of distance, time, manner, or frequency, as appropriate.

1. How often does Steve go to Mirror Lake? →
    He goes to Mirror Lake as often as he can get away.
2. How far does he drive the first day?
3. How fast does he drive?
4. How far did he drive last weekend?
5. How many times is he planning to go skiing this winter?

Clauses of Reason or Cause

13·13   Mrs. Perkins went downtown early **because she had a lot of shopping to do.
Since her husband needed the car,** she took the bus.

- Clauses introduced by **since** and **because** can occur at either the beginning or the end of the sentence.
- Notice the punctuation in the preceding examples. When **because** and **since** clauses occur at the beginning of the sentence, they are usually followed by a comma in writing. A comma does not usually precede **because** or **since** at the end of the sentence, however.
- **Since** clauses of reason should not be confused with **since** time clauses. *Compare:*

    She took a bus **since her husband needed the car.** (reason)
    It has been a long time **since I have seen her.** (time)

13·14 Mrs. Perkins went downtown early **because she had a lot of shopping to do.**

Mrs. Perkins had a lot of shopping to do; **therefore,** she went downtown early.

- Sentences with **because** and **since** clauses can be restated using **therefore.** Notice that **since** and **because** introduce the clause expressing *cause,* and **therefore** introduces the clause expressing *result* or consequences.

- **Thus** can be used in place of **therefore,** but it is generally more formal in tone.

- **Therefore** is preceded by a semicolon or a period and is usually followed by a comma. If **therefore** is not the first word in the sentence, it is usually set off by a pair of commas. *Compare:*

  Mrs. Perkins had a lot of shopping to do; therefore, she went downtown early.
  Mrs. Perkins had a lot of shopping to do. She, therefore, went downtown early.

- In restating **because** or **since** clauses, it is important to remember that the noun or proper noun occurs in the first clause and the pronoun in the second clause. *Compare:*

  Mrs. Perkins usually takes the bus **because she doesn't like to drive.**
  Mrs. Perkins doesn't like to drive; **therefore,** she usually takes the bus.

13·15 DRILL Combine the two sentences by making the second one a clause of reason or cause. Use *since* or *because* to introduce the clause.

1. Mrs. Perkins went to the bank first. She wanted to cash a check. →
   Mrs. Perkins went to the bank first because she wanted to cash a check.
2. The bank wasn't crowded. It was early.
3. She went to Bell's Department Store. She wanted to look at some sweaters.
4. The streets were still wet. It had rained that morning.
5. She walked carefully. The streets were slippery.

13·16 DRILL Restate each sentence in Drill 13.15. This time, place the adverbial clause at the beginning of the sentence. Use a comma after the adverbial clause. *Example:*

Because Mrs. Perkins wanted to cash a check, she went to the bank first.

13·17 DRILL Restate the sentences you produced in Drill 13.16, using *therefore.* Be sure to use a semicolon before, and a comma after, *therefore. Example:*

Mrs. Perkins wanted to cash a check; therefore, she went to the bank first.

13·18 Senator Blake's overwhelming defeat is surprising **inasmuch as the opinion polls indicated a close race for the senatorial seat.**

Walter Corbin's victory is virtually assured **in that all but 5 percent of the votes have been counted.**

- **Inasmuch as** and **in that** also introduce clauses of reason, but they are not so common as **because** or **since,** especially in informal speech and writing. Notice that there is no comma before **inasmuch as** or **in that.**

13·19   Senator Blake's overwhelming defeat is surprising **in that the polls indicated a close race.**

The polls indicated a close race; **therefore,** Senator Blake's overwhelming defeat is surprising.

- Like **since** and **because** clauses, sentences introduced by **in that** and **inasmuch as** can be restated using **therefore** or **thus.** *Compare:*

   Senator Blake's supporters were bitterly disappointed **in that** (**because**) they were confident of victory.

   Senator Blake's supporters were confident of victory; **therefore,** they were bitterly disappointed.

13·20   DRILL   Combine the two sentences by making the second one a clause of reason introduced by *inasmuch as* or *in that.*

1. Senator Blake's supporters were disappointed.}
   They were confident of victory.   →

   Senator Blake's supporters were disappointed inasmuch as they were confident of victory.

2. His campaign was a failure.
   He failed to get 30 percent of the vote.

3. Senator Blake was at a disadvantage on television.
   He is not a striking or colorful personality.

4. His choice of Samuel Baker as his campaign manager was unfortunate.
   Mr. Baker is not popular with the labor unions.

5. Walter Corbin's victory was largely a personal one.
   He did not receive the support of the major newspapers.

13·21   DRILL   Restate the sentences you produced in Drill 13.20, using *therefore* or *thus.* Remember to use the noun or proper noun in the first clause and the pronoun in the second clause. *Example:*

Senator Blake's supporters were confident of victory; therefore, they were disappointed.

Clauses of Result

13·22   Mrs. Perkins was very hungry. She decided to have lunch early.
   Mrs. Perkins was **so** hungry **that** she decided to have lunch early.

   It was a windy day. She decided to take a taxi to the restaurant.
   It was **such a** windy day **that** she decided to take a taxi to the restaurant.

- Notice that **so** or **such** is attached to the clause that expresses *cause* or *reason:* **that** introduces the *result* clause. The word **that** is often omitted. *Example:*

   Mrs. Perkins was so hungry she decided to have lunch early.

- The following patterns can occur between **so ... that:**

    1) She was **so hungry that** she had lunch early.   (*adjective*)

    2) The wind blew **so hard that** she lost her hat.   (*adverb*)

    3) There were **so few people** in the restaurant **that** she   (**few**/ **many** + *plural noun*)
    didn't have to wait for a table.

    4) She ordered **so much food that** she couldn't eat it all.   (**much**/ **little** + *noncount noun*)

- The following patterns can occur between **such ... that:**

    1) The waitress gave **such good service that**   (*adjective* + *noncount*
    she received a large tip.   *or plural count noun*)

    2) She has **such a friendly manner that** customers   (**a/an** + *adjective* + *singular*
    like her very much.   *count noun*)

13·23 DRILL Fill in the blanks with *so, such,* or *such a/an,* as appropriate.

1. She had _____ excellent lunch at the Bristol Restaurant that she would like to

   go there sometime for dinner.

2. The restaurant has _____ good reputation that it is usually necessary to make

   a reservation for dinner.

3. Everything on the menu seems _____ delicious it is difficult to make a choice.

4. The restaurant gives _____ good service that it is a pleasure to dine there.

5. The restaurant is _____ expensive that one can't go there very often, however.

13·24 DRILL Wherever (+) appears, substitute *many* or *much,* as appropriate; wherever (−) appears, substitute *few* or *little.*

1. She had so (+) packages that she decided to check them.

2. There were so (−) customers that the waitress was able to give excellent service.

3. She had spent so (+) money already that she decided not to order a complete luncheon.

4. She had so (−) money left that she couldn't buy the sweater she liked.

5. She saw so (+) beautiful dresses that she was tempted to buy one.

13·25 Mrs. Perkins decided not to buy a dress **because** she had already spent **so** much money.

Mrs. Perkins had already spent **so** much money **that** she decided not to buy a dress.

- Sentences with **because** and **since** clauses can frequently be restated using **so ... that** or **such ... that** clauses, as shown in the preceding example.

- The **so** in the **because** clause is an *intensifier* (**so much money**). The **so** in the **so ...** **that** clause serves to introduce the clause; it does not function as an intensifier. It is possible, of course, to have intensifiers in **so ... that** clauses.

13·26   DRILL   Convert the clauses (*because/ since*) to clauses of result (*so . . . that/ such . . . that*). Be careful of noun–pronoun placement.

1. Mrs. Perkins decided to go home because she was very tired. →
    Mrs. Perkins was so (very) tired that she decided to go home.

2. She decided to take a taxi because the buses were very crowded.

3. She was lucky to get a taxi because there were so many people waiting for one.

4. Since there was very heavy traffic on the main boulevard, the driver took a side street.

5. She asked him to go through the park because it was a very nice drive.

6. She gave the driver a generous tip because he was very pleasant and courteous.

13·27   It was **so** (very) late **that** Mrs. Perkins took a taxi home.
It was **very** late; **therefore,** Mrs. Perkins took a taxi home.

There was **such a** (great) demand for taxis **that** Mrs. Perkins had a difficult time getting one.
There was a **great** demand for taxis; **therefore,** Mrs. Perkins had a difficult time getting one.

■   Like **because** and **since** clauses, **so . . . that** and **such . . . that** clauses can be restated with **therefore** and **thus.** How does the punctuation differ?

13·28   DRILL   Restate these sentences, using *therefore* as a connector.

1. Mrs. Perkins was so tired that she decided to go home. →
    Mrs. Perkins was very tired; therefore, she decided to go home.

2. She had bought so many things that she didn't have much money left.

3. There was such a long line of people waiting for the bus that she decided to take a taxi.

4. She had so much to carry that she couldn't have got on a bus anyway.

5. It was so warm in the taxi that she opened the windows.

Clauses of Purpose

13·29   Mrs. Perkins turned on the TV **because she wanted to listen to the election results.**
Mrs. Perkins turned on the TV **so that she could listen to the election results.**

■   **Because** and **since** clauses can be restated as **so (that)** clauses. Notice that **because/since/so that** introduce the clause expressing cause, reason, or purpose; the main clause indicates effect or result.

■   **So (that)** clauses frequently contain verb forms with an auxiliary like **could, would, should, might,** and so on.

13·30 The regular program was canceled **so (that) the election results could be broadcast.** The regular program was canceled **in order that the election results could be broadcast.**

- **In order that** clauses are usually more formal in tone than those introduced by **so (that).** However, **in order to** + *verb* as an expression of purpose is very common in both formal and informal speech and writing.°

 The program was canceled **in order to** broadcast the election returns.

13·31 The major networks canceled all regular programs between six and seven o'clock **in order that the election results could be broadcast.**
Because the major networks wanted to present the results of the election, they canceled all other programs between six and seven o'clock.
The major networks wanted to broadcast the results of the election; **therefore,** they canceled all scheduled programs between six and seven o'clock.

- Notice the changes necessary to restate the sentence when using **because** and then **therefore.** In the second sentence, the **because** clause could also occur at the end.

13·32 DRILL Change the *because* clauses to *so that* clauses. Remember that *so that* clauses frequently have an auxiliary like *could, would,* or *might.*
1. She turned on the radio because she wanted to hear the news. →
 She turned on the radio so that she could hear the report on the election.
2. She turned up the volume because she wanted to listen to the newscast in the kitchen.
3. She turned on the oven because she wanted to cook a roast.
4. She opened the window because she didn't want the kitchen to get too warm.
5. She set the table because she wanted everything to be ready for dinner at seven o'clock.

13·33 DRILL Change the sentences with *so that* clauses produced in Drill 13.32 to sentences connected by *therefore. Example:*
 She wanted to hear the election returns; therefore, she turned on the radio.

Clauses of Contrast and Concession

13·34 **Because San Carlos is an industrial city,** it is not as attractive to tourists as San Remos.
Although San Remos is not a large city, there are many interesting things for a tourist to see.

- **Because** and **since** introduce clauses that express cause or reason; these clauses are joined to main clauses that express result or effect. *Example:*

 Because (Since) San Carlos is an industrial city, it is not as attractive to tourists as San Remos.

° See also §9.42 and 9.43 (on adverbials with **for** + *noun* and **in order to** + *verb*).

- **Although, even though,** and **though,** on the other hand, combine with main clauses to express contrast or concession. *Examples:*

  Although (Even though/ Though) young people like San Carlos, older people generally prefer San Remos. (Contrast)

  Although (Even though/ Though) San Remos is smaller than San Carlos, it is a more interesting place to visit. (Concession)

13·35   **DRILL**   Fill in the blanks with *because/ since* or *although/ even though,* as appropriate.

1. ___*Although*___ San Remos has a population of only 110,000, there are several museums.

2. Tourists like San Remos _____ it is picturesque.

3. It is a good idea to hire a guide _____ the streets are not clearly marked.

4. We have been to San Remos several times _____ we have not gone in summer.

5. San Remos is popular in winter _____ it is sunny and mild.

6. The streets are clean _____ they are swept every morning.

7. The marketplace is interesting _____ it is surprisingly small.

8. _____ farmers bring their produce to market every morning, the fruit and vegetables are always fresh.

13·36   San Remos has a large number of hotels and inns **although it is a small city.**
San Remos is a small city, **but** it has a large number of hotels and inns.
San Remos is a small city; **however,** it has a large number of hotels and inns.

- Sentences with **although/ even though/ though** clauses can be restated using **but, however,** or **nevertheless.** Notice the punctuation in the three sentences above.

  1) **Although/ even though/ though** clauses are usually followed by a comma when they occur at the beginning of a sentence; these clauses are not usually preceded by a comma when they occur at the end of a sentence. *Compare:*

  San Remos has a large number of hotels and inns **although (even though/though)** it is . . . .
  Although (Even though/Though) San Remos is a small city, it has a large number . . . .

  2) When **but** connects two sentences, it is usually preceded by a comma. **But** can also follow a period. *Compare:*

  San Remos is a small city, **but** it has a large number . . . .
  San Remos is a small city. **But** it has a large number . . . .

  Note: The rule sometimes cited that a sentence should not begin with **and** or **but** is a matter of usage or style rather than correctness or incorrectness.

  3) **However/ nevertheless,** like **therefore/ thus,** are preceded by a semicolon or a period and are usually followed by a comma. *Compare:*

  San Remos is a small city; **however (nevertheless),** it has a large number . . . .
  San Remos is a small city. **However (Nevertheless),** it has a large number . . . .

Also, like **therefore** and **thus, however** and **nevertheless** are set off by commas if they do not occur at the beginning of the sentence.

San Remos is a small city; it has, **however,** a large number . . . .

San Remos is a small city. It has a large number of hotels, **however.**

13·37

We prefer the Hotel Sol $\left\{\begin{array}{l}\textbf{though}\\ \textbf{although}\\ \textbf{even though}\\ \textbf{even if}\end{array}\right\}$ it is not the most luxurious.

We prefer the Hotel Sol; it is not the most luxurious, $\left\{\begin{array}{l}\textbf{though.}\\ \textbf{however.}\end{array}\right.$

■ Compare the use of **though** in the two preceding sentences. In the first sentence, **though** introduces the concession clause and could be replaced by **although, even though,** or **even if.** In the second sentence, it could be replaced by **however** but not by **although, even though,** or **even if.**

13·38   DRILL   Restate these sentences using *although, even though, even if*, or *though.*

1. San Remos is crowded in the summer, but it is relatively uncrowded the rest of the year. →
   Although San Remos is crowded in the summer, it is relatively uncrowded the rest of the year.

2. It is expensive, but hire a local guide.

3. The city is very old, but there are many modern buildings.

4. The population is over 100,000, but the city seems very small.

5. You may be able to stay only a short time, but you will find the visit worth your while.

6. You may plan to stay only a week, but you will probably stay longer.

13·39   DRILL   Restate the sentences you produced in Drill 13.38, using *however* or *nevertheless. Example:*

San Remos is crowded in the summer; however, it is relatively uncrowded the rest of the year.

13·40

You should see San Remos $\left\{\begin{array}{l}\textbf{although}\\ \textbf{even though}\\ \textbf{even if}\end{array}\right\}$ your visit is a short one.

You should see San Remos, $\left\{\begin{array}{l}\textbf{no matter how}\\ \textbf{however}\end{array}\right\}$ short your visit may be.

■ The meaning of the two preceding sentences is essentially the same. Notice that **however** in the second sentence has about the same meaning as **no matter how;** in this sentence, **however** could not be replaced by **but.**

13·41   DRILL   Restate the idea expressed in the following sentences, using *even though* or *even if.* You will have to add information, as is done in the first one.

1. No matter how long you stay in San Remos, you will want to stay longer. →
   Even if you stay a month in San Remos, you will want to stay longer.

2. It will be difficult to get reservations at the best hotels whatever time of year you go there.

3. The food in San Remos is excellent no matter how inexpensive the meal is.

4. The weather will be sunny no matter what time of year you go there.

5. The people of San Remos will listen to you courteously no matter how poorly you speak Spanish.

Adverbial Clauses and Participial Phrases

13·42   **As we were approaching San Remos,** we were stopped by two policemen.
Approaching San Remos, we were stopped by two policemen.

Since we didn't understand Spanish, we tried to speak to them in English.
Not understanding Spanish, we tried to speak to them in English.

I showed them my driver's license **because I thought that was what they wanted.**
I showed them my driver's license, **thinking that was what they wanted.**

- Adverbial clauses like those in the preceding group of examples can be changed to participial phrases by omitting the subordinators **as, since,** and **because** and the subject. In order to make this change, however, the subjects of both clauses must refer to the same person. *Compare:*

  As **the policeman** approached our car, **he** took a notebook out of his pocket.

  Approaching our car, **the policeman** took a notebook out of his pocket.
  (Notice that the noun and pronoun refer to the same person; also notice that the noun replaces the pronoun in the main clause.)

  As **the policeman** approached our car, **we** saw him take a notebook out of his pocket.
  Here the change to a participial phrase is not possible because the subjects refer to different persons. "Approaching the car, we saw the policeman take out a notebook" means that *we* were approaching the car. This type of faulty sentence is often called a *dangling modifier.*)

- Notice that a comma follows the phrase at the beginning and precedes the phrase at the end of the sentence.

13·43   DRILL   Change the adverbial clauses to participial phrases *whenever possible.*

1. As we showed the policemen our passports, they backed away. →
   (The change is not possible. Why?)

2. Since the policemen didn't understand English, they were baffled by our conversation. →
   Not understanding English, the policemen were baffled by our conversation.

3. Mr. Martin offered the policemen money because he thought that was what they wanted.

4. When the policemen saw the money, they became very angry.

5. As they approached Mr. Martin, he put his money in his pocket.

6. As we looked down the road, we saw a herd of cattle coming toward us.

7. We got back in the car because we thought that was the sensible thing to do.

13·44 **While the cattle were going by the car,** they raised clouds of dust.
Going by the car, the cattle raised clouds of dust.

After the cattle had passed the car, they broke into a run.
Having passed the car, the cattle broke into a run.

- The first pair of sentences expresses simultaneous action; the second pair indicates that one action precedes the other. How do the participial forms differ?

- **While** and **when,** unlike **as, since,** and **because** (see §13.42), can be retained in phrases expressing simultaneous action. *Compare:*

   While going by the car,⎫
      Going by the car,⎬ the cattle broke into a run.

- **After** can be retained in phrases indicating that one action precedes the other. *Compare:*

   Having passed the car,⎫
   After passing the car,⎬ the cattle broke into a run.

- **Before** is retained in participial phrases like the one below.

   Before we opened the windows, we waited for the dust to settle.
   Before opening the windows, we waited for the dust to settle.

- The change to a participle can take place without an adverbial clause. *Example:*

   The cowboy grinned and (he) rode on.
   Grinning, the cowboy rode on.

13·45 DRILL Change the *italicized* clauses to participial phrases *whenever possible.*

1. *After the policemen got in their car,* they motioned us to go on. →
   After getting in their car, the policemen motioned us to go on.
   OR: *Having got in their car, the policemen motioned us to go on.*

2. *We smiled* and drove away. → *Smiling, we drove away.*

3. I drove slowly *because I thought the policemen were watching us.*

4. *After the policemen had followed us for several miles,* they turned off on another road.

5. *When we saw them turn off,* we breathed a great sigh of relief.

6. *Since we had not met anyone there who didn't speak a little English,* we were totally unprepared for our experience with the policemen.

7. *After we had talked it over,* however, we felt much better.

8. *As we drove into San Remos,* the sun was setting and all was well with the world.

1 Combine the following pairs of sentences by making an adverbial clause of the sentence preceded by an *italicized* word or words. Change verb forms, as appropriate. If you write the exercise, use a comma after an adverbial clause beginning a sentence.

1. (*when*) I'll go to the library today. I'll complete the bibliography for my term paper. →
    When I go to the library today, I'll complete the bibliography for my term paper.

2. I'll check the dates of some of the books. (*while*) I'll verify the authors and titles of the books.

3. (*although*) I try to be accurate from the start. I always find a few mistakes.

4. I have always found mistakes. (*whenever*) I have checked the references.

5. I'll work hard to eliminate the errors. (*because*) I'll want my bibliography to be perfect this time.

6. I want the information to be accurate. (*so that*) I can use it in the future.

7. (*after*) I'll finish at the library. I'll join you for dinner.

8. (*since*) The cafeteria will be crowded. Maybe you'll want to go to a restaurant.

9. (*such . . . that*) There's always a crowd in the cafeteria. It takes forever to get through the line.

10. (*so . . . that*) There are always many people. It is difficult to find an empty table.

11. (*after*) We'll have dinner. Perhaps we can go to a movie.

12. (*so that*) I'll work hard to finish my checking. I'll have the evening free.

13. (*by the time*) I'll finish this paper. I'll be ready to relax.

14. I enjoy doing term papers. (*even though*) They take a lot of time.

15. I find I learn a lot. (*because*) I have to read so much material.

2 Look at the sentences in Ex. 1 and decide in which ones the adverbial clauses can be changed to participial phrases. Make the changes wherever possible.

3 Here are two groups of connectors: (1) *although, even though, since, because;* (2) *therefore, thus, however, nevertheless.* In the following paragraphs, change group 1 connectors to group 2 connectors, and vice versa. Make other changes, if appropriate, to improve the paragraphs. Punctuate appropriately.

1.   Both sound and sight are part of our experience; *therefore,* the addition of sound to picture greatly increases the effectiveness of film. *Although* sound film is, of course, more trouble to shoot and edit, the results are more than worth the effort. Viewers become more a part of the experience conveyed by the film with the addition of music or of the sound of wind, honking horns, knocking at doors, or human laughter; *thus,* the filmmaker is well advised to think as much about the sound as the visual elements in approaching each new motion picture he makes.

2.   *Although* the industrial revolution in the nineteenth century stimulated international trade, it also brought about international tension as nations competed for markets and raw materials. The industrial revolution raised the standard of living of some people; *however,* it created terrible living and working conditions for others. *Since* many laborers could not support their families and were ill-housed and often sick, they inevitably became dissatisfied with their lot in life. *Because* the working class felt more and more exploited during that time of prosperity, labor eventually demanded the right to organize and to fight for a better share of the economic goods.

3.   Scientists the world over have long tried to determine what causes stuttering, a common communication disorder; *nevertheless,* no one has come up with a definitive answer so far. *Because* many of the findings are contradictory, the answer is difficult at best. Some researchers claim that the cause is psychological; *however,* others contend that stuttering is a physiological disorder. Still others take the stand that it is fruitless to distinguish between emotional and physical causes *since* they feel the dividing line is not very clear. There are fortunately some findings that are clearer; for instance, investigators can point out that stuttering tends to run in certain families and that it occurs more frequently in males than in females. *Even though,* like causes, the "cure" of stuttering is often uncertain, many individuals, through clinical guidance and their own persistence, have largely overcome this disability.

4 Read the following paragraph, and then complete the exercises below.

Plato described Atlantis in the *Timaeus.* Since then that mythical island has captured man's imagination. According to Plato, a great civilization existed on Atlantis. Its armies conquered most of the lands around the Mediterranean, and only Athens managed to resist their power. Eventually, a great earthquake shook it to its foundation; then it supposedly sank into the sea within 24 hours. Throughout the centuries men have speculated about the location of Atlantis. After Columbus's discovery of America, some people thought that the New World might be the lost Atlantis.

1. Answer these questions; give full sentences, including adverbial clauses in your answers.

    a) How long has the mythical island of Atlantis captured man's imagination? (Begin the answer with "Ever since Plato . . .")

    b) Against what odds did Athens resist the armies of Atlantis? (Begin your answer with "Although the armies of Atlantis . . .")

    c) When did Atlantis sink into the sea?

    d) After Columbus discovered America, what did some people think?

2. Construct a paragraph by completing the adverbial clauses in this model.

    Ever since (time clause) . . . , that mythical island has captured man's imagination. According to Plato, a great civilization existed on Atlantis. *Although* its armies (reason clause) . . . , Athens managed to resist their power. Atlantis supposedly sank into the sea within 24 hours *after* (time clause) . . . . *After* (time clause) . . . , some people thought that the New World was the lost Atlantis.

5   Read the following paragraphs, and then do the exercises below.

    The rocks that compose the earth's surface are constantly under pressure from forces within the earth. *The strain sometimes becomes intense, and the rocks cannot withstand the pressure;* then the rocks rupture and may cause an earthquake. These ruptures in the rocks are called faults. *Most earthquake faults lie beneath the surface of the earth,* but some are visible on the surface.

    Great earthquakes that occur near coasts may produce enormous waves, often erroneously called tidal waves. *They are not caused by tides,* but they may be caused by undersea landslides. *These waves approach shore at high speeds;* they sometimes increase to 90 feet or more in height.

    Seismographs can record the number and intensity of shocks; no mechanism can yet predict the occurrence of earthquakes with any degree of accuracy. *Supposing scientists could predict for sure that severe earthquakes would occur within five years in a certain area.* Do you believe that many people would give up their homes and relocate?

1. Copy or read the paragraphs aloud, but convert the *italicized* portions into adverbial clauses. Use the adverbial connectors listed below:

    Paragraph 1: ... *so intense that* ..../ *Although* ....
    Paragraph 2: ... *Although* ..../ *As* ....
    Paragraph 3: *While* ..../ *Even if* ....

2. Now write questions and answers based on the paragraphs that you have written. Your questions should be formed to produce adverbials (words, phrases, or clauses) in your answers. *Examples:*

    Q: What causes the rocks on the earth's surface to be constantly under pressure?

    A: There are forces within the earth causing the rocks on its surface to be constantly under pressure.

    Q: Does the strain sometimes become so intense that the rocks cannot withstand the pressure?

    A: Yes; and when that happens, the rocks rupture and may cause an earthquake.

6   Write an original report of 150–200 words on one of the topics below. You may need an encyclopedia or other sources of information. If so, give the sources at the end of your report (that is, give the author, title, publisher, date, and pages of the material, in that order). Pay particular attention to the use of adverbials and adverbial clauses as you write.

1. Description of an earthquake (a flood, a fire, a car accident, etc.)

2. The pleasures and problems of mountain climbing (sailing, etc.)

3. Information about the destruction of Pompeii (the Krakatoa earthquake, the Arctic, outer space, etc.)

COMPARISONS

14

THE SAME AS/ DIFFERENT FROM/ LIKE/ UNLIKE/ SIMILAR TO

14·1 — Is Washington, D.C., **the same as** the District of Columbia?
— Yes, it is. It is **different from** the state of Washington, though.
— Is the climate of California **similar to** the climate of other states?
— Well, it's somewhat **like** the climate of Florida, but it's quite **unlike** that of Massachusetts.

■ Notice the boldfaced comparatives in the sentences above. Could we substitute **the same as** for **like** in the last sentence? Which comparative could we use instead of **like?** Which one could we use instead of **unlike?**

14·2 DRILL Make sentences with comparisons using *the same as, different from, like, unlike,* or *similar to.* You might also add items to the list.

1. Washington, D.C./ District of Columbia →
Washington, D.C. is the same as the District of Columbia.

2. Iraq/ Iran → *Iraq is different from Iran.*

3. Korea/ Chosen
4. Russia/ the Soviet Union
5. Holland/ the Netherlands
6. Nippon/ Japan

7. an Austrian/ an Australian
8. a Mexican/ a Spaniard
9. a Siamese/ a Thai
10. a Persian/ an Iranian

14·3 — Are Washington, D.C., and the District of Columbia **the same?**
— Yes, they are. Washington, D.C., and the state of Washington are **different,** though.
— Are the climates of California and Italy **alike?**
— Yes, they are quite **similar.**

■ These sentences make the same kinds of comparisons as those in the first set of examples. Compare the two sets of examples. How do they differ?

14·4   DRILL   Using the lists in Drill 14.2, ask questions and give answers. *Examples:*

— Are Washington, D.C., and the District of Columbia the same?
— Yes, they are.
— Are Iraq and Iran the same?
— No, they're different.

14·5   The climate of California is **quite similar to** the climate of Florida.
The climate of Hawaii is **rather similar to** that of Tahiti.

- ■   Words like **quite, rather, exactly, almost, very,** and **somewhat** can specify degrees of sameness, difference, likeness, and similarity.

- ■   Notice that **that of** replaces **the climate of** in the second sentence.

14·6   DRILL   Use *similar to* to make comparisons of the climates of various places. Use *very, quite, somewhat,* or *rather* to specify degrees of similarity, as appropriate. (If you are not familiar with some of the places on the list, add places that you can talk about.)

1. California ➔ *The climate of California is quite similar to the climate of Italy.*
   OR: *The climate of California is quite similar to that of Italy.*

2. Hong Kong   5. Cuba   8. Copenhagen   11. Mexico City
3. the Philippines   6. Rio de Janeiro   9. Bangkok   12. Djakarta
4. Liberia   7. Cairo   10. Morocco   13. Kathmandu

14·7   DRILL   Ask questions about the climate of places on the list in Drill 14.6 using *(anything) like.* If you wish, qualify your answers with *very much, somewhat, something (anything— negative). Example:*

Is the climate of California anything like the climate of Italy?
Yes, the climate of California is very much like that of Italy.

14·8   — Are both nylon and Dacron **the same?**
— No, they're not, but nylon is **similar to** Dacron.
— In what way?
— **Both** nylon **and** Dacron are synthetic fabrics.
— What about silk and cotton?
— **Neither** silk **nor** cotton is a synthetic fabric.

- ■   **Both ... and** obviously indicates similarity or likeness; **neither ... nor** indicates dissimilarity or unlikeness.

- ■   In formal English, the verb agrees with the (pro)noun following **nor.** *Compare:*

  Neither these dresses nor this shirt **is** silk.
  Neither this shirt nor these dresses **are** silk.

  In less formal English, however, one often sees and hears a plural verb following **nor** + singular noun.

14·9   DRILL   Make sentences using *both . . . and.*

1. nylon and Dacron/ synthetic fabrics → *Both nylon and Dacron are synthetic fabrics.*

2. spaghetti and macaroni/ pastas
3. jam and jelly/ fruit preserves
4. limes and lemons/ citrus fruits
5. coffee and tea/ hot drinks

6. gravel and sand/ building materials
7. Coca-Cola and Pepsi-Cola/ cold drinks
8. potatoes and beans/ vegetables
9. recorder and flute/ wind instruments

14·10   DRILL   Make sentences using *neither . . . nor.*

1. silk and cotton/ a synthetic fabric → *Neither silk nor cotton is a synthetic fabric.*

2. limes and lemons/ vegetables? → *Neither limes nor lemons are vegetables.*

3. rice and corn/ a pasta
4. potatoes and beans/ fruits
5. jam and jelly/ a cold drink

6. kerosene and gasoline/ a building material
7. fruit juices and soft drinks/ alcoholic beverages
8. nylon and Dacron/ a natural fabric

14·11   DRILL   Make sentences using *similar to/similar* and *the same.*

1. nylon/ Dacron → *Nylon is similar to Dacron, but it isn't the same.*
   OR: *Nylon and Dacron are similar, but they aren't the same.*

2. jam/ jelly
3. limes/ lemons
4. Coca-Cola/ Pepsi-Cola

5. spaghetti/ macaroni
6. cocoa/ chocolate
7. kerosene/ gasoline

14·12   — How does Jorge drive?
— He drives **like the wind.**
— What is his car like?
— His blue Ford looks and sounds **like a racing car.**

- **Like** + *noun* functions as an adverbial of manner after some verbs ("drives like the wind" = drives very fast).

- **Like** + *noun* also follows **look, sound, taste, feel, smell,** as well as a form of **be,** which can replace the other five (His blue Ford **looks and sounds** like a racing car = His blue Ford **is** like a racing car).

14·13   DRILL   Make sentences comparing an actual or imaginary person to an actress, a professional, etc.

1. look/ an actress → *That girl looks like an actress.*

2. dance/ a professional → *She also dances like a professional.*

3. act/ a computer
4. look/ a gentleman

5. sound/ a bore
6. eat/ a connoisseur

7. live/ fatalist
8. work/ a horse

14·14   It sounded **like a bell.**   It was **bell-like.**
         The trees looked **like ghosts.**   The trees looked **ghóstlike.**
         Her manner was **like a lady's.**   Her manner was **ládylike.**
         Her manner was **like** that of **a lady.**   She had a **ládylike** manner.

   ■   The suffix **like** is added to some nouns to form adjectives (**bell-like, lifelike, businesslike**). The noun receives heavier stress than **like.** What are the changes in spelling?

14·15   DRILL   Restate these sentences.

   1. His hair was *like straw.* → *His hair was strawlike.* OR: *He had strawlike hair.*
   2. The shape of the dish was *like a shell.* →
   3. The polished tabletop was *like a mirror.*
   4. Her manner was *like* that of *a child.*
   5. Her voice had a quality *like* that of *a bell.*
   6. The air was *like velvet.*

AS . . . AS/ -ER THAN/ MORE . . . THAN/ -EST OF ALL/ MOST . . . OF ALL

14·16   — Is Texas **as large as** California?
         — Texas is **larger than** California in area, but California is **more densely populated.**
         — Texas isn't **as large as** Alaska, is it?
         — Well, Alaska is much **larger than** Texas, but it's much **less densely populated.**

   ■   The comparatives have these meanings:

         as . . . as = at least equal to
         -er or **more** (**. . . than**) = plus degree
         not as (so) . . . as and **less** (**. . . than**) = minus degree

14·17   DRILL   Compare the following states to California in area and population. Use *-er than* and *more (less) . . . than* structures. *Example:*

         Alaska is larger than California in area, but California is more densely populated.

	Square miles	Population (1970 census)
California	156,803	19,953,134
Alaska	571,065	302,173
Arizona	113,580	1,772,482
Illinois	55,877	11,113,976
Mississippi	47,358	2,216,912
New York	47,929	18,190,740
Rhode Island	1,058	949,729
Texas	263,644	11,196,730

14·18   New York is **closer to** Boston **than** it is to Chicago.

New York is**n't as close** to Chicago **as** it is to Boston.

- In the preceding examples, notice that the distance from one place is compared to two other places (that is, the distance between New York and Chicago is compared with the distance between New York and Boston).

- Besides **not as . . . as,** you will also hear **not so . . . as.**

14·19   DRILL   Using the information below, compare the highway distances between New York and two other cities. Use both *closer . . . than* and *not as (so) close . . . as* structures. (See the examples in §14.18.)

	Distance from New York		*Distance from New York*
Philadelphia	91 miles	Chicago	840 miles
Boston	219 miles	Miami	1,331 miles
Washington, D.C.	224 miles	Dallas	1,595 miles
Cleveland	509 miles	Seattle	2,916 miles

14·20   It is **farther** from Los Angeles to San Francisco **than** it is from New York to Boston.

It is**n't as** far from New York to Boston **as** it is from Los Angeles to San Francisco.

- In the preceding examples, notice that the distance between two cities is compared with the distance between two other cities (that is, the distance between Los Angeles and San Francisco is compared with the distance between New York and Boston.)

14·21   DRILL   Using the information below, compare the air distance between two cities with the air distance between two other cities. Use both *farther . . . than* and *not as (so) far . . . as* structures. (See §14.20 for examples.)

	Distance in air miles		*Distance in air miles*
New York/ Boston	188	Tokyo/ Rome	6,135
Los Angeles/ San Francisco	347	Capetown/ Caracas	6,365
Washington, D.C./ Moscow	4,858	New Delhi/ Rio de Janeiro	8,753
Paris/ Peking	5,120	Montreal/ Melbourne	10,395

14·22   — Which continent is **the largest** in area? Which continent is **the smallest?**

— Asia is **the largest,** and Australia is **the smallest.**

— Which has **the most** population and which has **the least** population?

— Asia has **the most** and Antarctica has **the least.**

- The superlatives have these meanings:

  the most (+ *noun*) = highest degree of the members of a group
  the least (+ *noun*) = lowest degree
  the -est = highest or lowest degree, depending on the adjective (**the largest/the smallest**).

■ **The** can be omitted if **-est** or **most** is not followed by a noun. *Compare:*

Which is **the** highest mountain on the North American continent?
Which mountain on the North American continent is (**the**) highest?
Mount McKinley is (**the**) highest.

14·23   DRILL   Using the information about continents below, make comparisons of the population per square mile, the highest point, and the lowest point. Use *-est* and *most/least* structures. *Example:*

Australia has the least population per square mile of any populated continent; its highest point is Mount Kosciusko at 7,316′ and its lowest point is Lake Eyre at 38′ below sea level.

Continent	Population per square mile	Highest point	Lowest point
Africa	25	Mt. Kilimanjaro, 19,340′	Qattara Depression, 440′ below sea level
Antarctica	—	Vinson Massif, 16,863′	Sea level
Asia	109	Mt. Everest, 29,028′	Dead Sea, 1,290′ below sea level
Australia	4	Mt. Kosciusko, 7,316′	Lake Eyre, 38′ below sea level
Europe	153	Mt. Elbrus, 18,481′	Caspian Sea, 96′ below sea level
North America	30	Mt. McKinley, 20,320′	Death Valley, 282′ below sea level
South America	23	Mt. Aconcagua, 23,034′	Salina Grande, 131′ below sea level

14·24   — Is Boston **as large a city as** Chicago?
— No, Boston is **a smaller city than** Chicago.

■ In the preceding examples, notice that a noun follows **large** and **smaller** and that **a** precedes the noun (NOT: Boston is smaller city than Chicago).

14·25   — Which is **the largest city** in the United States?
— New York is **the largest city.**
— Which is (**the**) **largest**: London, Paris, or Rome?
— London is (**the**) **largest.**

14·26   DRILL   Use appropriate nouns in the comparison structures.

1. London is *larger than* Paris. → *London is a larger city than Paris.*
2. Tokyo is *the largest.* → *Tokyo is the largest city in the world.*
3. Is Rome as interesting as Paris? → *Is Rome as interesting a city as Paris?*

4. Spain is *less expensive* for a tourist *than* Sweden.

5. China is *much larger than* Japan.

6. The Pacific is *larger than* the Atlantic.

7. Shakespeare is *more famous than* Marlowe. (dramatist)

8. Wolfgang Amadeus Mozart is *more famous than* his father. (composer)

9. Mercury is *closest* to the Sun.

10. Mount Everest is *highest*.

11. Is Japan *as industrialized as* the United States?

12. Is Cairo *as fascinating as* some people say it is?

14·27 He's stubborn. He's **like** a mule.   He's **as** stubborn **as** a mule.
This bed is hard. It's **like** a rock.   This bed is **as** hard **as** a rock.

■ Many comparisons of persons, animals, and things have become fixed expressions. Most of them are regarded as clichés, expressions once fresh and original but now commonplace. These expressions are part of everyday speech. They become ridiculous, however, when used by a person who thinks he is saying something very original or clever. For example, a naïve young man who tells a sophisticated young woman that her "eyes are like stars" is likely to be cut off with the comment "You've got to be kidding." Also, a student who uses a lot of clichés in his compositions is likely to receive a comment from his instructor to "Avoid clichés."

■ Some native speakers of English omit the first **as.** *Example:*

He's **as** stubborn **as** a mule. OR: He's stubborn **as** a mule.

14·28 DRILL   Change the pairs of sentences to sentences with (*as*) . . . *as* comparisons.

1. The linen is white. It's like snow. → *The linen is as white as snow.*

2. This chili is hot. It's like fire.

3. The noise is very loud. It's like thunder.

4. The meat is tough. It's like shoe leather.

5. This place is quiet. It's like a church.

6. The fruit is sweet. It's like candy.

7. She's timid. She's like a mouse.

8. She looks fresh. She's like a daisy.

14·29 Wait **no longer than** twenty minutes.
Don't wait **longer than** twenty minutes.
Twenty minutes is **as long as** you should wait.

He saw **no more than** five persons.
Five persons are **as many as** he saw.

- Notice these things about the preceding examples:
    1) **Twenty minutes** and **five persons** are in subject position in the **as . . . as** constructions.
    2) The sentences containing the **as . . . as** constructions are affirmative rather than negative.
    3) The verb following **twenty minutes** is singular (twenty, thirty, forty minutes = a period of time). A sum of money (five, ten, fifteen dollars) would also be followed by a singular verb.

14·30   DRILL   Restate the sentences using the *as . . . as* construction.

1. Mr. Browning can't interview *(any) more than* three persons this afternoon. →
    Three persons are as many as Mr. Browning can interview this afternoon.

2. Each interview will last *no longer than* fifteen minutes. →
    Fifteen minutes is as long as each interview will last.

3. He doesn't have jobs for *more than* two persons.

4. He will pay *no more than* $600 a month for a secretary.

5. He won't pay *any more than* $450 a month for a file clerk.

6. The secretary cannot be *older than* twenty-six.

14·31   Jeffrey is **a better guitarist than** either Jack or Bill (is).

Jeffrey plays the guitar **better than** either Jack or Bill (does).

He is **a more skillful classical guitarist than** they (are).

He plays the classical guitar **more skillfully than** they (do).

He is also **the best singer** of the three.

He also sings **the best** of the three.

- In the examples on the left, adjectives occur in the comparative and superlative constructions; on the right, adverbs occur in these constructions. Auxiliaries and **be**-forms are optional in comparative constructions but are used more frequently after a pronoun than after a noun.

14·32   DRILL   Restate the sentences, using an adjective in a comparative or superlative construction.

1. Diane works harder than Karen (does). → *Diane is a harder worker than Karen (is).*

2. In fact, she works harder than anyone I know. →
    In fact, she is the hardest worker I know.

3. She studies more efficiently than Karen and Paul (do).

4. She also reads her assignments more carefully than they do.

5. Paul reads faster than Diane, however.

6. As a matter of fact, he reads the fastest of anyone I've ever known.

14·33   DRILL   Restate the sentences, using an adverb in the comparative or superlative construction.

1. Alex is a better tennis player than Olga (is). →
   Alex plays tennis better than she (does).
2. She's a better swimmer than anyone in the group.
3. Steve is a faster reader than David (is).
4. Steve is a slower reader than Don (is).
5. Harry is the fastest reader of anyone in the class.
6. Portney Wells is a less colorful writer than Elvis Dillingworth (is).

14·34   The brown shoes **lasted longer than** the white shoes.
The brown shoes **outlasted** the white shoes.

We did **more than** the others to make them feel at home.
We **outdid** the others in making them feel at home.

- Comparisons containing adverbs can often be restated, as shown in the preceding examples. The meanings are the same.

14·35   DRILL   Restate the sentences.

1. We bid more for the antique chair than the others did. →
   We outbid the others for the antique chair.
2. For once we were smarter than they were. → *For once we outsmarted them.*
3. Mr. Axel sold more furniture than the other dealers sold.
4. Cotton lasts longer than silk.
5. Factory A produced more silk than Factory B produced.
6. This leather bag will last longer than that plastic one.
7. A colonel ranks higher than a major.
8. They guessed more accurately than we did.
9. They maneuvered more skillfully than we did.
10. Old Mr. Richbanks lived longer than his heirs.

14·36   William Saroyan's Uncle Melik was **more** of a poet **than** he was a farmer.
He was **more** imaginative **than** (he was) practical.
His farm was **more** a dream **than** (it was) a reality.
The land was **as** dry **as** it was lonely.

- In the preceding examples, two qualities or features are contrasted in relation to one person or thing.

14·37   Uncle Melik had **more** intelligence **than** people gave him credit for.

He was **more** intelligent **than** people gave him credit for.

He wasn't **as** stupid **as** people thought he was.

■   Notice that a clause follows **than** and **as** in the examples.

14·38   DRILL   Restate the sentences using a comparison construction.

1. She is nice, and she is also attractive. →
   She is as nice as she is attractive.
2. She was very generous, but she shouldn't have been. →
   She was more generous than she should have been.
3. He has a lot of time, but he doesn't have enough money.
4. He has only a few relatives, but he has a lot of friends.
5. He is very clever, but people don't realize it.
6. He's a good businessman, but people don't give him credit for it.
7. He is only fairly intelligent, but he's exceptionally shrewd.
8. He isn't very theoretical, but he's very practical.
9. He's hard working, and he's honest.
10. He's accurate at details, and he's thorough in checking them.

14·39   If they have **more,** they want **more.**   **The more** they have, **the more** they want.

If the task is **harder,** he likes it better.   **The harder** the task, **the better** he likes it.

If you invest **more** money, your income is **greater.**   **The more** money you invest, **the greater** your income.

As you get **older,** you become **more cautious.**   **The older** you get, **the more cautious** you become.

FORMATION OF THE COMPARATIVE AND THE SUPERLATIVE

One-syllable adjectives and their adverb counterparts take **-er/-est** endings.

slow/slower/(the) slowest	soft/softer/(the) softest	loud/louder/(the) loudest
fast/faster/(the) fastest	hard/harder/(the) hardest	quick/quicker/(the) quickest

In writing, double a final single consonant letter preceded by a single vowel letter. *Compare:*

mad/madder/maddest	late/later/latest
big/bigger/biggest	soon/sooner/soonest

Two-syllable adjectives and adverbs ending in the letter **y** take **-er/-est** endings.

pretty/prettier/(the) prettiest	early/earlier/(the) earliest

In writing, change final **y** before a consonant letter to **i.** Other examples:

heavy/heavier/(the) heaviest	ugly/uglier/(the) ugliest

14·40   DRILL   Restate the following sentences.

1. If they are bigger, they fall harder. →
   The bigger they are, the harder they fall.

2. If the pearl is larger, it is more valuable. →
   The larger the pearl, the more valuable it is.

3. If we work harder, the rewards will be greater.

4. If we study more, we learn more.

5. As he gets older, he remembers less.

6. If you talk more, he will understand less.

7. As it gets colder, we use more fuel.

8. When we are younger, we are more hopeful.

14·41   He has no **heart**.   He's **héartless**.

His advice is not **worth** anything.   His advice is **wórthless**.

They don't have **jobs**.   They are **jóbless**.

■   In the preceding examples, the negative sentences on the left are restated as sentences with *noun* + **less** adjectives. In these combinations, the noun has heavier stress than **less**. The plural **s** is deleted when **less** is added, so that we have **jobless** (NOT: jobs less).

14·42   DRILL   Restate these sentences.

1. The old dog has no *teeth*. →
   The old dog is toothless. OR: *He's toothless.* OR: *He's a toothless old dog.*

2. The children don't have *homes*.

3. They don't have a *penny*.

4. They have no *mother*.

5. Their plan made no *sense* at all.

6. Their idea had no *meaning*.

Many two-syllable adjectives and adverbs can either take **-er/-est** endings or occur with **more/most** or **less/least**.

cleverer/(the) **cleverest** OR **more** clever/(the) **most** clever OR **less** clever/(the) **least** clever
stupider/(the) **stupidest** OR **more** stupid/(the) **most** stupid OR **less** stupid/(the) **least** stupid
lonelier/(the) **lonliest** OR **more** lonely/(the) **most** lonely OR **less** lonely/(the) **least** lonely

Adjectives and adverbs not included in the preceding sections occur with **more/most** or **less/least**.

more interesting/(the) **most** interesting	**more** slowly/(the) **most** slowly
more brilliant/(the) **most** brilliant	**more** rapidly/(the) **most** rapidly
less interesting/(the) **least** interesting	**less** slowly/(the) **least** slowly
less brilliant/(the) **least** brilliant	**less** rapidly/(the) **least** rapidly

14·43   He's a man without **mercy.**   {He's **merciless.**
                                                             {He's a **merciless** man.

- In the sentences on the right, **-less** has essentially the same meaning as "without."

14·44   DRILL   Change *italicized* phrases to phrases with *noun + less* and then use the phrases in sentences.

1. a personality *without color* → *a colorless personality* →
   She has a colorless personality.
2. *without tact* → *tactless* → *She was a tactless person.*
3. a man *without humor*   7. a flower *without odor*
4. *without a time limitation*   8. a remark *without taste*
5. *without limits*   9. *without weight*
6. a situation *without hope*   10. *without a hat*

SIMILARLY / ON THE OTHER HAND

14·45   Some Americans like European cars better than American cars. **Similarly,** some Europeans prefer American cars to European cars.

- **Similarly** relates the second sentence to the first. **Likewise, also,** and **too** are other signals that can be used in place of **similarly** in the example sentence.

14·46   European cars are still quite popular in the United States. **On the other hand,** American cars do not seem to be as popular in Europe as they once were.

- **On the other hand** is a comparison signal of difference or contrast; it relates the second sentence to the first. **Conversely, in contrast, however,** and **but** are also signals of difference or contrast. All of them can be used in place of **on the other hand** in the example sentence but not in all situations.

14·47   DRILL   Discuss the cars listed below. Tell how *economical* or *uneconomical* they are to operate, how *expensive* or *inexpensive* they are, how *large* or *small* they are, how *attractive* or *unattractive* they are, and how *comfortable* or *uncomfortable* they are. *Examples:*
A Volkswagen is less expensive than a Mercedes-Benz. It is also more economical to operate.
A Volkswagen is more economical to operate than a Mercedes-Benz. On the other hand, it is not as comfortable to ride in.

Cadillac	Rolls-Royce	Alfa-Romeo	Peugeot	Ford	Oldsmobile
Volkswagen	Toyota	Mercedes-Benz	Chevrolet	Fiat	MG

14·48 A Cadillac is more comfortable than a Toyota. **On the other hand,** a Toyota is more economical to operate.

While (Although) a Cadillac is more comfortable than a Toyota, a Toyota is more economical to operate.

A Toyota is more economical to operate than a Cadillac **although (while)** the Toyota is less comfortable.

- Sentences with signals of contrast such as **on the other hand, however,** and **but** can usually be restated with a **while** or **although** clause. A comma usually follows a **while** or **although** clause but does not usually precede it.

14·49 DRILL Restate the following sentences using a *while* or *although* clause.

1. A Toyota is smaller than a Chevrolet; however, a Volkswagen is even smaller than a Toyota. →
   Although (While) a Toyota is smaller than a Chevrolet, a Volkswagen is even smaller than a Toyota.

2. A pickup truck is more practical for hauling things than an ordinary car, but it isn't as comfortable.

3. A Jeep is more expensive than a Ford. On the other hand, it is less expensive than a Ferrari.

4. A Chevrolet is not as expensive as some cars, but it is more expensive than a Volkswagen.

5. A Volkswagen is one of the least expensive cars; however, it is one of the most underpowered cars.

14·50 A Jaguar is quite an expensive car. **In contrast,** a Toyota is quite inexpensive.
In contrast to a Jaguar, a Toyota is quite inexpensive.

- Sentences with **in contrast** signaling difference or contrast can be restated in one sentence with **in contrast to.**

14·51 DRILL Restate these sentences using *in contrast to.*

1. A Volkswagen is an inexpensive car. In contrast, a Porsche is quite expensive. →
   In contrast to a Volkswagen, a Porsche is quite expensive.
   OR: *In contrast to a Porsche, a Volkswagen is quite inexpensive.*

2. A Porsche is a fairly small sports car. In contrast, a Chevrolet Corvette is quite large.

3. A Volkswagen is economical to operate. In contrast, a Porsche is not very economical.

4. A Volkswagen is somewhat uncomfortable to ride in. In contrast, a BMW is exceptionally comfortable.

5. Most American cars are quite large. In contrast, most European cars are small.

1 Make comparisons based on the information given below. Use any of the structures of comparison that are applicable. *Example:*

Joe and Peter are the same height, but they aren't the same weight. Joe had a higher grade point average than Peter. On the other hand, Peter is a much better student than either Henry or John.

	Height	Weight	Age	Class	Major subject	Grade point average°
Joe	5'11"	168	21	Junior	Engineering	3.8
Henry	5'10"	167	21	Junior	English	2.6
Frank	6'	175	21	Senior	Engineering	3.8
Peter	5'11"	175	20	Sophomore	Engineering	3.0
John	5'10"	167	20	Sophomore	English	2.0

2 Describe everyday situations in which you might hear some of the following clichés. *Example:*

I was in my English class when that earthquake hit. Everybody was really scared, but old Professor Wilson was as cool as a cucumber.

1. as cool as a cucumber
2. as slow as molasses in January
3. as fat as a goose
4. as hungry as a wolf
5. as sound as a dollar
6. as weak as a kitten
7. as pale as a ghost
8. as rich as Midas
9. as poor as a church mouse
10. as mean as a snake
11. as wise as an owl
12. as green as grass
13. as fat as a pig
14. as red as a beet
15. as bald as an eagle
16. as hairy as an ape
17. as soft as a feather
18. as round as a dollar
19. as dark as pitch
20. as smart as a whip

Now rewrite your descriptions using a more formal style and tone. Your descriptions should *not* contain clichés. *Example:*

I was in my English class when the earthquake occurred this morning. The students were frightened, but Professor Wilson remained calm.

3 Develop situations in which the following adjectives might be used; you may want to add other adjectives with *like* and *less* suffixes. You may also want to use *as . . . as* and *more . . . than* and other structures that indicate comparison relationships. *Example:*

Mr. Penn was reasonably kind to his family, but he showed no mercy to his employees or business associates. In his talks with them, he was as heartless a man as I ever met.

1. heartless
2. ghostlike
3. colorless
4. hopeless
5. penniless
6. ladylike
7. birdlike
8. worthless
9. childlike
10. childless
11. businesslike
12. dreamlike

° *Grade point average* = the numerical average of a student's grades. For example, if $A = 4$ points, $B = 3$ points, $C = 2$ points, Joe's G.P.A. is about an $A-$; Henry's is about a $C+$, etc.

4 Write paragraphs on the following topics. Indicate comparison relationships by using *similarly, on the other hand, however, but,* and other signals between sentences as well as comparison structures (*as . . . as, more than, less than,* and *-er than*) within sentences.

1. Compare a typical North American meal (breakfast, lunch, or dinner) with a typical meal in another country.

2. Compare the behavior of women in the United States with the behavior of women in another country.

3. Compare the behavior of businessmen from the United States with the behavior of businessmen from another country.

4. Compare the yearly (or seasonal) climate of one country or area with the climate of another.

5. Compare your home city or town with another city or town in respect to location, population, and chief industries.

6. Compare your home city or town with another city or town in respect to type of architecture and major places of interest.

7. Compare the word order of statements in English with the word order of statements in another language.

8. Compare the word order of questions in English with the word order of questions in another language.

9. Compare the alphabet used in English with the alphabet (or other writing system such as a syllabary) used in another language.

10. Compare the consonant sounds in English with the consonant sounds in another language.

5 Choose a topic in Ex. 4 that interests you most and develop a 250–300-word composition.

NOUN CLAUSES

Position of Noun Clauses

15·1   Noun clauses are used in the position of nouns or nouns and their modifiers. They may occur in almost any position where a noun may be used. *Examples:*

Subject Position

Friendship
What he has done so far ⎱ is good.
That he is coming ⎰

Object Position

She asked ⎰ a question.
⎱ if he was coming.
⎱ when he was arriving.

WH-Clauses

WH-QUESTIONS

15·2   *Mary:*

Where's Bill?

When did he leave?

How long will he be gone?

INCLUDED WH-CLAUSES OR QUESTIONS

Peter:

Does anyone ever know **where Bill is?**

I have no idea **when he left.**

How long he'll be gone no one knows.

■   In **wh**-clauses the word order is *subject* + *verb. Example:*

Does anyone know where **Bill is?**
(NOT: Does anyone know where is Bill?)

15·3   DRILL   Read the examples and then complete the drill.

Mary:

1. Where's the post office?
2. Which bus should I take?
3. Where's the nearest bus stop?
4. How long does it take to get there?
5. Who borrowed his car?
6. How far is it to the Royal Theater?

Peter:

I don't know where it is.

I don't know which one you should take.

15·4   DRILL   Read the examples and then complete the drill.

Mary: *Peter:*
1. Where's Maximo's Cafe?   *I have no idea. Ask Fred where it is.*
2. How far is it to the restaurant?   *I have no idea. Ask Fred how far it is.*
3. How long will it take to get there?
4. When does the concert begin?
5. What time will the concert be over?
6. Who° is she going to the concert with?

15·5   DRILL   Read the examples and then complete the drill.

Mary: *Peter:*
1. What did he say?   *What he said is confidential.*
2. When is he leaving?   *When he is leaving is confidential.*
3. Who is going with him?
4. Why is he going?
5. How long will he be away?
6. What did he tell Mr. Brown?

15·6   Do you remember {which day Mr. Craigie is leaving for the sales conference?
                             {**the day (that)** Mr. Craigie is leaving for the sales conference?

Did he tell you {when his plane takes off?
                {**the time (that)** his plane takes off?

Do you know {where he plans to stay?
            {**the place** {**(that)**   } he plans to stay?
                           {**(where)** }

■ In the examples above, *wh*-clause objects are restated, using the expressions **the day (that),
   the time (that),** etc.

15·7   DRILL   Restate the sentences, using *the day (that), the time (that), the place (that* or *where),
the way (that),* and *the reason (that* or *why).*

1. Can you remember *which day* Mr. Craigie called us? →
   Can you remember the day (that) Mr. Craigie called us?
2. Can you remember *which day* the business meeting will be held?
3. Do you know *when* the meeting is scheduled?
4. Don't forget to let me know *where* the meeting will be held.
5. Tell me *how* you would like the business meeting to be conducted.

°**Who** is generally acceptable as an object in all but formal written English.

15·8   Mr. Craigie is going to leave **on Wednesday.**

The day (that) Mr. Craigie is going to leave is **Wednesday.**

Wednesday's the day (that) Mr. Craigie is going to leave.

He plans to stay **at the Chilton Hotel.**

The place (that) he plans to stay is **the Chilton Hotel.**

The Chilton Hotel is the place **(that)** he plans to stay.

■ Adverbials of *time, place, reason,* and *manner* can be restated as shown in the preceding examples.

15·9   DRILL   Restate the sentences, using *the time (that), the place (that* or *where), the reason (that* or *why),* and *the way (that).*

1. The sales conference starts *on Thursday.* →

   Thursday is the day (that) the sales conference starts.
   OR: *The day (that) the sales conference starts is Thursday.*

2. The delegates will register *from eight to nine o'clock.*

3. The conference is being held *at the Chilton Hotel.*

4. Mr. Craigie has to be there a day early *to attend a program committee meeting.*

5. Mr. Craigie prefers to conduct business meetings *informally.*

WH-QUESTION	WH + EVER CLAUSE
15·10 Where shall we meet?	I'll meet you **wherever you say.**
What shall I do?	**Whatever you do** is all right with me.

■ **Who, which, what, where, when, how + ever** means "any person, thing, place, time, or way at all." **However** used to introduce a noun clause should not be confused with the sequence signal **however,** meaning "but." *Compare:*

However you do it is all right with me.

He is willing to help you. **However, (But)** you must remember to call him a day in advance.

15·11   DRILL   Read the examples and complete the drill.

Olga:	*Steve:*
1. What should I say?	*Say whatever seems appropriate.*
2. When should I call her?	*Call her whenever you think best.*
3. Which telephone should I use?	
4. Who(m) should I invite to the party?	
5. What should I tell them?	
6. How should I arrange these flowers?	

15·12   DRILL   Read the examples and complete the drill. (If the drill is written, do not use a comma before *is*.)

Ann:

1. She wants to know when you want her to serve dinner.

2. She wants to know how you'd like your steak cooked.

3. She wants to know how you'd like her to set the table.

4. She wants to know which tablecloth you'd like her to use.

5. She wants to know where you want her to put the flowers.

6. They want to know who you'd like to sit next to, Mary.

Mary:

Whenever she serves dinner is all right with me.

However she cooks it is all right with me.

15·13

WH-QUESTION	REPORTED WH-QUESTION°
Kathleen to Dan:	*Dan to Ray (on the telephone):*
Where was Dr. Arnold last week?	She asked **where Dr. Arnold was last week.**
What is he doing this week?	She asked **what he was doing this week.**
Which day next week will he be able to see Mr. Rex?	She asked **which day next week he would be able to see Mr. Rex.**

■ After **asked,** the verb in the **wh**-clause may be past in form even though present or future time is indicated. However, a present form to indicate present or future time is customary with some speakers, especially when the question is repeated or reported immediately. *Example:*

Jane: Where are you going now?
Jim: What did she say?
Bill: She asked **where you're going now.**

■ Time expressions may change when the report is made at a much later time. *Compare:*

Conversation
Jane: Where is Dr. Arnold now?
Jim: He's in Italy now, but he'll be in France next week.

Immediate report
Jane asked Jim where Dr. Arnold was **now.**
Jim said that he was in Italy **now** but that he would be in France **next week.**

Report at a much later time
Jane asked Jim where Dr. Arnold was **then** (at that time).
Jim said that he was in Italy **at that time** but that he would be in France **the following week.**

°Reported questions are often called *indirect address* or *indirect speech.*

- The present is also common in reporting or repeating questions about general states, conditions, or situations. *Example:*

Jim: How old is Dr. Arnold?
Bill: What did he say?
Jim: He asked you how old Dr. Arnold **is.**

Variations in usage are mentioned here in order to indicate the range of possibilities. It is suggested, however, that *past forms* be used after **asked** unless there is a clear reason for doing otherwise. In other words, make past forms after **asked** the rule and present forms the exception.

15·14   DRILL   Read the examples and then complete the drill.

The receptionist to Daniel:	*Daniel to Tom later that day:*
1. Who(m) do you want to see?	*The receptionist asked me who I wanted to see.*
2. Which vice-president do you want to see?	*She asked me which vice-president I wanted to see.*
3. What do you want to see him about?	
4. When would you like to make an appointment?	
5. What day will be best for you?	
6. What time can you be here Wednesday afternoon?	
7. Where can you be reached during the day?	

IF or WHETHER Clauses

15·15   YES/NO QUESTIONS
Mr. Watanabe:
Will Mr. Ross be at the meeting?
Was he at the last meeting?
Will he accept the proposal?

INCLUDED YES/NO QUESTIONS
Mr. Esmali:
I don't know **whether he'll be there (or not).**
I don't know **if he was there (or not).**
Whether (or not) he will accept the proposal remains to be seen.

- If and **whether** are usually interchangeable in noun clauses that occur in the predicate, although **whether** is often preferred in formal written English.
- **Whether (or not)** is used in clauses at the beginning of the sentence; **or not** may also be used immediately after **whether** at the end of the clause. *Compare:*

Whether (or not) he will agree to the proposal, I cannot say.
Whether he will sign the contract (**or not**) depends on several factors.

15·16   DRILL   Complete the drill.

Mr. Watanabe:

1. Are they planning to meet Mr. Ross at the airport?

2. Should Mr. Moore call him?

3. Can you find out by tomorrow?

4. Will you be able to call on him next Saturday?

5. Did Mr. Ross put off his trip to New York?

Mr. Esmali:

I don't know if they're planning to meet him (or not).

15·17   DRILL   Complete the drill.

Mrs. Long:

1. Did your friend like the play?

2. Do Margaret and Sally want to see the play?

3. Are good seats still available?

4. Do you agree with Mr. Chapman's review of the play?

5. Do they have confidence in Mr. Chapman's judgment?

Mrs. Short:

I don't know whether she liked it (or not).

15·18   DRILL   Take information from the questions on the left to complete statements on the right.

Mr. Black asks Mr. Green:

1. Does Mr. Roberts plan to attend the conference?

2. Would you be willing to speak at one of the meetings?

3. Is Mr. Gale planning to resign?

4. Has the chairman scheduled a meeting of the board of directors?

5. Do all members intend to be present?

6. Are the arrangements for the meeting satisfactory?

7. Will the first meeting be held Friday afternoon?

8. Do you approve of our current financial policy?

Mr. Green writes to Mr. Roberts:

Please let us know *whether (or not) you plan to attend the conference.*

Please let us know

We should like to know

Do you know

Please let me know

Mr. Black would like to know

I should like to know

Please let us know

15·19

YES/NO QUESTION	REPORTED QUESTION
Mr. Sanchez to Mr. Lopez:	*Mr. Lopez to Mr. Green (on the telephone):*
Were they here yesterday?	Mr. Sanchez asked **if they were here yesterday.**
Are they working on the project now?	He asked **whether they were working on the project now.**
Will they still be working on it next month?	He asked **whether they would still be working on it next month.**
Did they leave last night?	He asked **if they left (had left) last night.**

- The verbs in the clause following **asked** may be past in form even though present or future time is indicated. (See also the explanation in §15.13.)

- A simple past tense customarily becomes past perfect in reported speech, especially if the report is made at a much later time. *Compare:*

  Jim: Did they arrive this morning?

  Jim asked **if they arrived this morning.** (Immediate report)

  Jim asked **if they had arrived that morning.** (Much later report)

  Notice that **this morning** becomes **that morning** when the person reporting no longer remembers or attaches importance to the exact day of the conversation.

- In addition to **this morning**, time expressions like **yesterday, now, tomorrow,** or **next month** and place expressions like **here** change in a report made at a much later time and in a different place. *Compare:*

Immediate report:	*Report at a later date in a different place:*
Jim asked if they were **here yesterday.**	Jim asked if they had been **there the day before.**
He asked if they were working on the project **now.**	He asked if they were working on the project **at that time (then).**
He asked whether they would still be working on it **next month.**	He asked whether they would still be working on it **the following month.**
He asked if we had seen them **today.**	He asked if we had seen them **that day.**

15·20   DRILL   Read the examples and then complete the drill, using *if* to introduce an informal or conversational style of clause.

Sue to Larry:	*Larry to Dan (on the telephone):*
1. Is tomorrow Catherine's birthday?	*Sue asked me if tomorrow was Catherine's birthday.*
2. Have you bought her a present?	*She asked me if I had bought her a present.*
3. Will she be 19 or 20 years old?	
4. Shall we have a party for her?	
5. Can we have the party at your house?	

6. Shall we make it a surprise party?

7. Do we have to invite Frank or Harold?

8. Did you see Frank this morning?

9. Have you seen John today?

10. Did you call him last night?

15·21 DRILL   Assume that the questions in Drill 15.20 were reported by Dan in a different place at a much later date. *Example:*

Sue asked Larry if the next day was Catherine's birthday.

THAT-Clauses

15·22

STATEMENT	INCLUDED STATEMENT
Helen was absent today.	I noticed **(that) Helen was absent today.**
She has a bad cold.	I believe **(that) she has a bad cold.**
I'll call her tonight.	I thought **(that) I would call her tonight.**

- **That** can be omitted in most noun clauses occurring in the predicate.
- When the main verb is past, verbs in clauses that follow are usually past in form even though the meaning may not be past time, as in the last of the preceding examples.

15·23 DRILL   Use the information in the first statement to complete the information in the second statement of each pair below. Remember to use the past tense after a past main verb.

1. Sylvia was wearing an engagement ring. →
   I noticed *that Sylvia was wearing an engagement ring.*

2. Her parents approve of the engagement. →
   I know *that her parents approve of the engagement.*

3. She announced her engagement last Sunday.
   I heard

4. Her fiancé is very wealthy.
   I understand

5. She met him in college.
   I believe

6. She will be married in June.
   Margaret said she thought

7. Her sister will be maid-of-honor.
   Do you suppose

8. Her cousins will give a bridal shower for her.
   Her cousins thought

15·24   STATEMENT

Miss Al-Faud to Mr. Jabbour:

Mr. Lee and Mr. Bell could not agree on a date for the meeting.

I agree with Mr. Lee.

Mr. Lee is not in his office.

Mr. Lee will call you tomorrow.

REPORTED STATEMENT

Mr. Jabbour to Mr. Rezian (on the telephone):

Miss Al-Faud says **(that) Mr. Lee and Mr. Bell could not agree on a date for the meeting.**

She says **(that) she agrees with Mr. Lee.**

She said **(that) Mr. Lee was not in his office.**

She told me **(that) Mr. Lee would call me tomorrow.**

- Speech may be reported from either a present or past point of view. When the reporting verb is present (**say, tell**), the verb in the following clause can be either present or past depending on the situation. However, when the reporting verb is past (**said, told**), the verb in the following clause is usually past in form even though present or future time is indicated. Exceptions to the *past–past* sequence occur in these instances:

  1) When the report closely follows the original statement in point of time:

  Alice: I'm leaving now.
  Tom: What did you say?
  Alice: I **said I'm leaving** now.

  The matter of immediacy is also discussed in relation to reported questions (see §15.13).

  2) When a historical fact or general truth is reported:

  He **said** that Baguio **is** the summer capital of the Philippines.

- Notice that **told** is followed by an object (**me**). *Example:*

  She told **me** that . . . . (NOT: She told that . . . .)

  Said does not require an object. If an object is present, it is preceded by **to**.

  She said **to me** that Mr. Lee was not there. (NOT: She said me that . . . .)

15·25   DRILL   Use either *said* or *told* as reporting verbs.

Ahmad to Ali:

1. I can't attend the meeting today.

2. I have an appointment this afternoon.

3. I'm sorry I can't be there.

4. Mrs. Smith will probably be there.

5. She can tell me about the meeting.

6. I'll call her tonight.

Ali to George (on the telephone) later that day:

Ahmad said (that) he couldn't attend the meeting today.

15·26 STATEMENT

Mr. Lee in a press interview:

I am not a presidential candidate.

I have often been misquoted.

There are too many candidates already.

There is not enough time to answer all of your questions.

REPORTED STATEMENT

Newspaper report:

Mr. Lee declared **that he was not a presidential candidate.**

He stated **that he had often been misquoted.**

He commented **that there were too many candidates already.**

He observed **that there was not enough time to answer all of the questions of the news reporters.**

■ Verbs like **state, declare, comment, remark, observe, reply, answer** are used along with the more common verbs **say, tell, ask** in more formal spoken and written reports. **That** is usually retained in clauses following these verbs.

15·27 DRILL Use reporting verbs like *replied, answered, stated, commented, observed, remarked, declared.*

1. *Mr. Lee:* The committee has not been able to reach an agreement. →
   Mr. Lee stated that the committee had not been able to reach an agreement.

2. *Mr. Smith:* We must have a decision soon.

3. *Mr. King:* I am in favor of asking the chairman of the committee to meet with us.

4. *Mr. Lee:* The chairman will be out of town until Tuesday.

5. *Mr. King:* We could discuss the matter with him by telephone.

6. *Mr. Lee:* It might be difficult to reach him.

7. *Mr. Smith:* It is getting late.

8. *Mr. Lee:* We still have several important matters to discuss.

9. *Mr. King:* I am in favor of postponing our discussion until tomorrow.

10. *Mr. Smith:* I also favor postponing discussion.

15·28 QUOTED SPEECH

"What have you been doing?" Fred asked Don.

"I've been writing letters," Don answered. "Do you have any stamps?"

"Sure. I just got some," Fred replied. "How many do you want?"

"Do you have both airmail and regular?" Don asked. "I need two of each."

REPORTED SPEECH

Fred asked Don **what he had been doing.**

Don answered **that he had been writing letters and asked if Fred had any stamps.**

Fred told him **he had just got some and asked how many he wanted.**

Don asked **if he had both airmail and regular stamps and told him that he needed two of each.**

- Quoted dialog with speaker identification tags can be changed to reported speech in much the same manner as speech in the dialog format. *Compare:*

"What have you been doing?" Fred asked Don.   ⎰ Fred asked Don **what he had**
Fred (to Don): What have you been doing?   ⎱ **been doing.**

- Notice that the statement and question are combined in the last three sentences in the reported speech column.

- Speaker identification tags can be placed either before or after the quoted material. *Compare and notice the punctuation:*

Fred asked Don, "What have you been doing?"   **Don answered,** "I've been writing letters."
"What have you been doing?" **Fred asked Don.**   "I've been writing letters," **Don answered.**

- There are two possible orders for the end-of-sentence speaker tags with noun subjects. *Compare:*

"I've been writing letters," ⎰ **Don answered.**
                             ⎱ **answered Don.**

However, when the speaker tag is at the beginning of a sentence or when the subject is a pronoun, the order is *subject + verb. Examples:*

Fred said, "I've just got some stamps."   (NOT: Said Fred, "I've . . . .")
"How many do you want?" **he asked.**   (NOT: "How . . . ?" asked he.)

15·29   DRILL   Change to reported speech and combine the sentences (with *and*). Make the reporting verbs past.

1. "I can't find the dictionary. Where did you put it?" Harley asked Jim. →
   Harley said he couldn't find the dictionary and asked Jim where he had put it.
   OR: *Harley told Jim he couldn't find the dictionary and asked where he had put it.*

2. "When does the mail arrive? I'm expecting an important letter," Jerry announced.

3. "Does anyone know Gregory's address? I want to send him an invitation," Brian stated.

4. Dorothy said to Konrad, "There's a meeting this afternoon. Do you know where it is?"

5. Konrad replied, "It's in Mr. Leisy's office. Do you know who'll be there?"

6. The secretary said, "There's a Mr. McDaniel waiting for you, Mr. Greenberg. Shall I send him in?"

7. "Show him in right away. I'm very anxious to see him," Mr. Greenberg replied.

15·30   QUOTATION   PARAPHRASE

"No man can answer for his courage   La Rochefoucauld, the noted French
who has never been in danger."—   author, **once commented** that no one
La Rochefoucauld, French author.   knows whether he is courageous until
                                          he has faced danger.

- In writing papers and discussing subjects, we often paraphrase (that is, put in our own words) what someone has said, rather than quote the person directly. When we paraphrase, we often make use of the same verbs and noun clause structures that we use in reporting and summarizing conversation or dialog.

■ The reporting verbs (**tell, say, ask, remark, comment, declare, point out, think, feel, believe,** etc.) may be either present or past. The choice is one of appropriateness. If we are paraphrasing a statement that someone made in the past and wish to set it in the past, a past reporting verb may be more appropriate, as in the preceding example of paraphrasing. If we wish to make a general statement, however, we may use **says** (we can do so even though La Rochefoucauld is no longer living). *Example:*

La Rochefoucauld **says** that no one knows whether he is courageous until he has faced danger.

■ Perhaps the main difference between paraphrasing and reporting speech is that we do not stick as closely to the wording of the speaker or writer in paraphrasing as we do in reporting speech. That is, in paraphrasing, we attempt to put the ideas of the speaker or writer in our own words. In doing so, we must be careful not to omit important information or to change the ideas of the speaker or writer.

15·31   DRILL   Paraphrase the following quoted statements. Use verbs like *remark, feel, think,* and *believe;* make the reporting verbs past or present, as appropriate.

1. "It will profit us nothing to brood over the past or blame this party or that."—Mahatma Gandhi, Indian leader. →
   The great Indian leader Mahatma Gandhi once stated that it did no good to brood over the past or to blame others.
   OR: *Mahatma Gandhi says that it does no good to brood over the past or to blame others.*

2. "I had climbed my mountain, but I must still live my life."—Norgay Tenzing, Sherpa mountaineer and conquerer of Mount Everest.

3. "I have often remarked that whereas men say there is a limit beyond which a man may not run or swim, may not raise a tower or dig a pit, I have never heard it said that there is a limit to wisdom."—Thornton Wilder, American playwright and novelist, in *The Ides of March.*

4. "There is one expression that continually comes to my mind whenever I think of the English language and compare it with others: it seems to me positively and expressly *masculine.*"—Otto Jespersen, Danish linguist, in *Growth and Structure of the English Language.*

5. "The eye of man serves to photograph the invisible, just as his ears record the echo of silence."—Machado de Assis, Brazilian author, in *Esau and Jacob.*

15·32   It is unfortunate (**that**) **the weather is bad.**   **That the weather is bad** is unfortunate.

It is unlikely (**that**) **the parade will be held.**   **That the parade will be held** is unlikely.

■ **That**-clauses occur at either the end or the beginning of the sentence. Notice that the word **that** is not optional in clauses at the beginning of the sentence.

15·33   DRILL   Complete the drill.

    1. He is going to resign. It's true. → *It's true (that) he's going to resign.*

    2. She did not believe him. It's unfortunate.

    3. She wasn't convinced. It's apparent.

    4. He's unhappy. It's obvious.

    5. I'll see him today. It's unlikely.

    6. I'll see him tomorrow. It's possible.

15·34   DRILL   Shift the *that*-clause to the beginning of the sentence. (If the drill is written, do not use a comma in these sentences.)

    1. It's surprising that he isn't more interested in world affairs. →
    That he isn't more interested in world affairs is surprising.

    2. It's unfortunate that we see him so seldom.

    3. It's unlikely that he will call on us Sunday.

    4. It's obvious that he has been very busy lately.

    5. It's possible that he prefers to be alone.

    6. It's apparent that he doesn't like large social gatherings.

15·35   We cannot **be certain of our success.**   We cannot **be certain that we will succeed.**

We shouldn't **be afraid of failure.**   We shouldn't **be afraid that we will fail.**

■   Some **be** + *adjective* + *preposition* combinations like **be certain of, be afraid of, be aware of,** and **be delighted with** can be restated using **that**-clauses. Notice that the preposition **(of)** is omitted in the preceding examples when a **that**-clause follows.

15·36   DRILL   Omit the preposition after the *italicized* word and change the rest of the sentence to a *that*-clause.

    1. He is *aware* of his mistakes in pronunciation. →
    He is aware that he makes mistakes in pronunciation.

    2. He is *afraid* of making a mistake.

    3. She is *happy* about his progress in learning English.

    4. She is *delighted* with his success.

    5. She was *surprised* by his enthusiasm.

    6. Mr. Bell is *worried* about losing his job.

    7. He is *aware* of his lack of experience.

    8. He was *disappointed* in his sales record.

    9. He is *unhappy* about having to work overtime.

    10. He was *angry* about having to work on Saturday.

1 This exercise is in three parts.

1. Read this conversation:

   Mary: Are Jane and Bill going to help you collect funds for the hospitality center?

   Joe: No, they aren't. Would you like to help me?

   Mary: I'm sorry, but I can't help you until next week.

   Helen: I can help you this week if you want me to.

   Joe: I can certainly use your help.

   Helen: Does Bob have a date for next Saturday?

   Joe: I don't think so. Why do you want to know?

   Helen: I'm just curious.

   Mary: Curiosity killed the cat.

   Helen: I think one should be curious. Don't you agree with me, Joe?

   Joe: It depends on what one means by curiosity. What is your definition of curiosity?

   Helen: I don't think I have ever tried to define the term. To me, curiosity is the desire to find out all you can about something.

   Joe: That isn't a bad definition.

   Mary: I don't think people should be curious about things that don't concern them. Do you like people to pry into your private affairs?

   Joe: No, I don't, but you're looking at curiosity from a negative point of view.

   Helen: I agree. Many important discoveries have been made because people were curious.

   Mary: That's true. Curiosity can be dangerous, however.

   Joe: It certainly can. Curious people often find out things that are very upsetting to other people.

   Helen: Galileo's discoveries forced man to change his idea of the universe and his place in it.

   Mary: Do you mean Galileo's curiosity led to these discoveries?

   Helen: That's exactly what I mean.

   Mary: Would you give me your definition of curiosity again?

   Helen: Curiosity is a desire to find the truth about something.

2. Change the conversation to reported speech. Use past tense for the reporting verbs. Assume that the report is being made at a much later date. *Examples:*

   Mary asked Joe if Jane and Bill were going to help him collect funds for the hospitality center.

   Joe said they weren't and asked Mary if she would like to help him.

3. Summarize the conversation. Use verbs like *remark, feel, think,* and *believe.* In summarizing we often use present verbs instead of past; the verb in the *that*-clauses may be either present or past depending on the situation.

   Your summary should be shorter than the reported speech version. You should be careful, however, to include all essential information. You should also be careful not to change the ideas expressed by the speakers in the dialog.

2   Take notes in class or at a meeting or conference.

1. From your notes construct a dialog of about ten exchanges of remarks or questions and answers.

2. Change the conversation (dialog) to reported speech.

3. Write a summary—in paragraph form—of the reported speech version of the conversation.

3   Paraphrase the following statements about women's roles and liberation. Remember that in paraphrasing you do not stick as closely to the wording of the speaker or writer as you do in reported speech. Use words like *say, remark, report, declare, think, believe,* and *comment;* use present or past, as appropriate. (See §15.30.)

1. "Women can get ahead more easily in underdeveloped countries."—Alva Myrdal, in an address at a women's conference in Ceylon in 1960.

   During an address given at a women's conference in Ceylon in 1960, Alva Myrdal stated that he believed that there were more opportunities for women to get ahead in underdeveloped countries.

   OR: *Alva Myrdal offers an opinion that it is easier for women to get ahead in underdeveloped countries.*

2. "It's a man's world. Woman's place is in the home."—Old saying.

3. "I have a feeling that man's fear of women comes from having first seen her as a mother, creator of men."—Anais Nin, in her diary published in 1966.

4. "Every step forward in work as a successful American regardless of sex means a step backward as a woman."—Margaret Mead, noted anthropologist.

5. "When we become conscious of the many subtle mechanisms of social control . . . it is not hard to see why girls who are better at almost everything in childhood do not excel at much of anything as adults."—Jo Freeman, women's liberation leader.

6. "If women understand by emancipation the adoption of the masculine role, then we are lost indeed. If women can supply no counterbalance to the blindness of male drive, the aggressive society will run to its lunatic extremes at ever-escalating speed."—Germaine Greer, in her book *The Female Eunuch.*

4   From current newspapers, magazines, or books, collect statements on the following subjects and write paraphrases of the statements.

1. Women's roles and liberation

2. Peace, pollution, world economy, racial discrimination, or any other subject that interests you

5   Write a composition (200–250 words) or prepare a speech on the subject of women's roles and liberation or on another subject for which you collected statements in Ex. 4. Quote or paraphrase some of the statements in the development of your ideas.

RELATIVE CLAUSES

16

Position and Function of Relative Clauses

16·1 — The man **who lives in that house** is a surgeon.

— Do you know the architect **who designed the house?**

- Relative clauses are used as noun modifiers. In the first sentence above, the relative clause modifies the *subject* of the sentence (**the man**); in the second sentence, the clause modifies the *object* of the sentence (**the man**).

16·2 — I can't remember the name of the architect **who designed the house.** Can you?

— Mr. King, **who owns the house,** told me the architect was Gary Mills.

- Relative clauses can be restrictive or nonrestrictive. A clause is *restrictive* when it limits or identifies the noun it modifies, as in the first sentence; it is *nonrestrictive* when the noun is already identified and the clause merely adds information about the noun, as in the second example.

Restrictive Clauses

16·3 The architect ⎹ **the architect** designed this hotel ⎹ is a friend of ours.

The architect (**who**) designed this hotel is a friend of ours.

It's the hotel ⎹ **the hotel** won the architects' annual award ⎹ .

It's the hotel (**which**) won the architects' annual award.

- In the preceding examples, the *relative pronoun* replaces the subject of the boxed clause (**the architect/the hotel**).

- **That** can replace either **who** or **which** in restrictive relative clauses. Many people, however, prefer **who** to **that** for persons and **that** to **which** for things. *Examples:*

  The architect **who** (that) designed the hotel is a friend of ours.
  There is the hotel **that** (which) won the architectural award.

- Notice that restrictive clauses are *not* set off by commas in writing.

16·4   DRILL   Make the sentences in brackets into restrictive clauses.

1. The house [The house is for sale] is on First Street. →
   The house that is for sale is on First Street.
2. Do you want to see the house [The house is for sale]?
3. The woman [The woman owns the house] is moving to Florida.
4. Do you know the real estate agent [The real estate agent is handling the transaction]?
5. Everyone [Everyone has done business with him] seems to like him very much.
6. Is that the realty company [The realty company has such a good reputation]?
7. A house [A house costs over $30,000] should have enough room for a family of four.
8. We talked to a woman [A woman said she had seen the house].

16·5   The man | you should see **the man** | is Mr. Grove.

The man (who(m)) you should see is Mr. Grove.

Mr. Grove owns the printing firm | I told you about **the printing firm** |.

Mr. Grove owns the printing firm (which) I told you about.

- In the preceding examples, the *relative pronoun* is an object. It is the direct object of the clause in the first example and the object of the preposition **about** in the second.

16·6   The man **you should see** is Mr. Grove.
Mr. Grove owns the printing firm **I told you about.**

- Relative objects are often omitted. When they are included, **that** is common for both persons and things. Other choices are **which** for things and **who** or **whom** for persons. **Whom** is rare, however, in restrictive relative clauses in spoken American English.

16·7   The man **that** Mr. Bond spoke to is Mr. Grove.
The man **whom** Mr. Bond spoke to is Mr. Grove.
The man **to whom** Mr. Bond spoke is Mr. Grove.

The room **that** the conference was held in had poor acoustics.
The room **which** the conference was held in had poor acoustics.
The room **in which** the conference was held had poor acoustics.

■ **That** cannot replace **whom** or **which** when the preposition and relative pronoun occur together. In long sentences the relative pronoun and preposition are often kept together to prevent misreading. *Example:*

The room which the committee for the preservation of historical monuments met in was on the fifth floor.

16·8 DRILL   Make the sentences in brackets into relative clauses.

1. The investment company [Mr. Eldredge works for the investment company] has three branch offices. →
   The investment company (that) Mr. Eldredge works for has three branch offices.
2. The office [Mr. Eldredge used to have the office] is much smaller than the one he has now.
3. Is that the secretary [Mr. Eldredge hired the secretary]?
4. The secretary [Mr. Eldredge hired the secretary] is very efficient.
5. Where are the supplies [The secretary ordered the supplies]?
6. The supplies [The secretary ordered the supplies] haven't arrived yet.

16·9   The hotel (**that was**) designed by Mr. Mills has a roof garden.
The hotel **designed by Mr. Mills** has a roof garden.

The man (**who is**) talking to Mr. Mills is Mr. Grove.
The man **talking to Mr. Mills** is Mr. Grove.

The woman (**who is**) next to him is Mrs. Mills.
The woman **next to him** is Mrs. Mills.

■ In restrictive clauses, **who/ which/ that** + the form of **be** can usually be omitted.

16·10   DRILL   Delete the relative pronouns and forms of *be* wherever possible.

1. The man who is sitting over there is an interior decorator. →
   The man sitting over there is an interior decorator.
2. The woman who invited him is also an interior decorator.
3. We liked the furniture that was designed by Mr. Rosenthal.
4. The furniture we liked best was designed by Saib Medhi.
5. The bowl that is on the center table is a priceless antique.
6. The people who are looking at the bowl are art students.
7. Exhibits that are arranged by Mr. Davies are always worth seeing.
8. The exhibit that is scheduled for next month seems particularly interesting.

16·11   Is that the man | **the man's** son is an astronaut | ?

Is that the man (**whose**) son is an astronaut?

Are you sure that is the astronaut | we saw **his** picture in the newspaper | ?

Are you sure that is the astronaut (**whose**) picture we saw in the newspaper?

■   Notice that **whose** replaces **the man's** in the first example and **his** in the second. **Whose** replaces possessive modifiers of noun subjects and objects, not the noun subjects and objects themselves.

SOME INFORMATION ON POSSESSIVE RELATIONSHIPS

Of-phrases are not generally used with animate nouns to express kinship or ownership, particularly with proper nouns.

Usually: **Mr. Lee's son**   *Rarely:* the son of Mr. Lee
         Mr. Kim's house   the house of Mr. Kim

Of-phrases are quite commonly used in expressing other relationships. *Examples:*

the (an) astronaut's picture   OR: the (a) picture of the astronaut
the president's secretary   the secretary of the president

(See the shaded area on page 120 for information on possessive 's with animate nouns.)

Inanimate nouns like **table, chair,** and **house** do not generally occur with **'s.** Common exceptions are **a day's work, a nickel's worth, a month's pay,** and **life's joys and sorrows.**

A "part of" or "belonging to" relationship is expressed by **of** + *noun. Examples:*

The top is part of the table.   → the top of the table
The leg is part of the chair.   → the leg of the chair
The roof is part of the house. → the roof of the house

The **of** + *noun* construction can often be restated as follows:

the top of the table   → the table top
the leg of the chair   → the chair leg
the back of the chair → the chair back

What are some other examples? People do not tend to say "the house roof" or "the building roof," but they do say "the gymnasium roof" as well as "the roof of the gymnasium" and "the garage door" as well as "the door of the garage."

A *purpose* relationship is expressed by **for** + *noun* in these examples:

the pot is for coffee   → the coffeepot
the knife is for steak   → the steak knife
the net is for the hair.   → the hairnet
the laboratory for (the) chemistry (class) → the chemistry laboratory
the textbook for (the) history (course)   → the history textbook

A *directional* relationship is expressed by **to** + *noun* in these examples:

the door that goes to the kitchen   → the door to the kitchen   → the kitchen door
the stairs that go to the basement → the stairs to the basement → the basement stairs
the road that goes to the mill   → the road to the mill   → the mill road

16·12   Are you sure that is the astronaut | we saw **a** picture **of the astronaut** in the paper | ?

Are you sure that is the astronaut (**whose**) picture we saw in the paper?

- Notice the relative **whose** replaces **a** before **picture** and the possessive phrase **of the astronaut.** (See the shaded area for more information on possessive relationships.)

16·13

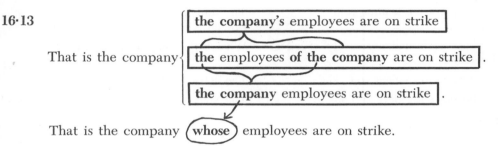

That is the company { | **the company's** employees are on strike |

| **the** employees **of the company** are on strike | .

| **the company** employees are on strike | .

That is the company (**whose**) employees are on strike.

- In some contexts, the possessive relationship can be indicated in three ways with nouns such as **company, committee, union, team, club, university; whose** can replace all three forms.

16·14   DRILL   Change the sentences in brackets to relative clauses introduced by *whose. Situation:* The ABC Company will hold a meeting on Tuesday afternoon to discuss plans for the construction of a new warehouse.

1. The man [*The man's* office will be used for the meeting] is on vacation. →
    The man whose office will be used for the meeting is on vacation.

2. The secretary [It is *the secretary's* duty to record the minutes of the meeting] is ill.

3. Mr. Able is the man [It is *the man's* responsibility to find a replacement].

4. Do you know the lawyer [*The lawyer's* firm represents the ABC Company]?

5. What is the advertising agency [The ABC Company will use the services *of the advertising agency*]?

6. A representative of the construction company [*The construction company's* bid was accepted] will attend the meeting.

7. The architect [*The architect's* plan will be discussed] will not be able to attend the meeting.

8. The department heads [*The department heads'* work will be affected by the construction of the warehouse] will attend the meeting.

9. Representatives of unions [*Union* members will be involved in the construction of the warehouse] will also attend the meeting.

10. A citizen's committee [*The committee* members oppose construction of the warehouse] has requested permission to attend the meeting.

16·15   DRILL   Attach the relative clauses at the left to nouns in the sentences at the right.

1. that Russell wants to see
   The Italian film is playing at Cinema 21. →

   The Italian film that Russell wants to see is playing at Cinema 21.

2. that is playing at the Tivoli
   Last night Steve and Herb saw the new Italian film.

3. who like Italian movies
   Many people will recommend the film to their friends.

4. who plays the leading role
   The Italian actor is related to the French actress.

5. whose performance received excellent reviews
   What is the name of the actress?

6. whose performance you liked
   The actress is French.

7. who plays the part of a spy
   The young woman is related to the blond actor.

8. that was held last week
   Gary went to a preview.

16·16   The table ⎡ **the table has a marble top** ⎤ costs $200.

The table **that has a marble top** costs $200.

The table **with a marble top** costs $200.

- **Whose** is rarely used with inanimate nouns to express a possessive relationship. The relationship meaning "part of" or "belonging to" can be expressed as shown in the examples. Notice that the relative clause changes to a phrase in the last sentence. (See the shaded area for more information on possessive relationships with inanimate nouns.)

16·17   DRILL   Change the relative clauses to *with*-phrases.

1. The house that has an excellent location costs $60,000. →
   The house with the excellent location costs $60,000.

2. The Lees do not want the inexpensive house that has a poor location. →
   The Lees do not want the inexpensive house with the poor location.

3. Mrs. Lee likes the stucco house that has a flat roof.

4. The two-story brick house that has a panoramic view is not for sale.

5. Mr. Lee likes the old wooden house that has a large backyard.

6. Chin Lee bought a new car that has black upholstery.

7. His sister Ming wanted him to buy a car that had red upholstery.

8. Ming Lee would like a car that has red upholstery.

16·18   Constance recommended a hotel. We stayed there.

Constance recommended **the** hotel **where we stayed.**

- Notice that the relative **where** replaces an adverb of place (**there**) rather than a noun phrase. Also notice that **a hotel** becomes **the hotel** when the relative clause follows. Can you think of a reason for this?

16·19   DRILL   Change one of the sentences to a clause introduced by *where* and include it in the other sentence.

1. Helen and Paul had dinner at an Italian restaurant. Spaghetti pomodoro was the speciality *there.* →

   Helen and Paul had dinner at an Italian restaurant where spaghetti pomodoro was the speciality.

2. We celebrated Jim's birthday *at an Italian restaurant.* Was that the Italian restaurant?

3. Alice and John wanted to go to a Japanese restaurant. They had dinner *there* the week before.

4. Northern Chinese food is served *in some restaurants.* Do you know of any restaurants?

5. Excellent curry is served *in some local Indian restaurants.* Would you like to go to one of the local Indian restaurants?

Nonrestrictive Clauses

16·20   My Aunt Jane was a noted photographer, **and she gave me my first camera** .

My Aunt Jane, **who gave me my first camera,** was a noted photographer.

The camera was the envy of my friends, **and it took excellent pictures** .

The camera, **which took excellent pictures,** was the envy of my friends.

- In these sentences, the main noun phrase (**my Aunt Jane,** etc.) is completely clear. The relative clause does not limit or identify; it merely adds information about the noun phrase. Relative clauses of this type are called *nonrestrictive,* and they are separated from the rest of the sentence by commas in writing and by pauses in speech.

- **That** cannot replace **who, whom,** or **which** in nonrestrictive clauses.

- Relative pronoun objects (**that/ whom/ which**) can be omitted in restrictive clauses, but **which** and **who(m)** cannot be omitted in nonrestrictive clauses. *Compare:*

  The woman **you spoke to** is Ken's aunt.
  Mrs. Parker, **whom you are going to meet,** is Ken's aunt.

- As an object, **who** instead of **whom** is fairly common, but **whom** is generally preferred in formal writing and speech.

16·21   John has three brothers but only one sister. His sister, **who is in high school,** speaks French and Italian fluently.

John has two Aunt Annes. His Aunt Anne **who lives in New York** is his father's sister. His Aunt Anne **who lives in Chicago** is his mother's sister.

- When the clause is attached to a noun phrase that is clearly identified, it is not difficult to distinguish a restrictive from a nonrestrictive clause. In the first example, the clause is not necessary to tell us which sister, since the sentence makes it clear that he has only one sister. The clause merely adds information about John's sister and is, therefore, *nonrestrictive.* In the second example, the relative clauses tell us *which* Aunt Anne—the one who lives in New York or the one who lives in Chicago. They are, therefore, *restrictive.*

16·22   My Uncle Bertrand, **whom** Senator Lang asked to be introduced **to,** had a reputation for being very frank.

My Uncle Bertrand, **to whom** Senator Lang asked to be introduced, had a reputation for being very frank.

- As with restrictive clauses, prepositions can be separated from the relative pronoun. Prepositions and relative pronouns most often occur together in formal speech and writing, however.

16·23   Centerville, **where he was born,** has a population of about 10,000.
The house **where he was born** has been torn down.

- **Where,** as a relative pronoun, occurs in nonrestrictive as well as restrictive clauses.

16·24   DRILL   Make the second clause nonrestrictive, using *who, whom, which,* or *whose,* as appropriate. Be sure to set off the nonrestrictive clauses with commas in writing and pauses in speaking.

1. He introduced us to his brothers, and both of his brothers work at the Ritz Hotel. →
   He introduced us to his brothers, both of whom work at the Ritz Hotel.
2. The Lenox Hotel is one of the favorite hotels of businessmen, and it has good conference facilities.
3. The hotel is fortunate to have a manager like Mr. Connors, and he has had years of experience in the hotel business.
4. Mr. Wong is head chef of the Pagoda Room, and he received his training in Shanghai.
5. The Pagoda Room is popular with theater goers, and it is open until 2 A.M.
6. Only men are served from 11 A.M. to 2 P.M. in the Athenian Restaurant, and it specializes in lunches for businessmen.
7. John Kalogeropolos is part owner of the Athenian Restaurant, and his uncle is a famous chef.
8. John is very popular with the customers, and everyone calls him Kall.

16·25 DRILL Rewrite the sentences so that your final sentences contain nonrestrictive clauses.

1. Ted is usually very punctual, but he was late to the theater. →
   Ted, who was late to the theater, is usually very punctual.
2. We're going to see *Hamlet*, and it's Ted's favorite Shakespearean play.
3. The Fox Theater was built in 1927, but it is still in excellent condition.
4. After the play we went to Adolph's, and it's an excellent restaurant.
5. We ordered a French wine, and everyone liked it very much.
6. Don's brother Tom is an engineer, and he often helps us with our math problems.
7. Don failed the last math test, but he's a good student.
8. Don is majoring in political science, and he is an excellent debater.

16·26 Michael Strong, **who is a well-known stock market analyst,** gave a lecture at Hertz Hall last Tuesday evening.

Michael Strong, **a well-known stock market analyst,** gave a lecture at Hertz Hall last Tuesday evening.

Mr. Strong, **who was expecting a small crowd,** was amazed by the large turnout.

Mr. Strong, **expecting a small crowd,** was amazed by the large turnout.

Mr. Strong, **who was pleased by the enthusiastic response of the audience,** answered questions for forty-five minutes after the lecture.

Mr. Strong, **pleased by the enthusiastic response of the audience,** answered questions for forty-five minutes after the lecture.

- Like restrictive clauses, the relative pronoun and a form of **be** can be omitted in nonrestrictive clauses.

16·27 Someone **who was expecting a small crowd**
Someone **expecting a small crowd** } would be surprised.

Mr. Strong, **who was expecting a small crowd,**
Mr. Strong, **expecting a small crowd,**
Expecting a small crowd, Mr. Strong } was surprised.

Someone **who was pleased by a remark of the speaker**
Someone **pleased by a remark of the speaker** } shouted "Bravo!"

Mr. Helm, **who was pleased by a remark of the speaker,**
Mr. Helm, **pleased by a remark of the speaker,**
Pleased by a remark of the speaker, Mr. Helm } shouted "Bravo!"

- Phrases resulting from deletion of the subject and a form of **be** in restrictive clauses cannot be shifted before the noun phrase; however, phrases resulting from a similar deletion in nonrestrictive clauses can, as illustrated in the examples.

16·28   Mr. Strong, **who is a dynamic speaker,**
 Mr. Strong, **a dynamic speaker,**   } is popular with audiences.
 A dynamic speaker, Mr. Strong

- Modifiers like "a dynamic speaker" are called *appositives*. Before the noun phrase, appositives are not as common as present or past participial phrases, but they can be shifted, as shown in the preceding example.

16·29   DRILL   Delete the relative pronoun and *be* in the relative clauses; do not delete the commas.

1. Mr. Reina, who is a druggist, is a leader in the Italian community.   →
   Mr. Reina, a druggist, is a leader in the Italian community.

2. Mr. Reina, who is greatly encouraged by community support, is optimistic about the proposed Italian cultural center.

3. Mrs. Cara, who is a social worker, is a member of the Planning Committee.

4. Mrs. Cara, who was annoyed by an article in the local newspaper *Figaro,* wrote a letter to the editor.

5. The editor of *Figaro,* who was impressed by Mrs. Cara's letter, printed her letter on the editorial page.

6. The Planning Committee, which is working hard for community solidarity, is understandably disturbed by the critical article.

Relative Clauses in Writing

16·30   Their Salt Lake City home was built fifty years ago, (which has ten rooms).

Their Salt Lake City home, **which has ten rooms,** was built fifty years ago.

- The relative clause should be placed as close as possible to the phrase it gives information about.

16·31   DRILL   Revise each sentence, placing the relative clause next to the noun phrase it modifies.

1. The car was his pride and joy, which was a Gullwing Mercedes.

2. Our next-door neighbor bought an Oriental rug in Turkey, who likes to travel, last summer.

3. The young man comes from Austria who is wearing the green sweater.

4. The play at the Star Theater is full of laughs, which we saw last weekend.

5. The actor often appears on television who plays the main part.

16·32   The professor postponed the quiz, which made us very happy.
 It rained on the day of the parade, which was unfortunate.
 Lois called us from Rome, which was a pleasant surprise.

■ In the preceding sentences, the relative clause is not attached to a noun phrase. The clause refers to the whole sentence or part of the sentence rather than a noun phrase. Phrases of this type are acceptable in speech, but are generally poor style in formal writing. In formal writing, the statements might be written as follows:

We were very happy because the professor postponed the examination.
It was unfortunate that it rained on the day of the parade.
Lois's telephone call from Rome was a pleasant surprise.

16·33 DRILL The relative clauses in the sentences below are not attached to a noun phrase. They would be quite acceptable in speech but might not be acceptable in formal writing. What might these statements be in formal writing?

1. The opera was completely sold out, which was not surprising. →
   It was not at all surprising that the opera was completely sold out.

2. The singers are world famous, which makes everyone want to hear them. →
   Everyone wants to hear the singers, who are world famous.
   OR: *Everyone wants to hear the world-famous singers.*

3. Joan Sutherland is one of the world's most celebrated sopranos, which everyone knows.

4. The singers respect the conductor, which makes them give a good performance.

5. The conductor is very demanding, which makes the orchestra play exceptionally well.

6. The opera ballet is excellent, which we appreciate.

16·34

Faulty statement	*Revised statement*
Ted's faculty advisor, who is a physics professor that recently received a Nobel Prize, which is annually awarded by the Swedish government, is a world-famous scientist, who is frequently called to Washington to advise the President.	Ted's faculty advisor, who is a physics professor, is a world-famous scientist and a recent Nobel Prize winner. He is frequently called to Washington to advise the President.

■ Written sentences that are overloaded with dependent clauses often seem heavy and unnecessarily complicated. Thus, it is a good practice to limit the number of relative clauses to one or two in a sentence.

16·35 DRILL Revise these overcomplicated sentences into two or more simpler sentences. Remove superfluous clauses (for instance, in the example in §16.34, the information that a Nobel Prize is "annually awarded by the Swedish government" is not relevant and is omitted in the revision).

1. Evelyn and Hans, who lead a very busy life, have a dachshund named Struppi, who lives with them in their beautiful house, which is modern in style and which is at the edge of town in a woods.

2. Every winter Evelyn and Hans, who are enthusiastic skiers, spend a month in the Dolomites in Italy, where they join their old friends the Barbers, who live in Switzerland, at a ski resort that they discovered several years ago, which they all like for its coziness and charm.

1 Combine the following sentences. The final sentences should contain either a restrictive or nonrestrictive clause. If the clause is nonrestrictive, it should be set off with commas. (It is possible that some clauses could be either restrictive or nonrestrictive, depending on your interpretation. In these instances, you should be able to explain why you use one or the other.)

1. George Orwell died in 1950. He wrote the novel *Animal Farm.* →
   George Orwell, who wrote the novel <u>Animal Farm</u>, died in 1950.

2. The title of the novel is *Animal Farm.* George Orwell wrote it in 1946.

3. *Animal Farm* is a story about some animals. These animals took over a farm.

4. In the same story, there is a group of aggressive pigs. They force the other animals into slavery.

5. George Orwell belongs to a group of authors. These authors hate authoritarianism and fear the loss of individuality.

6. George Orwell hated authoritarianism and feared any loss of individual freedom. He depicted his attitudes in *Animal Farm.*

7. Isaac Newton formulated a theory. The theory forms a part of everyone's picture of the universe.

8. Newton's law explained how the sun and planets stay in orbit by the force of gravitation. The law grew out of the hypotheses of earlier astronomers.

2 The following sentences contain nonrestrictive clauses. Separate the main clauses and the relative clauses and make the relative clauses into separate sentences.

1. Scientists before Newton had stated several hypotheses, none of which explained gravitation satisfactorily. →
   Scientists before Newton had stated several hypotheses. None of these hypotheses explained gravitation satisfactorily.

2. Newton's law of universal gravitation, which was based upon the work of earlier scientists, explained how the sun and planets stay in orbit.

3. According to the theory, gravitation, which is the force of mutual attraction, is a force that is proportional to the product of the masses of bodies attracted to one another and inversely proportional to the square of the distance between them.

4. About 1800 the German scientist Johann Wilhelm Ritter discovered that silver nitrate, which breaks down into metallic silver and becomes dark when exposed to blue or violet light, would break down even more rapidly when placed beyond the point in the spectrum where violet fades out.

5. Ritter thus discovered what we now call ultraviolet light, which is technically light beyond violet in the spectrum.

3 In these paragraphs, set off nonrestrictive relative clauses with commas; do not set off restrictive clauses, however. You may feel that some of the clauses can be considered either restrictive or nonrestrictive, depending on the interpretation. In these cases, be prepared to explain why you have or have not used commas.

1.   Like the giant redwood tree which was named as a tribute to him Sequoyah (1770?–1843) towered above his fellows. He was the son of an unknown white man and a Cherokee Indian woman who alone brought him up in a Cherokee village in Tennessee. Although he never attended school and did not know how to read, write, or speak English, he observed at an early age that the white man had a method of conveying messages by means of printed symbols. He decided to try to invent characters that would do the same thing for the red man.

2.   Sequoyah's quest which began with his studying printed matter and experimenting with symbols ended after many discouraging years of struggle with his invention of the Cherokee alphabet. This alphabet which consisted of 86 characters standing for syllables that could be combined into words was the work of a true genius.

3.   Sequoyah had yet to overcome the ridicule of his people who suspected him of witchcraft. In 1821 he submitted his alphabet to a public test before an assembly of Cherokee leaders. There, he and one of his sons who had learned the alphabet from him were placed at distances from each other. The members dictated sentences to one and took them to the other who read them aloud to the group. Thus the assembly tested and approved Sequoyah's system.

4.   Sequoyah's alphabet had a great effect upon the tribe whose members by the thousands learned to read and write in their own language within a year. Cherokees in Tennessee and Georgia could write letters to tribesmen who had moved to Arkansas. By 1827, as a result of the efforts of a missionary, a printing press was set up for the publication of the *Cherokee Phoenix* which was the first Cherokee newspaper.

5.   Sequoyah was honored in several ways which included the naming of a county in Oklahoma for him, the placing of a statue of him in the nation's Capitol, and giving his name to the California redwood tree (spelled *sequoia*). Most important of all, however, is the learning and culture the alphabet brought to the Cherokees whose advancement in society stems so directly from the work of Sequoyah's genius.

4 Revise these paragraphs, correcting poor uses and overuses of relative clauses. If necessary, punctuate the clauses that remain.

1.   Sequoyah who was the son of a Cherokee Indian woman and a white man whose name is not known for sure was a true genius who invented the Cherokee alphabet which had a great effect upon his tribe whose members by the thousands quickly learned to read and write.

2.   At an early age Sequoyah observed that there was magic in the "talking pages" of white men who were set apart from men who could not read and write. He decided to try to invent symbols for his people that would do the same thing.

5 Convert the list of sentences below into two or three well-organized paragraphs. You may want to change some sentences to adverbial or relative clauses and to combine them with other sentences or to form compound sentences by adding conjunctions like *and* and *but*. If you wish, delete words and phrases or add words and phrases like *therefore, however,* or *in addition*. Do whatever you think necessary to change the list of sentences into two or three well-written paragraphs.

1. The Bureau of Indian Affairs is a bureau of the U.S. Department of the Interior.

2. The Bureau of Indian Affairs is charged with the supervision and protection of the interests, welfare, and education of American Indians.

3. These Indians live on or near reservations.

4. Indian tribal officers maintain law and order.

5. The bureau assists these officers.

6. The Indian Arts and Crafts Board was established in 1935.

7. It was established within the Department of the Interior.

8. The purpose of the Indian Arts and Crafts Board is to maintain standards of Indian handmade products.

9. The Bureau of Indian Affairs operates in close cooperation with the Indian Arts and Crafts Board.

10. The Bureau of Indian Affairs provides agricultural guidance for the conservation and improvement of 53,000,000 acres of Indian land.

11. Some private industrial plants furnish jobs for Indians.

12. These Indians live on or near reservations.

13. The Bureau of Indian Affairs encourages the establishment of such plants.

14. Some Indians wish to relocate in urban areas away from the reservations.

15. The Bureau of Indian Affairs provides financial aid and guidance for them.

6 Write an original report (200–250 words) on a social organization to which you belong, on a governmental bureau or agency, or on a public services foundation with which you are familiar.

CONDITIONALS

HOPE versus WISH

17·1   Kahlil Tanous **hopes** that his parents **can visit** him in the United States soon. He **wishes** that he **could go** home to Lebanon in June, but he **can't** because he **has** to work. Sometimes he **wishes** that he **had enrolled** at the American University in Beirut, so that he **would have been able to spend his** vacations at home.

- ■ Compare the verbs after **hopes** and **wishes.** Here are some guidelines for tense sequence:

    1) **Hope** (present) is followed by a present verb form or auxiliary indicating present or future time.

    He **hopes** (that) they $\begin{Bmatrix} \textbf{can} \\ \textbf{will} \\ \textbf{are going to} \\ \textbf{—} \end{Bmatrix}$ visit him soon.

    2) **Hope** (present) can also be followed by the present perfect or past.

    He **hopes** (that) they **have gone.**
    I **hope** they **stopped** at the bookstore on the way home.

    3) **Wish** (present) is followed by two possible combinations:

    a) *A simple past verb or a past auxiliary + simple form*—if the wish is for something in the present or future.

    He **wishes** (that) his mother **was**° in the United States now.
    He **wishes** (that) he **could go** home this year (next year).

    b) **Had** + *past participle* or *past auxiliary* + **have** + *past participle*—if the wish is for something in past time.

    He **wishes** (that) he **had enrolled** at the American University.
    He **wishes** (that) he **had gone (could have gone)** home in June.

    Look at the second sentence in the opening paragraph. If **could have gone** instead of **could go** followed **wishes,** what else would have to be changed?

° Some people prefer **were** after **wish** for all persons, but **was** is generally acceptable in all but very formal writing. *Examples:*
He wishes he **were (was)** here. I wish I **was (were)** there.

- **Wish** is also used like this:

  Kahlil hopes that he can go home next year. We **wish** $\begin{cases} \text{him luck.} \\ \text{him the best.} \\ \text{the best for him.} \end{cases}$

- *Usage:* We generally **hope** for things that seem possible and **wish** for things that seem impossible or not present. Could we use **hopes** instead of **wishes** in sentence 2 of the opening paragraph? Why or why not?

17·2   DRILL   Choose the appropriate form in parentheses.

1. He _____ that he _____ home this summer, but he can't.
         (wishes, hopes)   (can go, could go)

2. He has to work, but he _____ that he _____.
                          (wishes, hopes)   (doesn't, didn't)

3. He _____ that he _____ home next summer.
      (wishes, hopes)   (can go, could go)

4. Sometimes his parents _____ that he _____ to the United
                         (hope, wish)   (hasn't gone, hadn't gone)

   States to study.

5. They _____ they _____ to visit him soon.
        (hope, wish)   (will be able, were able)

17·3   Kahlil Tanous **hoped** that his parents **could visit** him in the United States soon. He **wished** that he **could go** home to Lebanon in June, but he **couldn't** because he **had** to work. Sometimes he **wished** that he **had enrolled** at the American University in Beirut so that he **would have been able to spend** his vacations at home.

- Compare the verbs after **hoped** and **wished** with those after **hopes** and **wishes** in the previous section. Which verbs are different? Which verbs remain the same? Why? In the preceding paragraph, could we use **could have gone** instead of **could go** after **wished** in sentence 2? Would anything else have to be changed? What would the time reference be then?

- It is often necessary to change the verb form and time indicators (**this morning, yesterday,** etc.) to fit the situation. *Compare:*

  Time of "hoping" ⟶ *Result*

Tuesday, 10 A.M.	He **hopes** they **will call** him this morning.
Tuesday, 3 P.M.	He **hoped** they **would call** him this morning, but they **didn't.**
Wednesday, 11 A.M.	He **hoped** they **would call** him yesterday morning, but they **didn't.**

  Notice that in the preceding sentences **hoped** (past tense) refers to something that did not happen. This is not necessarily true, however, in past narration (storytelling) as in the following examples:

  As the school year went on, Kahlil became very homesick. He **hoped** that his parents would visit him soon. He also **hoped** that his brother would come with them.

Nor is it necessarily true in the case of reported speech (see §15.24). *Compare:*

He **hopes** they **will call** him tomorrow.
He **said** he **hoped** they **would call** him tomorrow.

17·4   DRILL   Change to past narration (that is, change *this summer* to *last summer, hope* to *hoped,* and *wish* to *wished*) and make whatever other changes are necessary.

Kahlil *hopes* he can get a good job this summer. He *wishes* he didn't have to work, but he needs more money to cover his expenses. He *wishes* he had been able to save enough money to go to summer school, but he had to spend all of his allowance this semester on books, food, and room rent.

17·5   DRILL   Change from past narration to present narration (that is, change *last semester* to *this semester,* as well as *wished* and *hoped* to *wishes, hopes, will hope,* etc.) and make whatever other changes are necessary.

Kahlil *hoped* that he would get good grades last semester. He *wished* that he could get A's in all his courses, but he realized that he had a lot of competition from other students. As the final examination period approached, he probably *wished* that he hadn't taken so many courses.

17·6   Kahlil **hopes to get a job** in an architect's office this summer. Yesterday he went downtown for an interview. Today the interviewer called and told Kahlil that the office manager **wished to see** him tomorrow morning.

■ Infinitives can replace **that**-clauses after **hope** only if the subject of the **that**-clause refers to the same person as the subject of the main clause. *Compare:*

He **wishes** {that **he** could leave now. / to leave now.

He **wishes** {that **she** would leave now. / **her** to leave now.

He **hopes** {that **he** will get the job. / to get the job.

He **hopes** that **she** will get the job.

17·7   DRILL   Change the *that*-clauses to infinitives wherever possible.

1. Kahlil hopes that he can get the job. → *Kahlil hopes to get the job.*

2. Kahlil hopes that he will hear from the interviewer.

3. The interviewer hoped that Kahlil would wait for an interview with the department supervisor.

4. Kahlil's faculty adviser wishes that he would get as much experience as possible this summer.

5. Kahlil wishes that he could get a good-paying job.

Conditional Sentences

17·8   If you **were** a taxidermist, **would you earn** your living by collecting taxes?

If you **had been born** in 1900, how old **would** you **have been** when Charles Lindbergh first flew nonstop across the Atlantic?

How old **would** you **be** now if you **had been born** on the same day and in the same year as Queen Elizabeth II of England?

Would you probably **have spent** years studying dentistry if you **were** an icthyologist?

- Notice that the **if**-clause can come at the beginning or end of a sentence. When it comes at the beginning, it is usually followed by a comma in writing.

- For your information: (1) If you were a taxidermist, you would not earn your living by collecting taxes; instead you would earn your living by preserving animal skins and stuffing them. (2) Lindbergh flew nonstop across the Atlantic in 1927. How old would you have been if you had been born in 1900? (3) Queen Elizabeth II was born on April 21, 1926. How old would you be now if you had been born at the same time? (4) If you were an icthyologist, you would be working with fish rather than teeth; therefore, you probably would not have spent years studying dentistry. Would you probably have studied marine biology?

- Compare the boldfaced verb forms in the examples. How do they differ? As the preceding examples reveal, a number of combinations of verb forms are possible. Here is a guide to possible sequences:

    1) *Regular conditional*

        a) *Present or future time*

        If he **goes**, I **go**.   If he **will go**, I **will go**.
        If he **goes**, I **will go**.   If he **has gone**, she **has gone**.

        b) *Past time*

        If he **was** there, then she **was** there.   If he **told** her to jump, she **jumped**.

    What are the verb forms in the **if**-clauses? What are the verb forms in the main clauses?

    2) *Hypothetical—contrary to fact*

        a) *Present or future time*

        If he **had** wings, he **could fly**.   If he **could fly**, he **would fly** away.

        b) *Past time*

        If you **had been born**° in 1930, how old **would** you **have been** when man first stepped on the moon?
        If you **had had** the opportunity to make the first trip to the moon, **would** you **have gone?**
        If you **could have gone, would** you **have gone?**

    What are the verb forms in the **if**-clauses? In the main clauses?

°The verb **had been born** is passive (**had** + **been** + *past participle*). Other examples: **had been taken, had been robbed, had been removed.**

■ As the sentences opening this section show, certain combinations are also possible.

   1) Examples of regular conditional combinations:

   If you **studied** the examples, you no doubt **understand** conditional sentences now.

   If you **don't understand** the examples now, you possibly **didn't read** them carefully.

   He probably **read** the text carefully if he **has done** the exercises perfectly.

   2) Examples of hypothetical or contrary-to-fact conditional combinations:

   If John Dunn **were°** an ornithologist, what **would** his college major probably **have been?**

   Would he **be** likely to be an ornithologist today if he **had majored** in electrical engineering?

17·9   DRILL   Answer the questions on the basis of your experience. For practice, use the *if-clause + main clause* in your answer.

1. If you are late, what do you say? → *If I'm late, I say, "I'm sorry."*

2. What do you say if you step on someone's toe?

3. If you want to get by someone in a crowded hall, what do you say?

4. What do you say if you want someone to go have coffee with you?

5. If you are visiting friends and you think it is time to go, what do you say?

6. What do they say if your friends don't want you to go?

17·10   DRILL   Ask questions using the terms below. Then answer, using both the *if-clause* and *main clause*. If you do not know the term, use your dictionary.

1. numismatist → *If you were a numismatist, what kind of work would you do?* → *If I were (was) a numismatist, I would collect, trade, and sell coins.*

2. *philatelist*	5. *ophthalmologist*	8. *anesthetist*
3. *entomologist*	6. *civil engineer*	9. *pediatrician*
4. *chiropodist*	7. *musicologist*	10. *plumber*

17·11   DRILL   Ask and answer questions, using the items below.

1. Celts → *If your ancestors had been Celts, where would they probably have lived?* → *If my ancestors had been Celts, they would probably have lived in Ireland, Scotland, Wales, or Brittany.*

2. Bedouins	4. Sherpas	6. Mongols	8. Moors	10. Ilocanos
3. Tartars	5. Vikings	7. Incas	9. Phoenicians	11. Navahos

°Some people prefer **were** for all persons in hypothetical conditional sentences, but **was** is generally acceptable in all but very formal writing. *Examples:*

If John Dunn **were** (**was**) an ornithologist, ...

If I **were** (**was**) an astronaut, ...

17·12 Suppose you **were** a taxidermist. **Would** you **earn** your living by collecting taxes?

Suppose you **had been born** in 1900. How old **would** you **have been** when Charles Lindbergh first flew nonstop across the Atlantic?

Suppose you **had been born** on the same day and in the same year as Queen Elizabeth II of England. How old **would** you **be** now?

Suppose you **were** an icthyologist. **Would** you probably **have spent** years studying dentistry?

■ Compare the preceding sentences with the **if**-sentences in §17.8. Are the verb forms the same?

17·13 DRILL Restate the questions, changing the *if-clause + main clause* to "Suppose . . . ." Answer the questions from your knowledge or experience. Use a dictionary if necessary.

1. If you were a podiatrist, what would your specialization be? →
   Q: Suppose you were a podiatrist. What would your specialization be?
   A: I would specialize in the treatment of feet.
      OR: *If I were (was) a podiatrist, I would specialize in the treatment of feet.*

2. If you were an obstetrician, what would your specialization be?

3. If you had been born in Zurich, Switzerland, what languages would you probably speak?

4. If you had been born in Tibet, what would your native language be?

5. If you lived in the largest city in Nepal, where would you live?

6. If you had been in high school in the 1930s, would you have studied about the United Nations?

7. If Mr. X lives in the largest city in the world, where does he live?

8. If Jane Young can remember the first landing on the moon, at least how old does she have to be?

1   Write a paragraph in which you tell several things that you hope you can do (*or* hope to do) within the next few years. Words like *first, also, next,* and *finally* can point out the sequence or series of things you plan to do. You might follow this outline:

> *In the next few years, I hope to do several things. First, I hope to . . . . I also hope . . . . Next, I hope that I . . . . Finally, I hope . . . .*

2   Write a paragraph in which you tell several things that you wish you could do in the near future. Use the following sequence if you wish.

> *I wish I could do the following things* (OR: *these three, four, etc., things*) *in the next few weeks* (*days, months, etc.*). *First, I wish I . . . . Next* (*second, also*), *I wish . . . . In addition* (*third, next*), *I wish . . . . Finally* (*fourth, last*), *I wish . . . .*

3   Write a paragraph in which you tell several things you wish you hadn't done or several things that you wish had been different in the past. You might begin like this:

> *There are several* (*three, four, etc.*) *things that I wish had been different about my life.*

4   Write paragraphs in which you develop the following situations.

1. Suppose you could live anywhere in the world. Where would you live? Give reasons for your choice. You might begin like this:

> *If I could live anywhere, I would choose . . . for these reasons. First, ... Second, ...*

2. If you were asked to name three of the most important people in the world today, which people would you choose and why?

3. If you were asked to name three of the most interesting people in the world today, which people would you choose? Why?

4. Suppose you could talk to historical figures of the past. Which three would you choose? Give reasons for your choices.

5   Write paragraphs in which you develop the following situations:

1. Tell what it would be like if airplanes suddenly were unable to fly because of some strange weather condition throughout the world.

2. Tell what would happen if it rained for forty days and nights in the city or town where you live.

3. Tell what would probably have happened if Christopher Columbus had had three airplanes instead of three ships.

4. In what way would the history of the United States probably have been different if the thirteen colonies had been settled by the Spanish instead of the British?

VERB FORMS

AS COMPLEMENTS

THAT-Clause/ TO + Verb

18·1   Mrs. Judd has decided **that she will vote for the liberal candidate** even though Mr. Judd has decided **to vote for the conservative candidate.**

- When the subjects of the main clause and the **that**-clause refer to the same person, an infinitive phrase can replace the **that**-clause after **decide, hope,** or **forget.**

  Mrs. Judd $\begin{Bmatrix} \text{decided} \\ \text{hoped} \\ \text{forgot} \end{Bmatrix}$ $\begin{matrix} \text{that she could vote early.} \\ \text{to vote early.} \end{matrix}$

18·2   **The liberal candidate** expected $\begin{cases} \text{that he would win.} \\ \text{to win.} \end{cases}$

Mrs. Judd expected $\begin{cases} \text{that he would win.} \\ \text{him to win.} \end{cases}$

- Notice that in the first example there is no pronoun before the **to** + *verb*. A pronoun is not necessary because **the liberal candidate** and **he** refer to the same person. Why is a pronoun necessary in the second example?

- **Promise, persuade,** and **remind** pattern somewhat differently from **expect.**

  1) **Mrs. Judd** promised $\begin{Bmatrix} \text{her husband} \\ \text{Nell McIntosh} \\ \text{herself} \end{Bmatrix}$ $\begin{matrix} \text{that she would vote early.} \\ \text{to vote early.} \end{matrix}$

  (**Mrs. Judd** and **she** refer to the same person.)

  2) Mrs. Judd $\begin{Bmatrix} \text{persuaded} \\ \text{reminded} \end{Bmatrix}$ **Mr. Whalen** $\begin{cases} \text{that he should vote early.} \\ \text{to vote early.} \end{cases}$

  (**Mr. Whalen** and **he** refer to the same person.)

  Mrs. Judd $\begin{Bmatrix} \text{persuaded} \\ \text{reminded} \end{Bmatrix}$ **Kay Thurber** $\begin{cases} \text{that she should vote early.} \\ \text{to vote early.} \end{cases}$

  (**Kay Thurber** and **she** refer to the same person.)

236

18·3   Mrs. Judd has decided **not to vote** for Mr. Lee.
Mrs. Bass **hasn't decided** to vote for Mr. Lee yet.

■ The first sentence above means that Mrs. Judd has decided something: she isn't going to vote for Mr. Lee. What does the second sentence mean? Has Mrs. Bass decided something? Does she know yet whether she is going to vote for Mr. Lee?

18·4   DRILL   Change the *that*-clauses to *to* + verb.

1. Mr. Judd has tried to *persuade* his wife that she should vote for his candidate. →
   Mr. Judd has tried to persuade his wife to vote for his candidate.

2. He *expects* that she will change her mind.

3. She has *decided* that she won't discuss politics with him.

4. He has *promised* her that he won't discuss politics during dinner.

5. She has to *remind* him that he shouldn't talk politics at the dinner table.

18·5   The Junior Chamber of Commerce has asked **that Mayor Lewis explain his position on the proposed city tax.**
The Conservation Club has asked **him to clarify his position on air pollution.**

■ Notice that the verb in the **that**-clause following **ask** is the simple form ("that Mayor Lewis **explain**"). The simple form also occurs in **that**-clauses following verbs like **advise, command, order, urge,** and **beg** (meaning "ask"). *Examples:*

They $\begin{Bmatrix} \text{advised} \\ \text{ordered} \\ \text{urged} \end{Bmatrix}$ that he **explain** his position.

■ **Suggest** is also followed by the simple form; however, **suggest** cannot be followed by **to** + *verb,* as can the other verbs in this group. *Compare:*

He urged **that she vote for Mr. Lee.**   He urged **her to vote** . . . .
He suggested **that she vote for Mr. Lee.**   —

18·6   DRILL   Change the *that*-clauses to *to* + verb wherever possible.

1. Mrs. Lenrow, a prominent civic leader, yesterday urged that all registered voters cast their ballots in Tuesday's election. →
   Mrs. Lenrow, a prominent civic leader, yesterday urged all registered voters to cast their ballots in Tuesday's election.

2. She advised that everyone read the ballot carefully.

3. She suggested that voters familiarize themselves with the voting procedure.

4. She begged that each person exercise his right to vote.

5. She suggested that neighbors offer to babysit for mothers of small children.

18·7   It is important **that the mayor explain his views on low-cost housing.**
It is important **for him to explain his position on reorganization of the police department.**

■ Notice that the verb in the **that**-clause is the simple form ("that the mayor **explain**").

■ Also notice that it is "important **for him** to explain" (NOT: "important him to explain"). **For** + *pronoun* also occurs after **essential, possible, impossible,** and **necessary**. *Example:*

It isn't $\begin{cases} \textbf{essential} \\ \textbf{possible} \\ \textbf{necessary} \end{cases}$ **for him** to explain everything.

■ When the pronoun after **for** is **you, me,** or **us,** the **for**-phrase can be omitted.

18·8   DRILL   Change from *that*-clauses to *to* + verb or the reverse, as appropriate.

1. It is important for the mayor to maintain a good image. →
   It is important that the mayor maintain a good image.
2. It is important that he clarify his views on housing.
3. It isn't necessary for him to explain everything.
4. It isn't possible that he explain everything.
5. It is impossible for him to please everybody.

18·9   **That the mayor explain his views on low-cost housing** is important.
For him to explain his position on reorganization of the police department is also important.

■ Compare these sentences with those in §18.7. How are they different?

■ In the second sentence, it is possible to omit **for** + (*pro*)*noun* or to place it at the end of the sentence.

To explain his position on reorganization of the police department is also important (for him).

18·10   DRILL   Go back to Drill 18.8 and put the *that*-clauses and the *to* + verb phrases in subject position. The first one is done for you. (*Note:* If you write out this drill, do *not* use a comma in these sentences.)

1. *For the mayor to maintain a good image is important.*
   OR: *To maintain a good image is important for the mayor.*

18·11   It seems **likely that Mayor Lewis will get the labor vote.** *
That he will get the Italian vote appears unlikely.
Even without the Italian vote, however, it is **almost certain that he will win the election.**

° **Labor vote** = the vote of members of labor unions; **Italian vote** = the vote of people of Italian descent.

Mayor Lewis seems **likely to get the labor vote.**

He appears **unlikely to get the Italian vote.**

Even without the Italian vote, he is **almost certain to win the election.**

- Notice that the **that**-clauses in the preceding examples cannot be changed directly to **to** + *verb* phrases. We do not say, "It seems likely for Mr. Lewis to get ..."; instead we say, "Mr. Lewis seems likely to get ..."

- **Happen** and **turn out** + **that**-clause undergo the same type of change in converting from a **that**-clause to **to** + *verb*. *Compare:*

It happens
It turns out $\Big\}$ **that he is a good speaker.**

He happens
He turns out $\Big\}$ **to be a good speaker.**

18·12   DRILL   Restate the sentences so that you have *to* + verb phrases rather than *that*-clauses.

1. That he will get the Italian vote appears unlikely. →
   He appears unlikely to get the Italian vote.

2. It is unlikely that he will hold a press conference.

3. It is more likely that he will make a TV appearance.

4. It happens that he has a good TV personality.

5. It turns out that he is very articulate.

6. It seems that he has acting talent.

7. It is certain that he will be a favorite with TV audiences.

8. It seems that he is popular with both old and young people.

18·13   It **seems** almost certain that Mayor Lewis **has won** the election.

It **is** unlikely, however, that his opponent **will concede*** the election at this time.

Mayor Lewis **seems** almost certain **to have won** the election.

His opponent, however, **is** unlikely **to concede** the election at this time.

- Compare the boldfaced verbs and infinitives in the preceding examples. Notice that **has won** becomes **to have won** (NOT: to win). This form of the infinitive is used to reflect the past action expressed by **has won.** *Compare:*

It $\left\{\begin{array}{l}\textbf{is}\\\textbf{was}\end{array}\right\}$ certain the he $\left\{\begin{array}{l}\textbf{will}\\\textbf{would}\end{array}\right\}$ win. → He $\left\{\begin{array}{l}\textbf{is}\\\textbf{was}\end{array}\right\}$ certain to win.

(**Is** and **was certain** express present and past prediction of an action to come.)

It seems that he $\left\{\begin{array}{l}\textbf{has won.}\\\textbf{won.}\end{array}\right\}$ → He $\left\{\begin{array}{l}\textbf{seems}\\\textbf{seemed}\end{array}\right\}$ to have won.

(The action in both cases has been completed.)

* To **concede** the election = to admit to losing the election.

18·14   DRILL   Change the *that*-clauses to infinitives.

1. It is more likely that he was scheduled for a TV appearance. →
   He is more likely to have been scheduled for a TV appearance.
2. It happens that he was scheduled for a TV appearance.
3. It is certain that he scheduled several TV appearances.
4. It is unlikely that he would schedule a rally.
5. It turns out that he was more popular than we thought at first.
6. It appears that he had training as an actor.

18·15   Mayor Lewis has learned **to handle hecklers in the audience.**
He invites them **to talk with him** after he has finished his speech.
He wants **to be fair to them,** and he wants **them to be fair to him.**

- Verbs like **learn, deserve, endeavor, mean,** and **plan** do not allow a noun or pronoun before the infinitive. *Example:*

  He has **learned to handle** them. (NOT: He has learned him to handle them.)

- Verbs like **invite, cause, encourage, get, instruct,** and **oblige** require a noun or pronoun before the infinitive. *Example:*

  He **invites them to talk** with him. (NOT: He invites to talk with him.)

- A noun or pronoun follows **want** when it refers to a person different from the subject. *Compare:*

  He wanted **to be fair.**
  He wanted **them to be fair.**

- The verbs listed in this section are not followed by **that**-clauses. "He learned that he could handle hecklers" *is* possible, but the meaning is "found out or discovered" rather than "learned how to" or "learned a way to" handle hecklers. We also have "He meant that the rule should apply to everyone" and its counterpart "He meant the rule to apply to everyone."

18·16   DRILL   Combine the two sentences by changing the second one to a *to* + verb phrase. Omit the *italicized* word, or words, in the first sentence.

1. The mayor wants *something*. The people will elect him. →
   The mayor wants the people to elect him.
2. He has learned *something*. He can handle hecklers. →
   He has learned to handle hecklers.
3. He invites *some people*. They talk to him after his speech.
4. He persuades *some people*. They are quiet.
5. He is planning *something*. He will make several TV appearances.

THAT-Clause/ Verb-ING

18·17   The candidate **admitted that he had accepted a legal fee from the ABC Company,** but he **denied taking a bribe.**

- A **that**-clause or a verb-**ing** can follow these verbs: **admit, deny, consider, imagine, resent, suggest.**

  A verb-**ing** can follow these verbs: **appreciate, avoid, enjoy, escape, finish, keep, miss, postpone, practice, quit.** *Example:*

  The candidate **avoided talking** about the fee.
  (NOT: The candidate avoided to talk about the fee.)

18·18   He is **looking forward to seeing** you.
He **objects to being called** dishonest.

- The verb-**ing** also follows phrases like **look forward to, object to, be opposed to, be used to,** and **be accustomed to.**

- In the phrases above, the **to** is like a preposition, and prepositions are followed by verb-**ing.** *Examples:*

  He is interested **in discussing** the issue.
  He convinced them **by stating** facts.
  He is used **to speaking** extemporaneously. (NOT: He is used to speak . . . .)

- Do not confuse **used to** and **be used to.** *Compare:*

  He **used to work** late at night.
  (past habitual action)

  He **is used to working** late at night.
  (is accustomed to working)

18·19   Does he mind **answering** questions?
Would you mind **explaining** that point?

- The verb-**ing** (NOT: **to** + *verb*) follows **Do (Would) you mind . . .**

18·20   DRILL   Change the *italicized* portion of the sentence so that it includes an *ing*-phrase; use the verb at the left. In some cases, you may have to change the wording somewhat.

see   1. They are looking forward to *Mr. Lee's TV appearance.* →
      They are looking forward to seeing Mr. Lee on TV.

enjoy   2. He *likes to talk* to a TV audience. →
        He enjoys talking to a TV audience.

answer   3. He doesn't mind *their questions.*

answer   4. He is used to *embarrassing questions.*

keep on   5. They *continue to ask* questions, and he *continues to answer* them.

discuss   6. Sometimes he avoids *controversial issues.*

receive   7. He appreciates *the support of the young voters.*

seek   8. He admits *that he wants their support.*

talk   9. He doesn't object to *reporters.*

have   10. They suggested *that he hold a press conference after the TV program.*

18·21   After the audience became quiet, Mayor Lewis **began to speak.**
He had said not more than a dozen words, however, when someone in the audience
began shouting insults at him.

- **To** + *verb* or verb-**ing** can follow verbs like **begin, continue, dislike, dread, intend, like, neglect, plan, prefer,** and **start** or phrases like **can't stand** or **can't bear** with essentially no change in meaning.

   Permit and **allow** also belong in this category but require a (pro)noun before the infinitive. *Compare:*

   They don't permit (allow) **us to smoke** in the TV studio.
   They don't permit (allow) **smoking** in the TV studio.

18·22   DRILL   Change the *to* + verb or verb-*ing*, as appropriate.

1. Some people like *to discuss* political issues with friends. →
   Some people like discussing political issues with friends.

2. Some people can't stand *listening* to political speeches. →
   Some people can't stand to listen to political speeches.

3. When the speaker appeared, the audience began *to clap.*

4. The band started *to play.*

5. Some speakers prefer *to begin* with a joke.

6. They intend *getting off* to a good start.

7. Sometimes they will continue *telling* jokes for a few minutes.

8. They like *to have* the audience in a good mood.

18·23   He **remembered** $\begin{Bmatrix} \textbf{to thank} \\ \textbf{thanking} \end{Bmatrix}$ his supporters.

He **stopped** $\begin{Bmatrix} \textbf{to talk} \\ \textbf{talking} \end{Bmatrix}$ to the man.

- With verbs like **remember** and **stop,** there is a change in meaning. For example, the meanings in the preceding examples are as follows:

   remembered to thank = didn't forget to thank
   remembered thanking = recalled the time when he thanked
   stopped to talk = stopped doing something else in order to talk
   stopped talking = ceased talking

18·24 DRILL Restate the sentences, using *remember* or *stop*. The meaning will determine whether you use verb-*ing* or *to* + verb.

1. Mr. King didn't forget to introduce her to Mayor Lewis. →
    Mr. King remembered to introduce her to Mayor Lewis.

2. She recalled that she had met Mayor Lewis. →
    She remembered meeting Mayor Lewis.

3. He didn't recall that he had met her.

4. He didn't forget to smile, however.

5. He finished his chat with her.

6. He paused so that he could talk with Mrs. Lenrow.

18·25 He admitted {that **he** said that. / **saying** that.   He admitted {that **they** said that. / **their saying** that.

- Compare the two examples. Notice that in the example on the right **their** precedes **saying**. Other verbs that pattern this way are **deny, consider, imagine, remember,** and **prefer.**

    With **imagine** and **remember,** the object pronoun as well as the possessive pronoun can be used. *Compare:*

    Imagine **his** saying that.   Imagine **him** saying that.
    I remember **his** saying that.   I remember **him** saying that.

18·26 DRILL Restate the sentences, using (pro)noun + verb-*ing:*

1. I can't imagine that he would say that. →
    I can't imagine his (OR: *him*) *saying that.*

2. She denies that he said it. → *She denies his saying it.*

3. I don't remember that he said anything.

4. He admits that we were right.

5. I recall that she questioned him.

6. He denies that she questioned him.

Passive and Perfect Infinitives and Verb-ING Forms

18·27 Mayor Lewis said that he **respected** the views of others, and he hoped his views **would be respected** by others.

He went on to say that it was as important **to respect** others as **to be respected** by others.

He also said **respecting** one's political opponents was important and **being respected** by one's rivals was equally important.

- Compare the active and passive constructions in the sentences above. How do they differ? When is Mayor Lewis the actor or agent? When is he the receiver?

18·28   DRILL   Complete the sentences by following the model set by the first two examples.

1. He likes to praise others, and he also likes *to be praised by others.*
2. He is used to criticizing others, and he is also used *to being criticized by others.*
3. He wants to respect others, and he wants
4. He doesn't offend others, and he doesn't want
5. He enjoys helping others, and he enjoys
6. He doesn't like to flatter others, and he doesn't like

18·29   When the mayor met Mrs. Lenrow, he said, "I am most happy **to meet** you at last."

When he was leaving, he said to Mrs. Lenrow, "I'm glad **to have met** you."

Mrs. Lenrow later said to a friend, "I so enjoyed **meeting** the mayor. I can't recall ever **having met** a more charming public figure."

■ Compare the boldfaced infinitives and verb-**ing** forms. The perfect forms indicate that the time of the action or situation is before the time of the action or situation expressed by the main verb. "I am glad **to have met** you" clearly means that the person has already met the person he is addressing ("I have already met you. I am glad"). "I can't recall ever **having met** . . ." clearly means that Mrs. Lenrow has never in the past met a more charming public figure, as far as she can recall.

■ Native speakers of English may seem inconsistent to you in using perfect forms. You will hear: "I don't recall ever **meeting** him before." You will also hear "I don't recall ever **having met** him before." However, in the sentence "I am glad **to have met** you," the perfect form is clearly called for.

18·30   DRILL   Complete the sentences with a perfect infinitive or verb-*ing* form.

1. The mayor met Mr. King at a political rally. When the mayor left he said, "I'm glad

   _____ you."

2. Mrs. Hall remembered that she had seen Mr. King at the last meeting. In fact, she

   remembered _____ him at several meetings before.

3. She heard the man say to the mayor, "I am honored to work with you on this campaign,

   and I am honored _____ with you on your past campaigns."

4. The mayor replied, "I am delighted to have you working with me on this campaign,

   and I am, indeed, fortunate _____ you working with me on the last campaign."

5. The mayor denied that he had said that taxes should be raised. In fact, he denied

   emphatically ever _____ it.

Adjective + Verb-ING or TO + Verb

18·31   — Don't throw these shoes away! **They're still good. You can hike in them.**

— You're right! **They're certainly still good to hike in.**

— **I could use that old knapsack. I could carry my extra equipment in it.**

— Yes. **You could use it for carrying your camera and binoculars.**

- Compare the boldfaced sentences in the first two utterances and the last two utterances. What would the sentence in the second utterance be if we used **for** instead of **to** + *verb?* What would the sentence in the last utterance be if we used **to** + *verb* instead of **for?**

- In the following examples, notice that **in order to** can be used only in the first example. *Compare:*

Why did he buy those boots?	He bought them **in order to go on hiking trips.**
	OR: He bought them **for hiking trips.**
	(NOT: He bought them for to go on hiking trips.)
What are those boots good for?	They're good **to hike in.**
	(NOT: . . . in order to hike in.)
	They're good **for hiking.**
What do you use these boots for?	I use them **to hike in.**
	(NOT: . . . in order to hike in.)
	I use them **for hiking.**

18·32   DRILL   Answer the questions, using *(in order) to* + verb, *for* + (pro)noun, or *for* + *ing*-form, as appropriate.

1. Why did Mrs. Hall go to the store? →

   She went (in order) to get some soap.   OR: *She went for some laundry soap.*

2. What does she use laundry soap for?

3. What is an iron good for?

4. Why do people press clothes?

5. Why do people take clothes to the dry cleaners?

6. What are clothes hangers used for?

7. What are pliers good for?

8. What are scissors good for?

Verb-ING and Verb-ED as Adjectives

18·33   The lecture **bored** the audience.

In fact, several **bored people** were put to sleep by the **boring lecture.**

- The verb-**ed** adjective indicates that the noun is the *receiver* of the action (the people were bored by the lecture); the verb-**ing** indicates that the noun is the *giver,* actor, or instigator of the action (the lecture was boring to the people).

18·34   DRILL   Restate the sentences. Change the *italicized* verb form to a verb-*ed* or verb-*ing* adjective and place it before the subject.

1. The tennis match, which obviously *interested* the spectators, lasted for nearly two hours. →

   The interesting tennis match lasted for nearly two hours.

2. The players, who were *tiring*, started to slow down.

3. The spectators, who *cheered* enthusiastically, inspired the players.

4. The players, who were obviously *inspired*, began to play better.

5. The player who *won* threw his racquet into the air.

6. The loser, who was very *tired*, managed to smile.

HAVE Someone DO Something/ HAVE Something DONE

18·35   On Monday Mr. Thomas **got** a student **to wash** his car.

On Tuesday he **had** the student **polish** the car.

He wants **to get** the car **greased** tomorrow.

He **had** the oil **changed** last week.

- In the first two sentences, who polished the car? In the third sentence, who is going to grease the car? In the last sentence, who changed the oil last week? Which sentences are active and which are passive?

- Notice that there are two grammatical patterns for active constructions but only one for passive. *Compare:*

    Active   *Passive*

    He $\left\{\begin{array}{l}\textbf{got} \text{ someone } \textbf{to wash} \\ \textbf{had} \text{ someone } \textbf{wash}\end{array}\right\}$ his car.   He $\left\{\begin{array}{l}\textbf{had} \\ \textbf{got}\end{array}\right\}$ his car **washed** (by someone).

18·36   DRILL   Change from active to passive.

1. John had someone wash his car. → *John had his car washed.*

2. He got someone to polish the car.

3. He had someone repair the windshield wiper.

4. He got someone to replace the seat covers.

5. He had someone clean the inside of the car.

18·37   DRILL   Change from passive to active.

1. Mrs. Mee had the lawn mowed. → *Mrs. Mee had someone mow the lawn.*

2. She had the hedge trimmed.

3. She got the fishpond cleaned.

4. She had the rosebushes sprayed.

5. She got the fence painted.

SEE/ HEAR/ FEEL Something MOVE/ MOVING

18·38   As we **watched** the log **burn** cheerily in the fireplace, we **heard** the rain **falling** on the roof.

- Either the **ing**-form or simple form of the verb can follow **see, hear, watch, feel, notice,** or **listen to.** *Compare:*

  The rain fell. We heard it.   We **heard** the rain **fall.**
  The rain was falling. We heard it.   We **heard** the rain **falling.**

- The two forms are not always interchangeable, however, in certain contexts. The **-ing** form suggests continuous action or action of limited duration, whereas the simple form suggests simultaneous action. *Compare:*

  Thunder rumbled in the distance. I heard it.   A bolt of lightning struck the tree. I saw it.

  I heard thunder $\begin{Bmatrix} \textbf{rumbling} \\ \textbf{rumble} \end{Bmatrix}$ in the distance.   I saw a bolt of lightning **strike** the tree.

18·39   DRILL   Complete the sentences with either an *ing*-form or simple form of an appropriate verb.

1. Except for the rain, it was quiet. Suddenly, I heard a car <u>*coming up the road.*</u>

2. I felt my chair _____ as my dog Lad bumped into it as he rushed to the door.

3. As the car stopped in front of the house, I heard _____.

4. I went to the window and saw a man and a small child _____.

5. I watched them _____.

HELP/ MAKE/ DO/ LET + (Pro)Noun + Simple Verb Form

18·40   The man knocked at the door and said, "Please **let** us **come** in. Please **help** me **take** care of this child. He seems to be lost, but I can't **make** him **tell** me his name or where he lives."

- The simple form follows **help, make, do,** or **let. To** + *verb* can follow **help** but not **make, do,** or **let,** as in "He **helped** us **(to) look** after the child."

18·41   DRILL   Complete the sentences, using a simple verb form.

1. The man's hat and coat were wet. I said, "Let me <u>*take your hat and coat."*</u>

2. The child's coat was wet. I helped him _____.

3. His shoes were also wet, but he wouldn't let me _____.

4. We told the child that we would help him _____.

5. It was twenty minutes or so before we could make him _____.

1 Rewrite the following paragraph, changing the verbs and verb phrases in *italics* so that they contain the verb on the right + infinitive (*to* + verb). For example, *called* becomes *decided to call.* In some cases, the change will necessitate a different verb form; for example, *didn't drive* becomes *hadn't learned to drive.*

When Helen Wells was in Chicago, she *called* a college   decide
classmate whom she hadn't seen in twenty years. She told
her friend, Margaret Ramos, that she *would have written*   mean
but that she *hadn't saved* the address on her last letter.   forget
Helen asked Margaret if she *would have* lunch with her at the   care
hotel. Margaret said she would be delighted. She *was going*   plan
downtown anyway. She added that she still *didn't drive,* so   learn
she would have to come by bus. She *would get* to the hotel   try
by one-thirty. Helen said that was all right because she
would do some shopping before she got there.   hope

2 Rewrite the following paragraph, changing the *italicized* portion to a verb-*ing* phrase. In some sentences, you will need to add verbs. In one or two cases, either *to* + verb or verb-*ing* is possible, but use the verb-*ing* for this exercise.

Mr. Carrie has both good and bad points as an employee. First, let's take the bad points. He will never admit *that he has made a mistake.* If he is asked about a letter which hasn't been answered, he will deny *that he has received it.* By the time that Carrie has finished *with his explanation,* the listener wants to avoid *further talk.* He simply cannot bear *any more excuses.*

Now let's consider his good points. He is used to *hard work,* and he never objects to *overtime.* He enjoys *office work,* and he likes *data processing.* He is opposed to *large social gatherings,* but he doesn't mind *office parties and picnics.* He won't consider *offers* from other companies because he prefers *his present position.* Can you imagine *an employee* like Mr. Carrie?

3 Read the following situations. Decide in each case what you would have done or what you would have someone do. Then write notes or letters to the persons concerned. (See §19.33 for a personal letter form.)

1.   Bill wants to sell his Ford sedan. The car is five years old, and he hasn't taken very good care of it. All the fenders have dents in them, the paint is peeling off in places, the back seat cover is dirty, the left rear window won't open, the front right window is cracked, one headlight is broken, and the engine sounds like a cement mixer. Bill naturally wants to get as much as he can for the car.
    What should he have done to the car in order to get a good price?

2.   Mr. and Mrs. Gonzalez are going to a banquet tonight. Mrs. Gonzalez has hired a babysitter for their two children, Carlos, age 5, and Nina, age 3.
    What will she probably have the babysitter do?

3.   The Katos have bought a house that has not been occupied for some time. The garden is full of weeds. All of the flowers are dead except the rosebushes, and they need to be sprayed. The grass in the front yard is a foot high and is covered with dead leaves and papers. The fishpond is filled with mud and dead leaves, and several branches of a large chestnut tree are dangerously close to the roof of the garage.

The house also needs attention. First of all, the roof leaks where several bricks have fallen off the chimney and cracked the shingles. The brick walls are in good condition, but the doors and window frames and sills need to be painted. Inside, the house is in fairly good condition. However, the floors should be waxed and the kitchen and bathroom walls should be washed. Mrs. Kato likes the off-white walls and ceilings of the living room, dining room, and study, but she doesn't care for the colors of the bedrooms. One is painted green, another bright orange, and the third a dark purple.

Mr. and Mrs. Kato are now living one hundred miles away, so they will have to get someone to do most of the work. You have offered to help them get the house in order, so they can move in. They have already hired a gardener.

Tell what you will have him do first. After that? And so on.

Now tell the Katos what you think they should have done to the house.

4 Imagine yourself in the following situations. Tell what you *see, hear, feel, are watching, notice,* and *are listening to.* Use verb + (pro)noun + verb-*ing* or simple verb.

1. You are standing on the corner of a busy street in a large city. *Examples:*
   I see a lot of people crossing the street.
   I hear a man hailing a taxi.

2. You are in a cafeteria.

3. You are watching a movie.

5 Write paragraphs on each of these five subjects.

1. Four things that you would like to do in the next few years. You might begin this way:
   There are several things I would like to do in the next few years. First, I would like to travel. I would visit Europe first and then explore the Middle East and Asia. Second, I would like to . . . .

2. Advice on doing certain things before buying a car (house, camera, or anything on which you feel qualified to advise). Use either "I advise that you . . ." or "I advise you to . . ."
   I would advise you to read a consumers' report before you buy a car, so that you can find out about the good points and defects of various makes and models. I would also advise you to . . . .

3. Several things that you *must remember to do* or *not forget to do* in the coming week.
   Next week I must remember to do a number of things. First, I must remember to pay my rent. It is due on Wednesday. Second, I mustn't forget to . . . .

4. What you are looking forward to doing, seeing, or hearing in the months ahead.
   I am looking forward to several things in the months ahead. First of all, I'm looking forward to seeing my parents. They will visit me next month. Second, I'm looking forward to . . . .

5. Your New Year's resolutions.
   I am planning to overcome several habits next year. First, I have promised myself to stop smoking. Second, I am going to control . . . .

PUNCTUATION

19

End-of-Sentence

19·1 — Do you know when Labor Day is?
— It's the first Monday in the month of September.
— Wow! That means we have another three-day holiday coming up.

■ The period and the question mark are the most common end-of-sentence punctuation marks. Exclamation marks are reserved for sentences and words that, in speech, would be uttered with surprise or some kind of strong emotion. *Examples:*

Look out! Oh! You frightened me! What a gorgeous day!   How lucky you are!

Between Sentences

19·2 Labor Day is a legal holiday in all fifty states, but Halloween is not.
Labor Day is a legal holiday. But Halloween is not a legal holiday in any state.
Labor Day is a legal holiday; but Halloween, May Day, and Leap Year Day are not legal holidays.

■ Two sentences joined by **but, and, or, for, so,** or **yet** are usually preceded by a comma. A period or a semicolon is also possible.

19·3 Halloween isn't a legal holiday; however, it is a favorite holiday of children.
Halloween isn't a legal holiday. However, it is a favorite holiday of children.

■ A semicolon or period is required with connectors like **however, therefore, nevertheless, moreover,** and **furthermore.**

19·4 Halloween isn't a legal holiday; however, it is a favorite holiday of children.
Halloween isn't a legal holiday; it is a favorite holiday of children, however.
Halloween isn't a legal holiday; it is, however, a favorite holiday of children.

- Connectors like **however, therefore,** etc., are usually followed by a comma if they occur at the beginning of the sentence and preceded by a comma if they occur at the end of the sentence. If they come in the middle of the sentence, they are usually set off by commas.

19·5   DRILL   Supply appropriate punctuation marks at the end of sentences and between sentences.

Ahmad: When is Halloween

Carol: It's October 31   It is on the eve of All Saints' Day, a feast day on which the Roman Catholic and Anglican churches commemorate all known and unknown saints of God

Ahmad: I always associate Halloween with black cats and witches   What have they to do with a Christian feast

Carol: Well, All Saints' Day dates from early Christian times   however   many of the customs and practices associated with Halloween originated with the Celts in England in pagan times
The Celts, it seems, celebrated the new year on the first of November   and the last night before the new year was thought to be the time when the souls of the dead were allowed to return to their homes   They also believed that witches, demons, and other evil spirits were allowed to come out on that night   therefore   they kept huge bonfires burning to keep them away
The early Celts were very superstitious   however, as time went on, these evenings of dancing around the fire with pitchforks to the tune of loud shouts turned into festivals for young people
In the United States today, many young people go to costume parties   and young children, wearing masks and costumes and carrying jack-o'-lanterns, go from house to house chanting "Trick or treat   "   The people who live in the house don't want the children to play a trick on them   so they give them candy, fruit, or nuts

Ahmad: What a strange custom   I suppose, though, that the children symbolize the evil spirits
They must be pacified in some way or they will bring harm to people   By the way, what are jack-o'-lanterns

Carol: They are hollowed-out pumpkins with lighted candles in them   The pumpkin is scooped out   then two triangular eyes, a triangular nose, and a large curving mouth full of long jagged teeth are carved on one side   They are made as grotesque as possible   for the idea is to frighten away the evil spirits   Of course, few people today believe in witches and goblins   but they are part of the Halloween tradition.

Adverbial Phrases and Clauses

19·6   In the United States, the celebration of holidays is determined by the individual states rather than the federal government.
The federal government can declare holidays for federal employees and agencies in the United States and its territories.

- An introductory adverbial phrase, especially if it is long, is often followed by a comma, but a phrase at the end of a sentence is usually not preceded by one.

19·7   Although February 22 is a legal holiday in all fifty states, many stores throughout the country are open for business.

Banks and schools are closed on the Monday or Friday closest to February 22 because Washington's birthday is a legal holiday in all fifty states.

- An introductory adverbial clause is usually followed by a comma, but an adverbial clause at the end of the sentence is usually not preceded by one. (See Chapter 13, especially §13.1, 13.13, 13.14, and 13.36, for further information on the punctuation of adverbial clauses.)

Relative Clauses

19·8   Two holidays that are widely celebrated in Christian countries throughout the world are Christmas and Easter.

Two holidays widely celebrated in Christian countries throughout the world are Christmas and Easter.

Christmas Day, which is on December 25, is one of the most important holidays in Christian countries.

Christmas Day, December 25, is one of the most important holidays in Christian countries.

- Restrictive clauses and phrases are not punctuated with commas, but nonrestrictive clauses and phrases are. (See Chapter 16, especially §16.3 and 16.20, for further information on the punctuation of relative clauses.)

19·9   DRILL   Supply appropriate punctuation marks for clauses and phrases in the following sentences.

1. Although Americans tend to think of Christmas Day and New Year's Day as part of the same holiday season   the two holidays actually have no relationship to each other. While Christmas Day is a religious holiday   New Year's Day marks nothing more than the beginning of a new year.

2. New Year's Day   the first day of the year   is celebrated on January 1 by countries that use the Gregorian calendar.

3. Chinese New Year   which falls sometime between January 10 and February 19 of the Gregorian calendar   is an important holiday for the Chinese.

4. On the day before the first day of the First Moon   the Chinese settle their debts because a person who has not settled his debts before the new year loses face.

5. The Jewish New Year is the first day of Tishri   which falls sometime in September or early October.

6. Muharram   the Moslem New Year   comes eleven days earlier each year because Moslems follow the lunar year. When thirty-five years have passed   Muharram   the first day of the year   will be on the same day again.

Within the Sentence

19·10   Abraham Lincoln, the sixteenth President of the United States, was born in Hardin County, Kentucky, on February 12, 1809.

     As Lincoln sat watching a performance at Ford's Theatre in Washington, D.C., on the night of April 14, 1865, he was shot by John Wilkes Booth, an actor who was thought to be insane. Lincoln's supporters and many of his opponents felt that his death on the morning of April 15, 1865, was, indeed, tragic for the nation.

- In the first line, the pair of commas separate a nonrestrictive phrase (an *appositive*) from the rest of the sentence. A restrictive appositive (that is, one that identified the noun phrase it was placed next to) would not be punctuated with commas. *Example:*

  Lincoln's son **Robert** was the only one of his four sons to survive to adulthood.

- Notice how dates are punctuated.

- Notice the punctuation of place names in the first two sentences.

- In the last sentence, notice that **indeed** is set off by commas. Expressions like **indeed, of course, naturally, by the way,** and **unfortunately,** which provide emphasis or serve to relate one sentence to a previous sentence, are customarily separated from the rest of the sentence by commas.

19·11   Many biographies, novels, and poems (including some of the finest American literature) have been written about Abraham Lincoln. Perhaps the most famous biography is Carl Sandburg's *Abraham Lincoln: The Prairie Years* (1926) and *Abraham Lincoln: The War Years* (1939).

- Parentheses are often used to separate related but nonessential material from the rest of the sentence. A pair of dashes or commas are sometimes used in place of parentheses. Commas, however, are not as strong separators as parentheses or dashes. *Examples:*

19·12   There are only seven legal holidays (that is, holidays on which banks and schools are closed and on which there are some restrictions on business transactions) observed by all fifty states. Some legal holidays—for example, Lincoln's Birthday—are not observed in all fifty states.

- Parentheses or a pair of dashes are frequently used to set off definitions, explanations, and examples that occur in the middle of a sentence. **That is** announces that an explanation or definition will follow; **for example** obviously announces that an example will follow. Both are followed by a comma.

- In writing that involves many explanations, definitions, and examples, **that is** and **for example** are often omitted. *Compare:*

  Some legal holidays—for example, Lincoln's Birthday—are not observed in all fifty states.

  Some legal holidays—including Lincoln's Birthday—are not observed in all fifty states.

- A pair of commas can be used in place of dashes or parentheses to set off examples or explanations. They are not as effective, however, when the sentence already has several commas.

19·13   Memorial Day is celebrated on different days in the North and the South—that is, it is celebrated at the end of May in the North but on various days in the South.

   ▪ A dash is commonly used to set off a definition, explanation, or example at the end of the sentence. Notice that a comma follows **that is.**

19·14   Some days are legal holidays in all fifty states; for example, Christmas Day, New Year's Day, and Labor Day.
   Some days are legal holidays in some states but not in others, for example, Columbus Day.

   ▪ Semicolons and commas are also used to set off examples, definitions, and the like at the end of the sentence. The semicolon is a stronger signal than a comma; a semicolon is generally preferred when there are other commas in a sentence.

19·15   Some holidays are legal in all fifty states: New Year's Day, George Washington's Birthday, the Fourth of July, Labor Day, Veterans Day, Thanksgiving Day, Christmas Day.

   ▪ A colon also is sometimes used to set off examples, explanations, and the like; it is a much stronger signal than the dash, semicolon, or comma.

19·16   The legal holidays observed by all fifty states are as follows: New Year's Day, George Washington's Birthday, the Fourth of July, Labor Day, Veterans Day, Thanksgiving, and Christmas Day.

   ▪ A series preceded by **as follows** or **the following** is commonly set off by a colon. A dash is also possible. *Example:*

   The legal holidays observed by all fifty states are as follows—New Year's Day . . . .

   ▪ Items in a series are separated by commas. Many stylists prefer a comma before **and** or **or** preceding the last member of the series; others do not. Those who favor a comma argue that it produces greater clarity.

   ▪ In some instances, items in a series are separated by semicolons, particularly when there are other commas within the items. *Example:*

   The following are legal holidays not observed in all fifty states: Lincoln's Birthday, February 12; Memorial Day, May 30; Columbus Day, October 12; and Election Day, the first Tuesday after the first Monday in November.

19·17   DRILL   Supply appropriate punctuation marks (including dashes and parentheses) between and within sentences.

   1. Proper names of people and things   including the names of days   months   countries   nationalities   languages   religions   and deities   are capitalized.
   2. Names of languages   French   Italian   Chinese   Japanese   Arabic   and names of

nationalities   Swiss   American   Brazilian   Mexican   Canadian   Indian   are also capitalized.

3. Names of religions   for example   Moslem   Christian   Buddhist   are capitalized.

4. Official titles of academic courses   English 902   Chemistry 305   Economics 110   are capitalized   however   names of general areas of study   economics   chemistry mathematics   physics   are not. Names of languages   of course   are capitalized whether they are part of a course title   Latin 1   Russian 101   Chinese 402   or whether they refer to an area of study   French   Russian   Japanese.

5. Names of the seasons   winter   spring   summer   fall   and directions   east west   north   south   are usually not capitalized   however   directional words are capitalized when they are part of a proper name   Southern California   the Deep South the Middle East   the Far East.

6. The Empire State Building   the United Nations   the University of Chicago   the College of Marin   the President of the United States   and the Secretary of State are all proper names   therefore   they are capitalized. Words like college   university   president and secretary are not capitalized   however   when they are not part of a proper name.

7. Articles   prepositions   conjunctions   and auxiliary verbs are not usually capitalized in proper names and titles   the University of California   the Joint Chiefs of Staff   *Life in the Tropics.* Of course, if the article   preposition   conjunction   or auxiliary verb begins a sentence   The President of the United States will address the nation   or is the first word in the title   *The Lazy Life in the Tropics*   it will be capitalized.

8. It is customary to underline titles of books   magazines   newspapers   pamphlets documents   and symphonies in typed or handwritten papers   <u>Reading for the Disadvantaged</u>   <u>Saturday Review</u>   <u>The New York Times</u>   however   these titles usually appear in italics in print   *Reading for the Disadvantaged*   *Saturday Review* *The New York Times.*

9. It is customary to enclose in quotation marks the titles of short stories or articles that appear in books   magazines   or newspapers   the article "Henry Miller: Rebel-Clown at Eighty" appeared in the December 11, 1971, issue of *Saturday Review.*

10. Titles of short poems   "Dover Beach"   and short musical compositions or parts of operas "Un Bel Di" from *Madame Butterfly*   are customarily put in quotation marks.

11. Foreign words or phrases are usually underlined in typed or handwritten papers   <u>à bientôt</u> and italicized in print   *à bientôt.*

Capitalization

19·18   Drill 19.17 contains guidelines for the use of capital letters in English. After you have completed Drill 19.17 and the exercise has been corrected, read it again and focus your attention on the use of capitals. When you have done so, go on to Drill 19.19.

19·19 DRILL Capitalize wherever capital letters are needed in the following passages. Underline or use quotation marks for foreign phrases and for titles of articles, books, and magazines, as appropriate.

1. Some people say that french food is the best in the world; others say that chinese food has no equal. If you like northern chinese food, you should try the mandarin restaurant on grant avenue. If you prefer parisian cuisine, you should try chez maurice. The chef is a graduate of the cordon bleu. Both restaurants are superb. I cannot decide for you. Chacun à son gout.

2. Mr. langdon had always dreamed of doing research in the middle east. For years he had studied arabic, persian, and hebrew. He had also taken the most advanced courses in anthropology and archeology. I first met him in the fall of 1970 in anthropology 902, which was taught by the distinguished turkish scholar yavuz nutku.

3. There is a review of the play The Sty of the Blind Pig in the december 4, 1971, issue of the new yorker.   Profiles,   an article in the same issue, is about francis t. p. plimpton.

4. Walter cronkite's book eye on the world contains the following chapters: can the world be saved?   ;   a beginning, a middle, and end(?)   ;   the state of the nation   ;   a generation gap   ;   women of the world, united!   ;   such interesting people.

Dialogs

19·20 Johnny said, "Open sesame!"
Gigi asked, "What does that mean?"
Johnny replied, "It's a magic phrase."

- Notice that the speaker tags (**Johnny said, Gigi asked**) are followed by a comma. Also notice that the exclamation point, question mark, and period go inside the quotation marks.

19·21 "Open sesame!" Johnny said.
"What does that mean?" asked Gigi.
"It's a magic phrase," he replied.

- Compare the punctuation of this dialog with the preceding dialog. How does it differ? Notice the position of the question mark and the periods and commas.

- The style generally followed in the United States is to place commas and periods inside quotation marks at all times. *Examples:*

  "It's a magic phrase," replied Johnny.
  Johnny replied, "It's a magic phrase."

  Question marks and exclamation points are placed inside when they are part of the material quoted and outside when they are not. *Compare:*

  Gigi asked, "What does the phrase mean?"
  Why did Johnny say "Open sesame"?

  Semicolons and colons are placed outside. *Example:*

  Johnny said, "Open sesame"; however, he did not draw the card he wanted.

- Speaker tags at the end can be either *noun + verb* or *verb + noun* (**Johnny said** or **said Johnny**), but the order is, with rare exceptions, *pronoun + verb* (**he said**).

19·22   "But why did you say it?" asked Gigi, still puzzled by the remark.

"Well," said Johnny, "it's supposed to make something happen that you want to happen. I said it before I drew a card because I need only the six of spades to win."

"Where does the phrase come from?" Gigi asked, "I wonder—"

"I believe," said Johnny, "that it comes from *The Arabian Nights Entertainments*. A poor woodchopper named Ali Baba," he continued after a slight hesitation, "was the hero of one of the tales. He used the magic phrase 'Open sesame' to open the door to the den of the Forty Thieves."

- Notice the punctuation of Johnny's speeches. What punctuation surrounds speaker tags in the middle of the sentence?

If the speeches were not interrupted, they would be punctuated like this:

Johnny said, "Well, it is supposed to make something happen that you . . ."

"I believe that it comes from *The Arabian Nights Entertainments*" said Johnny. He continued after a slight hesitation, "Ali Baba was the hero . . ."

- In the third paragraph, a dash is used to indicate an unfinished utterance—probably unfinished because the speaker has been interrupted.

- In writing dialog, it is customary to indent for each change of speaker, as illustrated in the dialog above.

19·23   DRILL   Punctuate the following dialog.

Who was Croesus   asked Cate.

I believe   Robert replied   that he was a ruler in Asia Minor in the sixth century B.C. Why?

I heard someone say that Aristotle Onassis was as rich as Croesus   said Cate   and I wondered what he meant

The person meant that Onassis is tremendously wealthy like Croesus   said Robert   Croesus was the first to issue coins of pure gold and silver   he added   and these coins were readily accepted in the world market at that time. You can imagine how wealthy he was

Quotations, Footnotes, and Bibliography

19·24   "I have offered the definition of a society as a group of unequal beings organized to meet common needs."[1]

- In writing papers, we frequently use quotations to support or illustrate points we wish to make. The quotation should be accurate (that is, it should contain the exact words of the speaker). The reader will know it is a quotation because it appears in quotation marks.

- In scholarly papers, it is customary to credit the source of quoted material in a footnote at the bottom of the page on which the quotation appears. Look at footnote 1 at the bottom of this page. Why is *The Social Contract* italicized? The footnote includes the following information: name of author (first name and last name), title of the book, place of publication, publisher, date of publication, and the page on which the quotation appears.

[1] Robert Ardrey, *The Social Contract* (New York: Atheneum, 1970), p. 67.

19·25   Liliuokalani, the last reigning queen of the Hawaiian Islands, by her refusal to recognize the constitutional reforms of 1887, precipitated a revolt that led to dethronement in 1893.[2]

- Quotation marks are not used with paraphrases. However, paraphrased material or a generous borrowing of material from one source is also acknowledged in a footnote in scholarly papers. Encyclopedia articles are frequently unsigned, but the source, nevertheless, is acknowledged, as in footnote 2.

- Footnote 2 contains the following information: the title of the article (the article is unsigned, so there is no author's name), the title of the encyclopedia in which the article appears, the edition of the encyclopedia, the date of publication, the page on which the paraphrased material appears.

19·26   "Women editors-in-chief are as rare in the book business today as ... were women chiefs in [American] Indian days."[3]

- Three dots in a quotation indicate that material has been omitted.

- Brackets indicate that material has been added to the original quotation.

- Look at footnote 3. What is the author's name? "Trade Winds" is the title of a column written by Cleveland Amory; *Saturday Review* is the name of the magazine in which the column regularly appears. Why is one title in quotation marks and the other italicized? What other information appears in the footnote?

19·27   "Housing Secretary George Romney, in a [1971] year-end report, conceded that 'Fragmented local governments, weakened state governments and too numerous and complex separately financed federal programs are not equal to the challenge [of the cities] .... Furthermore, the rotting of central cities is beginning to rot the surrounding suburbs.'"[4]

- A quotation within a quotation is punctuated by single quotation marks.

- Notice footnote 4. **Sec. B** is the section of the newspaper in which the article appeared. What other information is given in the footnote?

19·28   *Bibliography*

Amory, Cleveland. "Trade Winds," *Saturday Review* (December 11, 1971), pp. 16–17.

Ardrey, Robert. *The Social Contract.* New York: Atheneum, 1970.

"Liliuokalani," *The Columbia Encyclopedia,* 3rd ed. (1963), pp. 1217–1218.

Smothers, David. "Are Our Cities Really Worth Saving?" *San Francisco Sunday Examiner and Chronicle,* January 2, 1972, Sec. B., p. 9.

- Compare the items in the bibliography with the footnotes at the bottom of pages in this section. How do they differ?

---

[2] "Liliuokalani," *The Columbia Encyclopedia,* 3rd. ed. (1963), p. 1217.
[3] Cleveland Amory, "Trade Winds," *Saturday Review* (December 11, 1971), p. 16.
[4] David Smothers, "Are Our Cities Really Worth Saving?" *San Francisco Sunday Examiner and Chronicle,* January 2, 1972, Sec. B., p. 9.

19·29 DRILL Punctuate the footnotes below. Do not forget to underline the titles of books, magazines, and newspapers or to put quotation marks around titles of chapters, articles, or stories in books, magazines, and newspapers.

[1] John Connors   Over the Hill to the Poorhouse   Boston   Able & Sons 1973   p. 49

[2] Leon Edwards   What Are They Doing to Our Cities?   The People's Voice   October 12   1972   pp. 15–16

[3] Antonio Burget   Spending Ourselves out of Existence   San Francisco Courier   June 10   1972   Sec. C   p. 5

19·30 DRILL Arrange the items in Drill 19.29 in the form of a bibliography and punctuate appropriately. (See §19.28.)

Letters

19·31 *Business Letter* (Victoria Daniels writes the Admissions Office at Bear State University)

> 2345 Red Bluff Street   (1)
> Boulderville, Colorado 88088
> August 1, 1972

Office of Admissions
Bear State University
1924 Garden Drive   (2)
Barnsdale, California 98000

Gentlemen: (3)

 I am planning to apply for admission to your university   (4)
for the fall semester of 1974 as a graduate student in economics.
Please send me an application blank and whatever information
you have for prospective applicants. Thank you for your
attention to this request.

> Yours very truly,   (5)
> *Victoria Daniels*   (6)
> Victoria Daniels   (7)

- It is preferable to type business letters, but a clearly written letter is acceptable.
- Look at the sender's address (1). What is included and how is it punctuated? How many lines are used for the address and date?
- (2) is the receiver's address. When the receiver's name is known, it should be used.

   Mr. Lee Emerson, Director
   Office of Admissions, etc.

- When the receiver's name is unknown, "Dear Sir:" or "Gentlemen:" is used in the salutation (3). "Dear Madam" is not used unless it is definitely known that the receiver is a woman.

If the receiver's name is known, it should appear in the salutation (3)—for example, "Dear Mr. Emerson:" Notice that a colon follows the salutation in a business letter. (A comma, however, usually follows the name in a personal letter.)

- American business letters are usually brief and to the point (4). Courtesy is conveyed by the relative formality and by words and phrases such as "please" and "thank you."

- Look at the body of the letter (4). Are contractions and abbreviations used?

- In addition to "Yours very truly," there are several closing expressions (5) that would be suitable for a business letter like the one in the example. *Examples:*

Very truly yours,   Sincerely yours,   Yours sincerely,

- The letter is always signed in ink (6), and the sender's name is typed below (7). If the letter is handwritten, the name can be printed.

- The person answering Victoria Daniels' letter would use this salutation:

Dear Miss Daniels:

The envelope would be addressed as follows:

Miss Victoria Daniels°
2345 Red Bluff Street
Boulderville, Colorado 88088

19·32   DRILL   Assume that you work in the Admissions Office at Bear State University and have been assigned to answer Victoria Daniels' letter. You might tell Miss Daniels that you have just received her letter requesting an application blank. Also tell her what you are enclosing (an application blank, information leaflets, etc.). Your letter should be fairly brief; busy administrators do not have time to write long letters to hundreds or thousands of applicants.

19·33   *Personal Letter* (Vicki writes to her cousin David)

2345 Red Bluff Street   (1)
Boulderville, Colorado 88088
August 5, 1972

Dear David,   (2)

    This'll be a short letter because I'm way behind in my studies   (3)
and my work, but I promise to write a long letter soon.
    Last week I wrote to Bear State University for an application form.
I'd like to see a bulletin or list of courses, but I didn't quite know how
to go about asking for one. Could you get one and mail it to me? If
that's too much trouble, could you call a bookstore and find out the cost plus
postage, so I could send for one? Anything you do will be appreciated.
    I hope everything is well with you. Have you seen Jean Goodman
lately? Write soon.

Love,   (4)

Vicki   (5)

° Today *Ms.* is a form commonly appearing before the names of women, whether they are single or married.

- Compare the personal letter with the business letter. How do they differ?

- In a personal letter, the salutation (2) is usually followed by a comma rather than a colon.

- Are contractions common in personal letters?

- Closing expressions (4) are likely to be very personal. "Sincerely," is a middle-ground closing, being neither very formal nor very informal. "Affectionately," is warm but rather impersonal. "Yours," "Best," and "As ever," are other common closings.

19·34   DRILL   Answer the letter. Assume that you are Vicki's cousin David (or assume that the letter was written to a girl cousin, Karen, instead of David). David's (or Karen's) address is 269 Pine Lane, Barnsdale, California 98000. You might tell Vicki: (1) you were glad to hear from her; (2) whether or not you were able to get a Bear State bulletin or catalog for her; (3) what you have been doing lately; (4) whether or not you have seen Jean Goodman lately; (5) whatever else you want to tell her.

19·35   *A Social Letter* (A friend of Vicki's mother invites Vicki to a Bear State University luncheon)

1607 Bluestar Road   (1)
Boulderville, Colorado 88088
August 15, 1972

Dear Vicki,   (2)

    Your mother has told me that you are planning to do graduate   (3)
work at Bear State University. As you may know, I have been
active in the Colorado division of the Bear State Alumni
Association. On Saturday, August 26, the local alumni are having
a luncheon meeting at my house, and we would like you to be
our guest. You would have an opportunity to meet some of
the former graduates, and they would have the pleasure of talking
with a young person studying for an advanced degree. I do hope
you will be able to join us.

Cordially,   (4)

Genevieve Pulhaven   (5)

- Social letters are usually handwritten.

- Mrs. Pulhaven's salutation is "Dear Vicki," because she knows Vicki's mother and probably knows Vicki, too. "My dear Vicki," would be somewhat more formal. She would probably write "My Dear Miss Daniels," if she did not know Vicki or her mother.

- The tone of the letter is friendly but relatively formal. Mrs. Pulhaven is observing social amenities.

- Closing expressions (4) for letters of this kind, in addition to "Cordially," are as follows:

Cordially yours,
Very sincerely,
Affectionately, (used when the person knows the receiver rather well)

- Mrs. Pulhaven signs her own given name (Genevieve) rather than her husband's. However, she probably would use her husband's name for the return address on the envelope (Mrs. Harold J. Pulhaven, Jr.). When Vicki answers Mrs. Pulhaven's letter, the salutation will be as follows:

Dear Mrs. Pulhaven,

The envelope will be addressed as follows:

Mrs. Harold J. Pulhaven, Jr.
1607 Bluestar Road
Boulderville, Colorado 88088

19·36   DRILL   Answer the letter. Assume that you are Vicki or assume that the letter was written to Vicki's brother Charles. Here are some suggestions for the letter: (1) thank Mrs. Pulhaven for the invitation; (2) tell her how much you would like to meet some graduates of Bear State University; (3) tell her whether or not you will be able to accept the invitation; (4) tell her whatever else you want to; (5) thank her again for the invitation and tell her how much you are looking forward to the luncheon or how much you regret not being able to come.

1 Supply punctuation marks and capitalize words wherever necessary.

St. patrick's day is not a legal holiday in the united states   however   it is celebrated by many americans of irish descent. For many years americans associated the color green with ireland   so they made a point of wearing something green on st. patrick's day. In 1959 the president of the republic of ireland happened to be in washington   d.c.   on march 17 st. patrick's day. Virtually everyone turned out in green to greet him. People expected the irish president to be pleased   but he startled the nation when he announced   that evening at a banquet   that the irish people did not like green because it reminded them of ireland before it was free. He also reminded the american people that the flag of the republic of ireland is not solid green but green   white   and orange   furthermore   the irish president's flag is blue with a white harp.

2 Punctuate the following paragraphs.

1.   Modern man   particularly the type steeped in scientific method   likes to think that superstitions have no hold on him. Science has   of course   broken the iron grip of superstition by explaining and describing phenomena that once filled man with awe and terror   Nevertheless   the shadow of superstition hovers in the background. This is especially the case when it comes to omens of bad luck and misfortune. Observe sometime the number of people who will go out of their way to keep from walking under a ladder. Notice the look of horror on the face of a motorist who has just seen a black cat streak across his path. Listen to precocious children chant   Bread and butter   as they are separated by a lamppost or obstacle in their path   or watch the middle-aged lady with a no-nonsense look about her wince as she draws or is assigned number 13. See the smartly dressed, sophisticated young businessman who has just given a light to two companions hesitate before lighting his own cigarette. Watch the professorial-looking old gentleman furtively throw a pinch of salt over each shoulder when he upsets a saltshaker. Do you say all this is nonsense   Perhaps so. But what superstitions have you in their grip

2.   Man   in his ageless attempt at understanding man   has tried to classify his fellow beings into types. During the Greek period   Hippocrates speculated on the "humors" of the body and the effects of these on personality. As the science of psychology developed further attempts at classification occurred. One of the most recent systems was developed by William Sheldon   who tried to define a number of "temperamental" traits. In so doing he did not think of mutually exclusive body types but rather of relative but basic variables of body build. He defined three primary variables of body build   and he developed a 7-point scale for scoring individuals on each of the variables. The variables were as follows   (1) *endomorphy*   characterized by a roundness and softness of body   (2) *mesomorphy* typified by a squarish and muscular body   (3) *ectomorphy*   indicated by an elongated body of rather delicate structure.

3.   Peter Ilyich Tchaikovsky is so clearly identified with his symphonies and ballet music that it is often forgotten that he wrote a total of nine operas. The best known is Eugene Onegin   an opera in three acts   with the libretto by Tchaikovsky and Konstantin Shilovsky. The opera   which is based on a poem by Alexander Pushkin   was first performed in public by the students of the Imperial College of Music in Moscow on April 23   1881. It was

presented in the United States in concert form on February 1   1908. This performance was in English   but in the Metropolitan Opera première   which took place on March 24 1930   the roles were sung in Italian. Although Eugene Onegin is the most successful of Tchaikovsky's operas   it has never been consistently performed by opera companies outside Russia.

3   Punctuate the introduction, the footnote at the bottom of the page, and the excerpt from *Through the Looking Glass* that follows. Some punctuation marks in the excerpt have been retained because of unusual style in the original.

Lewis Carroll is the pseudonym of Charles Lutwidge Dodgson   English writer and mathematician. Although Mr. Dodgson lectured in mathematics at Christ Church College   Oxford from 1855 to 1881 and published a number of books on mathematics   he is chiefly remembered as Lewis Carroll   the author of the children's books Alice's Adventures in Wonderland and Through the Looking Glass   in which the famous poem   Jabberwocky   appears.

Dodgson developed these stories from the tales he told the children of the Dean of Christ Church   Dr. Henry George Liddell.   Liddell   incidentally   is pronounced with a heavier stress on the first syllable.   Alice's Adventures in Wonderland has its beginnings in a story Dodgson told Alice, Lorena, and Edith Liddell on a boat ride on the Cherwell River near Oxford on July 4   1862. He noted the story in his diary and later wrote it down   added illustrations   pasted a picture of Alice on the last page   and presented it to her. In 1865 an expanded version with illustrations by John Tenniel   a well-known humorist and illustrator   was published. Through the Looking Glass was published in 1872.

For children   these stories are pure fantasy   however   adults have read a great many symbolic and satiric meanings into them. Indeed   characters such as the Mad Hatter   the March Hare   the Cheshire Cat   the White Rabbit   the Red Queen   and the White Queen have found their way into sophisticated adult conversation and literature.

The following is an excerpt from *Through the Looking Glass*[1]

Here the Red Queen began again.   Can you answer useful questions   she said   How is bread made

I know *that*   Alice cried eagerly   you take some flour—

Where do you pick the flower   the White Queen asked   In a garden or in the hedges

Well   it isn't *picked* at all   Alice explained   it's *ground*—

How many acres of ground   said the White Queen   You musn't leave out so many things

Fan her head   the Red Queen anxiously interrupted   She'll be feverish after so much thinking   So they set to work and fanned her with bunches of leaves, till she had to beg them to leave off, it blew her hair about so.

She's all right again now   said the Red Queen   Do you know languages   What's the French for fiddle-de-dee

Fiddle-de-dee's not English   Alice replied gravely

---

[1]Lewis Carroll   Through the Looking Glass   Chap. IX (Queen Alice   ).

Whoever said it was   said the Red Queen

Alice thought she saw a way out of the difficulty this time. If you'll tell me what language fiddle-de-dee   is   I'll tell you the French for it   she explained triumphantly.

But the Red Queen drew herself up rather stiffly and said   Queens never make bargains

I wish Queens never asked questions   Alice thought to herself

Don't let us quarrel   the White Queen said in an anxious tone   What is the cause of lightning

The cause of lightning   Alice said very decidedly   for she felt very certain about this is the thunder—no, no!   she hastily corrected herself. I meant the other way

It's too late to correct it   said the Red Queen   when you've once said a thing   that fixes it   and you must take the consequences

Which reminds me   the White Queen said   looking down and nervously clasping and unclasping her hands   we had *such* a thunderstorm last Tuesday   I mean one of the last set of Tuesdays   you know

Alice was puzzled. In *our* country   she remarked   there's only one day at a time

The Red Queen said   that's a poor thin way of doing things   Now *here* we mostly have days and nights two or three at a time   and sometimes in the winter we take as many as five nights together   for warmth you know

Are five nights warmer than one night, then   Alice ventured to ask

Five times as warm   of course

But they should be five times as *cold* by the same rule

Just so   cried the Red Queen   Five times as warm *and* five times as cold   just as I'm five times as rich as you are, *and* five times as clever

Alice sighed and gave it up.   It's exactly like a riddle with no answer   she thought

ENGLISH

SPEECH SOUNDS

The sounds in the following list are represented by a set of pedagogical transcription symbols (*PTS*) and by symbols from *Funk and Wagnalls Standard College Dictionary* (*F&W*). (Some of the spellings that represent the sounds in written English are shown in the examples.)

CONSONANTS[1]

	Voiceless				Voiced	
PTS ___[2]	F&W ___[2]	Examples		PTS___	F&W ___	Examples
/p/	p	pin, apple, pipe		/b/	b	be, rubber, robe
/t/	t	tea, better, bite light, liked		/d/	d	do, sudden, rode, lived
/k/	k	key, can, occur, sick, bake, talk		/g/	g	go, egg
/f/	f	fan, offer, life, rough, photo		/v/	v	vote, give
/th/	th	thin, both		/ᴛh/	ᴛh	the, bathe
/s/	s	so, bless, horse, city, face		/z/	z	zoo, buzz, size, sees
/š/	sh	she, sure, session, nation, racial		/ž/	zh	measure, rouge, azure
/č/	ch	chest, catch, question		/j/	j	joy, age, edge, educate
/h/	h	he, who		. . . .		
/hw/	hw	why		/w/	w	we, one
. . . .			/l/	l	let, all, smile
. . . .			/r/	r	red, parrot, write
. . . .			/y/	y	you, use, million
. . . .			/m/	m	me, simmer, some, palm, limb
. . . .			/n/	n	no, dinner, done, know
. . . .			/ng/	ng	sing, sink

[1]Consonant sounds are classed as *voiceless* (without vibration of the vocal cords during articulation) and *voiced* (with vibration of the vocal cords during articulation). Many of the consonant sounds fall into pairs of voiceless and voiced sounds, as /p/ and /b/. Two sounds representing a pair are placed opposite each other on the list.
[2]These columns have been left blank to provide space for those who would like to add another set of symbols.

VOWELS AND DIPHTHONGS[3]

PTS	F&W	Examples	PTS	F&W	Examples
/iy/	ē	be, see, sea, field, deceit	/uw/	o͞o	too, rule, blew, true, shoe
/i/	i	it, city, money	/u/	o͝o	book, put, should
/ey/	ā	day, age, rain	/ow/	ō	go, blow, oat, toe
/e/	e	let, any, said	/ɔ/	ô	all, law, offer, ought
/æ/	a	cat, plaid	/a/	ä	calm, doll, heart
/ə/	u	up, done, tough	/ər/	û(r)	her, fur, girl, word, learn
/ə/ (unstressed)	ə	away, element, accident, circus, curious[4]	/ər/ (unstressed)	ər	letter, dollar, actor, treasure[5]
/ay/	ī	I, my, lie, buy	/ɔy/	oi	oil, boy
/aw/	ou	out, now, bough	/yuw/	yo͞o	few, you, view

[3] A diphthong is a blend of two vowel sounds into a sound considered to be a separate, distinctive sound, as /aw/ in out.
[4] /ə/ occurs very frequently as the vowel in unstressed syllables (alone, a day, the book, etc.)
[5] /ər/ is pronounced with little or no "r-flavor" by some speakers of English, particularly in eastern and southern sections of the United States. In such speech, the sounds in her and letter are usually symbolized by /ə/.

SUBJECT INDEX

References are to section numbers unless otherwise specified: footnote information is indexed by page number plus *n*, as p. 33*n*; shaded areas at bottom of text pages are indexed by page numbers plus (list), as pp. 194–195(list). Section numbers in the text can be quickly found in the margins.

A / an / some (*see* Indefinite
     articles; *see also* entries
     in Word Index)
Ability, auxiliaries expressing, 8.9
Abstract nouns, 10.8, 10.22
Accompaniment, adverbials
     indicating, 9.9, 9.36, 9.37
Active constructions, with *have*
     and *get,* 18.35
Additive signals, 9.6
Adjective + verb-*ing,* 18.31
Adjectives, in comparisons,
     14.31, pp. 194–195(list)
   describing weather, 2.26
   noun + -*less,* 14.41
   noun + -*like,* 14.14
   verb-*ing* and verb-*ed* as, 18.33
Adverbial clauses, of cause, 13.13
     to 13.21
   of concession, 13.24 to 13.41
   of contrast, 13.34 to 13.41
   of distance, 13.11
   of frequency, 13.11
   function of, 13.2
   of manner, 13.11
   and participial phrases, 13.42 to
     13.45
   of place, 13.9
   position of, 13.1, 13.3
   punctuation of, 13.1, 13.13,
     13.14, 13.18, 13.36, 19.6,
     19.7
   of purpose, 13.29 to 13.33
   of reason, 13.13 to 13.21
   of result, 13.22 to 13.28
   of time, 13.3 to 13.8
   verb tenses in, 13.3
Adverbial phrases, punctuation
     of, 19.6, 19.7
Adverbials, 9.1 to 9.48
   as additive signals, 9.6, 9.7
   ago, 9.25, 9.27, 9.29
   already, 9.20
   anymore, 9.22
   by + object, 9.37, 9.38
   and change in word order,
     9.11, 9.12
   with contractions, 9.15
   of degree, 9.45, 9.47,
     p. 105(list)
   during, 9.25, 9.26
   ever, 9.17
   expression of purpose, 9.42, 9.43
   for, 9.25, 9.29
   of frequency, 9.1, 9.9, 9.14
   indicating accompaniment,
     9.9, 9.36, 9.37
   indicating agent, 9.9, 9.36 to
     9.38

indicating instrument, 9.9, 9.36,
     9.38
in, on, at + noun phrases, 9.31,
     9.32
in + object, 9.36, 9.38
   of manner, 9.1, 9.9, 9.36 to
     9.38, 15.8
   as modifiers of adverbs and
     adjectives, 9.45, 9.47,
     p. 105(list)
   in negative sentences, 9.18
   *never, seldom, rarely, scarcely,
     hardly, barely,* 9.18
   order of, 9.9
   phrases, punctuation of, 19.6,
     19.7
   of place, 9.1, 9.9, 9.31, 9.32,
     9.40, 15.8
   placement for emphasis, 9.1
   position of, 9.1 to 9.16
   punctuation for, 9.2
   of reason, 15.8
   of sequence, 9.1
   as sequence signals, 9.1, 9.4
   since, 9.28, 9.29
   still, 9.22
   there (place), 9.40
   of time, 9.1, 9.9, 9.34, 15.8
   with + object, 9.36, 9.37
   yet, 9.20
   (*see also* Adverbial clauses)
Adverbs, in comparisons, 14.31,
     14.34, pp. 194–195(list)
Advice, and *yes / no* questions,
     1.11
Affirmative commands and
     requests, forms of, 5.1
Affirmative questions, use of
     still, 9.22
Affirmative sentences, *but* as
     connector, 4.10
   connectors with, 4.1
   and *much, many, a lot of,* 10.34
Affirmative statements, adverbials
     in, 9.14
   use of *already,* 9.20
   and contrastive questions, 3.13
   use of *still,* 9.22
   and tags, 3.2, 3.11
Affirmative tags, 3.4, 3.11
Agent, adverbials indicating, 9.9,
     9.36 to 9.38
Agreement, of subject with verb,
     1.6, 4.8, 10.29, 10.31
   with *a couple of,* 10.40
   with *a number of / the number
     of,* 10.40
   with collective nouns,
     p. 117(list)

with *each* and *every,* 10.29
   with *either* (*. . . or*) and *neither*
     (*. . . nor*), 4.8, 10.31, 14.8
   with *people* and *person,* 10.15
   with *there,* in subject position,
     1.6
Animate nouns (*see* Persons)
Appositives, 16.28, 19.10
Articles, capitalization of, 19.17
     (*see also* Definite articles,
     Indefinite articles,
     Prearticles)
Attached statements, 4.1 to 4.13
Auxiliaries, 8.1 to 8.18
   in adverbial clauses, 13.11
   and adverbials of frequency,
     9.14
   in attached statements, 4.1
   capitalization of, 19.17
   in comparative constructions,
     14.31
   contractions with, p. 3(list)
   in short responses, 1.12
   in *so* (*that*) clauses, 13.29
   in tag questions and responses,
     3.2
   in *yes / no* questions, 1.11, 1.12

Be (forms of), and adverbials
     of frequency, 9.14
   in attached statements, 4.1
   in comparative constructions,
     14.31
   contractions with *not,* 1.4,
     p. 3(list)
   contractions with pronouns,
     1.3, 1.4, p. 3(list)
   in passive verbs, 6.6
   in short responses, 1.1 to 1.10
   in tag questions and responses,
     3.2
   in *yes / no* questions, 1.1 to 1.10
Be (forms of) combinations,
     12.23, pp. 150–159(list)
   and *that*-clauses, 15.35
Bibliography, 19.28
Books and periodicals, titles of,
     19.17
Business letters, 19.31

Capability, auxiliaries expressing,
     8.9
Capitalization, guidelines for,
     19.17
Cardinal numbers, use of *the,*
     10.17
Cause, adverbial clauses of,
     13.13 to 13.21

Choice questions, 1.19
Cities, proper names of, 11.2,
    p. 138(list)
Clauses, in passive sentences,
    6.8, 6.9
    (see also Adverbial, If-, Main,
    Nonrestrictive, Noun,
    Relative, Restrictive,
    That-, Wh-, Whether-
    clauses)
Cleft sentences, 6.11
Clichés, 14.27
Collective nouns, agreement of
    verbs with, p. 117(list)
    plurals of, p. 117(list)
    and possessive relationships,
    16.13
Colon, 19.15, 19.16
    with quotation marks, 19.21
    after salutation of letters, 19.31
Commands, in giving directions,
    5.19
    affirmative, 5.1
    politeness of, 5.1
    reported, 5.21
    (see also Negative commands)
Commas, after adverbial, 9.2
    and adverbial clauses, 13.1,
    13.13, 13.14, 13.18, 13.36,
    19.7
    with adverbial phrases, 19.6
    with connectors, 19.4
    and if-clause, 17.8
    and nonrestrictive clauses,
    16.20, 19.8
    with nonrestrictive phrases,
    19.8 19.10
    and participial clauses, 13.42
    and participial phrases, 6.9
    in place of parentheses, 19.11
    with question marks, 19.20,
    19.21
    and restrictive clauses, 16.3
    after salutation of letters, 19.31,
    19.33
    between sentences, 19.2
    to separate items in series,
    19.16
    to set off examples, definitions,
    19.12, 19.14
    with speaker tags, 19.20, 19.22
    in tag questions, 3.13
    after that is, for example,
    19.12
    before too, p. 33n
Comparatives, 14.16 to 14.21,
    14.29, 14.31
    formation of, pp. 194–195(list)
Comparison signals, 14.45, 14.46,
    14.48, 14.50
Compound nouns, plurals of,
    p. 116(list)
Compound subjects, connected
    by neither . . . nor, 4.8,
    10.31
Concession, adverbial clauses of,
    13.34 to 13.41
Conditional sentences, 17.8 to
    17.13
Conjunctions (see Connectors)

Connectors, in attached
    statements, 4.1
    capitalization of, 19.17
    contrast and contradiction, 4.10
    in negative sentences, 4.4
    punctuation of, 19.2 to 19.4
Continents, proper names of,
    11.2, p. 138(list)
Contractions, p. 3(list)
    and adverbials, 9.15
    in letters, 19.31, 19.33
    in negative questions and
    responses, 1.21
    in short responses, 1.3, 1.4
    and still, 9.22
Contradictions, but as connector,
    4.10
    in long responses, 1.17
Contrast, adverbial clauses of,
    13.34 to 13.41
    but as connector, 4.10
    signals of, 14.46, 14.48, 14.50
    of since, for, ago, 9.29
Contrastive questions, 3.13
Conversation (see Spoken
    English)
Count nouns, with definite article,
    10.17
    and how many, 2.18
    indefinite articles with, 10.1
    to 10.16
    with many, a lot of, 10.33
    prearticles with, 10.33, 10.36,
    10.38, 10.40, 10.42
    referring to kind, type, variety,
    10.7
    referring to units, 10.6, 10.8,
    10.9
Countries, proper names of, 11.2,
    p. 138(list)

Dangling modifier, 13.42
Dashes, 19.11, 19.12, 19.13,
    19.16, 19.22
Dates, punctuation of, 19.10
Definite articles, 10.17 to 10.19
    with nouns referring to a group,
    10.20, 10.22
    with proper nouns, 11.1, 11.12,
    pp. 138–139(list)
    with superlatives, 14.22
Definitions, punctuation of, 19.12,
    19.13, 19.14
Degree, expression of, p. 105
    (list), 9.45 to 9.48, 13.25,
    14.5
Deserts, proper names of, 11.7,
    p. 138(list)
Dialog, paragraphs in, 19.22
    punctuation of, 19.20 to 19.23
    reported, 5.23 to 5.28
    (see also Quoted dialog)
Directions, command and
    request forms, 5.19
Directions (compass),
    capitalization of, 19.17
Direct objects, in active and
    passive sentences, 6.6
    defined, 6.1
    and object complements, 6.13

with two-word verbs, 12.1, 12.2,
    12.6, 12.10, 12.12, 12.15
Distance, adverbial clauses of,
    13.11
Do (forms of), in attached
    statements, 4.1
    in invitations, 5.15
    in predicate-type questions, 2.10
    in requests, 5.1
    in short responses, 1.15
    in tags, 3.3
    in yes/no questions, 1.14 to
    1.17

-ed suffix, p. 71(list), 18.33
Ellipsis, 19.26
Emphasis, in contrastive
    questions, 3.13
    in invitations, 5.15
    placement of adverbials, 9.1
    in requests, 5.1
    in tags, 3.13
    -er suffix, 14.16 to 14.21, 14.31,
    pp. 194–195(list)
    -es suffix, pp. 70, 114–118(lists)
    -est suffix, 14.22, 14.25,
    pp. 194–195(list)
Examples, punctuation of, 19.12,
    19.13, 19.14
Exclamation mark, 19.1
    with quotation marks, 19.20,
    19.21
Explanations, punctuation of,
    19.12, 19.13, 19.14

Footnotes, 19.24 to 19.27
    information in, 19.24, 19.25
    and paraphrasing, 19.25
For + indirect object, verbs used
    with, 6.1
For + (pro)noun, 18.7, 18.9
For + verb-ing, 18.31
Frequency, adverbial clauses of,
    13.11
    adverbials of, 9.1, 9.9, 9.14
Future continuous verbs, 7.20(fig.)
Future perfect verbs, 7.20(fig.)
Future verbs, 7.20(fig.)

Gerunds (see Verb-ing)

Habitual past activity, auxiliaries
    expressing, 8.17
Have (forms of), in active and
    passive constructions, 18.35
    combinations, 12.23,
    in tag questions, 3.3
    pp. 150–159(list)
Hypothetical conditional
    sentences, 17.8

Identity, establishment of, 10.17
Idioms (see Be (forms of)
    combinations; Have (forms
    of) combinations; Two-word
    verbs)
If-clauses, 15.15, 15.19
    position, punctuation, verb
    forms in, 17.8

Inanimate nouns (see Things)
Indefinite articles, 10.1 to 10.16
  with nouns referring to a group,
    10.20, 10.21
  with proper nouns, 11.11, 11.12
  stress on *some*, 10.49
Indefinite pronouns (see
    Prearticles)
Indirect objects, in active and
    passive sentences, 6.6
  defined, 6.1
  meanings with *to* and *for*, 6.1
  position in sentence, 6.1
Indirect speech, p. 203*n*
Infinitive, 18.1 to 18.16
  perfect and verb-*ing* forms,
    18.27 to 18.30
  (see also *To* + verb)
Information, asked in *wh*-
    questions, 2.1, 2.2, 2.4, 2.6
  in long responses, 1.17
-*ing* suffixes, p. 71(list)
  (see also Verb-*ing*)
Instrument, adverbials indicating,
    9.9, 9.36, 9.38
Intensifiers, p. 105(list), 9.45 to
    9.48, 13.25, 14.5
Interrogatives (see Wh-questions;
    Wh-words)
Intonation patterns, in choice
    questions, 1.19
  in invitations, 5.15
  in tag questions, 3.1, 3.9
  in *yes/no* questions, 1.1
Invitations, 5.1, 5.15
  information in responses, 1.17
  intonation patterns in, 5.15
  question vs. command form,
    5.15
  and *yes/no* questions, 1.11
Irregular verbs, principal parts,
    pp. 74–77(list)
Italics, use of, 19.17

Languages, capitalization of,
    19.17
-*less* suffix, 14.41, 14.43
Letters, 19.31 to 19.36
Likeness, 14.1 to 14.51
-*like* suffixes, 14.14
Listing signals, 9.6
Long responses, 1.17

Main clauses, verb tenses in, 13.3
Manner, adverbial clauses of,
    13.11
  adverbials of, 9.1, 9.9, 9.36 to
    9.38
Mass nouns, 10.6, 10.7, 10.22
  (see also Noncount nouns)
Measure words, 10.4, 10.14
Mental perceptions, verbs
    expressing, 7.1, 7.14
Modifiers, adverbials as, 9.45,
    9.47, p. 105(list)
  appositives, 16.28
  dangling, 13.42
  and position of adverbials, 9.9
  relative clauses as, 16.1

Nationalities, capitalization of,
    19.17
Necessity, auxiliaries expressing,
    8.5
Negative attached statements,
    4.5, 4.8
Negative commands, 5.6 to 5.9
  in reported speech, 5.21
Negative questions, 1.21
  use of *anymore* and *still*, 9.22
Negative requests, 5.6 to 5.9
  in reported speech, 5.21
Negative sentences, *but* as
    connector, 4.10
  connectors, 4.4
  and *much, many, a lot of*, 10.34
  negative adverbials, 9.18
  restricted with noun + -*less*
    adjectives, 14.41
  still and *yet* in, 7.8
Negative statements, contractions
    in, 1.21
  and tags, 3.2, 3.11
  use of *anymore* and *still*, 9.22
  use of *ever*, 9.17
  use of *yet*, 9.20
Negative tags, 3.4, 3.11
Noncount nouns, with definite
    article, 10.17
  and *how much*, 2.18
  indefinite articles with, 10.1 to
    10.16
  with *much, a lot of*, 10.33
  prearticles with, 10.33, 10.34,
    10.36, 10.38, 10.40, 10.42
  referring to abstractions, 10.8
  referring to material (mass),
    10.6, 10.7
  referring to portion or part,
    10.9
  referring to units, 10.10
Nonrestrictive clauses, 16.20 to
    16.29
  defined, 16.2
  punctuation of, 16.20, 19.8
Nonrestrictive phrases,
    punctuation of, 19.8
Not, contractions with auxiliaries,
    p. 3(list)
  contractions with *be* (forms of),
    1.4, p. 3(list)
  uncontracted in questions and
    statements, 1.21
Noun clauses, 15.1 to 15.36
  if and *whether* in, 15.15, 15.19,
    17.8
  position of, 15.1
  wh-clauses, 15.2 to 15.14
Noun phrases, in adverbials,
    9.31, 9.32
Nouns, in adverbial clauses,
    13.42
  agreement of verbs with, 1.6,
    4.8, 10.29, 10.31
  with comparatives, 14.24
  compound, plurals of, p. 116(list)
  in contrastive questions, 3.13
  foreign plurals, pp. 118–119(list)
  form with *each, every, neither,
    either, any*, 10.29

irregular plurals, p. 118(list)
  + -*less* to form adjectives, 14.41
  + -*like* to form adjectives, 14.14
  in main clause, 13.14
  with no singular form, 10.14
  plural possessives, pp. 120–121
    (list)
  plurals of, pp. 114–121(list)
  possessive modifiers of, 16.11,
    16.13
  regular plurals, pp. 114–116,
    119(lists)
  with reporting verbs, 5.21
  with superlatives, 14.22, 14.25
  in tag questions, 3.7
  (see also Collective, Count,
    Noncount, Plural nouns)
Noun subjects, in speaker tags,
    15.28, 19.21
  in *yes/no* questions, 1.2

Object complements, 6.13
Object position, noun clauses in,
    15.1
Objects, and position of
    adverbials, 9.9
  with *told* and *said*, 15.24
  who used as, 16.6, 16.20,
    p. 201*n*
  (see also Direct, Indirect
    objects)
Obligation, auxiliaries expressing,
    8.11
Oceans, proper names of, 11.7,
    p. 138(list)
Of-phrases, p. 218(list)
Orders, 5.1
  (see also Commands)

Paraphrasing, 15.30
  and footnotes, 19.25
Parentheses, 19.11, 19.12
Parks, proper names of, 11.2,
    p. 138(list)
Participial phrases, and adverbial
    clauses, 13.42 to 13.45
  punctuation of, 6.9, 13.42
  and relative clauses, 16.28
Passive constructions, with
    have and *get*, 18.35
Passive infinitive, and verb-*ing*
    forms, 18.27 to 18.30
Passive sentences, 6.4 to 6.10
  with two-word verbs, 12.8
Passive verbs, how formed, 6.6
Past continuous verbs, 7.16
Past participles, irregular verbs,
    pp. 74–77(list)
  with *must have*, 8.5
  in passive verbs, 6.6
  suffixes, p. 71(list)
Past perfect continuous verbs,
    7.18
Past perfect verbs, 7.18(fig.)
  in reported speech, 15.19
Past tenses (see Habitual past
    activity; Past continuous,
    Past perfect continuous,
    Past perfect, Simple past
    verbs)

270

Perceptions, verbs expressing, 7.1, 7.14
Perfect infinitives, and verb-*ing* forms, 18.27 to 18.30
Perfect tenses, with *since,* 9.28
 (*see also* Future perfect, Past perfect continuous, Past perfect, Present continuous perfect, Present perfect verbs)
Periods, 19.1, 19.2, 19.3
 and adverbial clauses, 13.36
 in contrastive questions, 3.13
Permission, auxiliaries expressing, 8.7
 requests for, 5.10 to 5.14
 and *yes/no* questions, 1.11
Personal letters, 19.33
Persons, comparisons of, 14.27
 in contrastive questions, 3.13
 it referring to, 1.8
 possessive relationships, p. 218(list)
 relative pronouns referring to, 16.3, 16.6
 in tags, 3.13
 what and *which* referring to, 2.7, 2.8
 who/whom/whose referring to, 2.6
Phrases, in passive sentences, 6.8, 6.9
 (*see also* Adverbial, Noun phrases; Object complements; *Of-,* Participial phrases)
Place, adverbial clauses of, 13.9
 adverbials of, 9.1, 9.9, 9.31, 9.32, 9.40, 15.8
Place names, articles with, 11.1 to 11.10, pp. 138–139(list)
 punctuation of, 19.10
Plural nouns, pp. 114–121(list)
 in *either* and *neither* constructions, 10.31
 irregular, pp. 118, 120–121(lists)
 proper nouns, p. 121(list)
Plural possessives, pp. 120–121(list)
Plural suffixes, pp. 114–121(list)
Politeness, in business letters, 19.31
 in commands and requests, 5.1, 5.4
 of responses, 5.4
 use of *can, may, could,* 8.7
Possessive pronouns, *whose,* 2.6
 in *yes/no* questions, 1.9
Possessive relationships, 16.11 to 16.17, p. 218(list)
Possessives, plurals of, pp. 120–121(list)
 of proper nouns, p. 121(list)
Possessive suffix, pp. 120–121, 218(lists)
Possibility, auxiliaries expressing, 8.1, 8.3
Prearticles, 10.24 to 10.51
 with count nouns, 10.33, 10.36 10.38, 10.40, 10.42, 10.47

definite and indefinite, 10.24
formal and informal, 10.34, 10.38
 with noncount nouns, 10.33, 10.36, 10.38, 10.40, 10.42, 10.47
 stress on *some,* 10.49
Predicates, and adverbial clauses, 13.1
 in attached statements, 4.1
 if and *whether* in, 15.15, 15.19
 and *much, many, a lot of,* 10.34
 position of object complement, 6.13
 wh-words in, 2.2
Predicate-type questions, 2.2
 interrogatives identifying, 2.10
Preference, auxiliaries expressing, 8.15
Prepositions, *at, in, on,* in adverbials, 9.31, 9.32
 by, in adverbials, 9.37, 9.38
 capitalization of, 19.17
 in, in adverbials, 9.36, 9.38
 and relative pronouns, 16.7, 16.22
 to and *for* with indirect objects, 6.1
 in two-word verbs, 12.1, 12.2, 12.14, 12.20
 and verb-*ing,* 18.18
 with in adverbials, 9.36, 9.37
 (*see also* To + verb; Two-word verbs)
Present continuous perfect verbs, 7.6(fig.), 7.7(fig.), 7.12
Present continuous verbs, 7.1(fig.) to 7.5, 7.6(fig.) to 7.7
 to express future time, 7.21
Present participle (*see* Verb-*ing*)
Present perfect verbs, 7.6, 7.7(fig.), 7.8(fig.), 7.10(fig.), 7.11(fig.), 7.12(fig.), 7.13(fig.)
Present tenses (*see* Present continuous perfect, Present perfect, Simple present verbs)
Probability, auxiliaries expressing, 8.1, 8.2
 must have + past participle, 8.5
Pronoun objects, 6.1
 with two-word verbs, 12.2
Pronouns, in adverbial clauses, 13.14
 agreement of verbs with, 1.6, 10.29
 contractions with auxiliaries, p. 3(list)
 contractions with *be* (forms of), 1.3, 1.4, p. 3(list)
 in contrastive questions, 3.13
 in main clauses, 13.42
 as objects, 6.1
 in reported speech, 5.21, 5.23
 with reporting verbs, 5.21, 5.23
 in short responses, 1.2, 1.3, 1.4, 1.8, 1.9

in tag questions, 3.2, 3.7
in *that*-clauses, 18.1
with verb-*ing,* 18.25
 (*see also* Possessive pronouns; Pronoun objects; Pronoun subjects; Relative pronouns)
Pronoun subjects, in speaker tags, 15.28, 19.21
 of *to* + verb, 18.2, 18.18, 18.21
 in *yes/no* questions, 1.3, 1.4, 1.9
Pronunciation, irregular plurals, p. 118(list)
 plural suffixes, pp. 114–121(list)
 verb suffixes, pp. 70–71(list)
Proper names, article usage with, pp. 138–139(list)
 capitalization of, 19.17
Proper nouns, articles with, 11.1 to 11.13
 expression of kinship or ownership, p. 218(list)
 in main clause, 13.14
 possessives of, pp. 121, 218(lists)
 (*see also* Place names)
Punctuation, 19.1 to 19.36
 of adverbial clauses, 13.1, 13.13, 13.14, 13.18, 13.36, 19.6, 19.7
 of adverbial phrases, 19.6, 19.7
 for adverbials, 9.2
 in business letters, 19.31
 of connectors, 19.2 to 19.4
 of contrastive questions, 3.13
 of dates, 19.10
 of dialog, 19.20 to 19.23
 of *if*-clauses, 17.8
 of nonrestrictive clauses, 16.20, 19.8
 of participial phrases, 6.9, 13.42
 of place names, 19.10
 of relative clauses, 19.8
 of restrictive clauses, 16.3, 19.8
 of sentences, 19.1, 19.2 to 19.5, 19.10 to 19.17
 of series, 19.16
Purpose, adverbial clauses of, 13.29 to 13.33
 adverbial phrases of, 9.42, 9.43
 expression of, with *to* + verb or *for* + verb-*ing,* 18.31
 of tag questions, 3.13

Qualifications, in long responses, 1.17
Qualifiers, p. 105(list), 9.45 to 9.48, 13.25, 14.5
Question mark, 19.1
 with quotation marks, 19.20, 19.21
Questions, and *much, many, a lot of,* 10.34
 as responses to tag questions, 3.4
 still and *yet* in, 7.8
 use of *should,* 8.11
 (*see also* Choice, Contrastive, Negative, Predicate-type, Reported, Reported *wh*-, Subject-type, Tag questions)

Quotation marks, with other
punctuation, 19.20, 19.21,
19.22
with quotations, 19.24
single, 19.27
for titles of short works, 19.17
Quotations, 19.24, 19.26, 19.27
omitted material, 19.26
within quotations, 19.27
use of three dots (ellipsis), 19.26
(*see also* Paraphrasing)
Quoted dialog, 5.23 to 5.28
punctuation of, 19.20 to 19.23
and reported speech, 15.28

Reason, adverbial clauses of,
13.13 to 13.21
adverbials of, 15.8
Regular verbs, past suffixes,
p. 71(list)
Rejoinders, 4.14 to 4.17
adverbials in, 9.14
so used in, 4.16
Relationships, expression of,
p. 218(list)
Relative clauses, 16.1 to 16.35
function of, 16.1, 16.2
in passive sentences, 6.8
position of, 16.1, 16.2
punctuation of, 19.8
in writing, 16.30 to 16.35
Relative pronouns, omission of,
16.6, 16.9, 16.20, 16.26,
16.27
and prepositions, 16.7, 16.22
in restrictive clauses, 16.3
to 16.19
Religions, capitalization of, 19.17
Remainders, words that indicate,
10.42, 10.43, 10.45, 10.50
Repeated past activity, auxiliaries
expressing, 8.17
(*see also* Present perfect,
Simple past)
Repeated statements, in tag
questions, 3.11
Reported dialog, 5.23 to 5.28
(*see also* Reported speech)
Reported questions, 15.19
Reported speech, 5.21 to 5.28
and quoted dialog, 15.28
time expressions in, 15.19
verbs in, 15.19
(*see also* Paraphrasing;
Reported dialog;
That-clauses)
Reported *wh*-questions, 15.13
Reporting verbs, 5.21
formal and informal, 15.26
in paraphrasing, 15.30
tense of, 15.24, 15.30
Requests, in asking directions,
5.19
information in response to, 1.17
for permission, 5.10 to 5.14
politeness of, 5.1, 5.4
reported, 5.21
(*see also* Affirmative commands
and requests; Invitations;
Negative requests)

Responses, formal and informal,
5.3, 5.4, 5.8, 5.11 to 5.13
to negative questions, 1.21
to negative requests, 5.8
politeness of, 5.4
to requests, 5.3, 5.4
to requests for permission,
5.11 to 5.14
to tag questions, 3.2, 3.4
to *yes/no* questions, 1.1 to
1.23
(*see also* Long responses;
Rejoinders; Short responses)
Restrictive clauses, 16.3 to 16.19
defined, 16.2
punctuation of, 16.3, 19.8
Restrictive phrases, punctuation
of, 19.8
Result, adverbial clauses of, 13.22
to 13.28
Rivers, proper names of, 11.7,
p. 138(list)

Seas, proper names of, 11.7,
p. 138(list)
Seasons, capitalization of, 19.17
Semicolons, and adverbial
clauses, 13.14, 13.36
with quotation marks, 19.21
between sentences, 19.2, 19.3
to separate items of series,
19.16
to set off examples, definitions,
19.14
Sensory perceptions, verbs
expressing, 7.1, 7.14
Sentence connectors (*see*
Connectors)
Sentences, position of adverbials,
9.1 to 9.16
punctuation of, 19.1 to 19.4,
19.10 to 19.17
(*see also* Affirmative, Cleft,
Conditional, Negative,
Passive sentences; Word
order)
Sequence signals, adverbials as,
9.1
however, 15.10
position of, 9.4
Series, punctuation of, 19.16
Short responses, 1.2, 1.3, 1.4, 1.5,
1.8, 1.9, 1.12, 1.15
adverbials in, 9.14
use of *should,* 8.11
Simple past verbs, 7.10(fig.),
7.11(fig.), 7.12, 7.13(fig.),
7.14, 7.16(fig.), 7.18(fig.)
with *ago,* 9.27
irregular verbs, pp. 74–77(list)
in reported speech, 15.19
suffixes, p. 71(list)
Simple present verbs, 7.1(fig.) to
7.5
to express future time, 7.21
irregular verbs, pp. 74–77(list)
Simple verb forms, 18.38, 18.40
following *Let's,* 8.13
following *suggest,* 5.17, 5.25,
18.5

irregular verbs, pp. 74–77(list)
with *may, might, could,* 8.1
in *that*-clauses, 18.5, 18.7
Speaker tags, 15.28
punctuation of, 19.21, 19.22
word order in, 19.21
Spelling, plural nouns, pp.
114–121(list)
verb suffixes, pp. 70–71(list)
Spoken English, attached
statements in, 4.1
contractions in, p. 3(list)
and *neither . . . nor,* 4.8
stress in responses, 1.22
use of *who* and *whom,* 2.6,
16.6, 16.20
-*s* suffix, pp. 70, 114–118(lists)
-*'s* suffix, pp. 120–121, 218(lists)
Statements (*see* Affirmative,
Attached, Negative
statements)
States, proper names of, 11.2,
11.3, p. 138(list)
Streets, proper names of, 11.2,
p. 138(list)
Subject position, and *much, many,
a lot of,* 10.34
noun clauses in, 15.1
Subjects, in adverbial clauses,
13.11
agreement of verb with, 1.6,
4.8, 10.29, 10.31
in contrastive questions, 3.13
in participial phrases, 6.9
in tags, 3.13
in *wh*-questions, 2.1, 2.6
in *yes/no* questions, 1.2, 1.3,
1.5, 1.6, 1.9, 1.11, 1.14
(*see also* Noun, Pronoun
subjects)
Subject-type questions, 2.1
Subjunctive forms (*see*
Hypothetical conditional
sentences; Simple verb
forms; Suggestions)
Subordinators, 13.2, 13.42
(*see also* Adverbial clauses)
Suffixes, -*ed,* p. 71(list)
-*er,* 14.16 to 14.21, 14.24,
14.29, 14.31, pp.
194–195(list)
-*es,* pp. 70, 114–118(lists)
-*est,* 14.22, 14.25, pp.
194–195(list)
-*ing,* p. 71(list)
-*less,* 14.41, 14.43
-*like,* 14.14
possessive, pp. 120–121,
218(lists)
-*s,* pp. 70, 114–118(lists)
-*'s,* pp. 120–121, 218(lists)
of verbs, pp. 70–71(list)
Suggestions, 5.1, 5.17
auxiliaries expressing, 8.13
in question form, 5.17
reported, 5.25
(*see also* Commands)
Superlatives, 14.22, 14.25, 14.31
formation of, pp. 194–195(list)
use of *the, a, an,* 10.17

Tag questions, 3.1 to 3.14
   intonation patterns, 3.1, 3.9, 3.11
   with *Let's* and *Let us,* 5.1
   in permission requests, 5.12
   punctuation of, 3.13
   and requests, 5.1
   verbal emphasis, 3.13
Tags (*see* Affirmative, Negative,
   Speaker tags)
*That-*clauses, 15.22 to 15.36
   with *happen* and *turn out,* 18.11
   after hope, 17.6
   omission of *that,* 15.22
   position of, 15.32
   after *suggest,* 5.17
   and *to* + verb, 18.1 to 18.16
Things, comparisons of, 14.27
   possessive relationships, 16.16,
      p. 218(list)
   pronouns referring to, 16.3,
      16.6
   what, which referring to, 2.7,
      2.8
   whose, referring to, 2.6
Three dots (ellipsis), 19.26
Time, adverbial clauses of, 13.3
      to 13.8
   adverbials of, 9.1, 9.9, 9.34,
      15.8
   statements about clock time,
      2.24
Time expressions, with ago, 9.27
   with *during,* 9.25, 9.26
   with *for,* 9.25
   with *hope,* 17.3
   on time and *in time,* 9.34
   with present continuous
      perfect verbs, 7.6
   with present continuous verbs,
      7.3, 7.7
   with present perfect verbs, 7.7,
      7.8, 7.10, 7.11
   in reported speech, 15.13, 15.19
   with simple past verbs, 7.10,
      7.11
   with simple present verbs, 7.3
   with *since,* 9.28
Titles of articles, short works,
   books, periodicals,
   punctuation of, 19.17

To + indirect object, verbs used
   with, 6.1
To + verb, 18.19, 18.21, 18.23,
      18.31, 18.40
   with reporting verbs, 5.21
   and *that-*clauses, 18.1 to 18.16
Two-word verbs, pp. 150–159(list)
   nonseparable, 12.14 to 12.22
   separable, 12.2 to 12.13
   structure and meaning, 12.1
   verbal stress in, 12.1, 12.2,
      12.20

Uncertainty, and *yes/no*
   questions, 1.11
Underlining, use of, 19.17

Verbals (*see To* + verb; Verb-*ing*)
Verb-*ed,* as adjective, 18.33
Verb-*ing,* 18.17 to 18.34, 18.38
   as adjective, 18.33
   following *be* and *have*
      combinations, 12.23
   following *mind,* 5.1
   following *object to,* 12.20
   following *suggest,* 5.17
   in participial phrases, 6.9,
      13.42 to 13.45
Verb phrases, in *yes/no*
   questions, 1.11
Verbs, 7.1 to 7.22
   in adverbial clauses, 13.11
   agreement with collective
      nouns, p. 117(list)
   agreement with subject, 1.6,
      4.8, 10.29, 10.31
   after *asked,* 15.13, 15.19
   with *either of the* + plural
      noun, 10.31
   expressing perceptions, 7.1,
      7.14
   followed by *for* + indirect
      object, 6.1
   followed by *to* + indirect
      object, 6.1
   following reporting verbs, 5.24
   after *hopes* and *wishes,* 17.1,
      17.3
   in *if-*clauses, 17.8
   and position of adverbials, 9.9

position in *yes/no* questions, 1.1
in reported speech, 5.21, 15.19
requiring preposition with
   indirect object, 6.1
in *so* (*that*) clauses, 13.29
in speaker tags, 15.28, 19.21
tenses in main and adverbial
   clauses, 13.3
in *that-*clauses, 15.22, 15.24,
   15.26
in *wh-*clauses, 15.13
Verb suffixes, pp. 70–71(list)

Weather, adjectives describing,
   2.26(list)
*Wh-*clauses, 15.2 to 15.14
*Whether-*clauses, 15.15, 15.19
*Wh-*questions and *wh-*clauses,
   15.2, 15.6, 15.10, 15.13
*Wh-*words, 2.6, 2.7, 2.8
   in the predicate, 2.2
   in subject position, 2.1
Word order, of adverbials, 9.9
   after *and neither,* 4.4
   following adverbial, 9.11, 9.12
   for speaker tags, 15.28, 19.21
   in *wh-*clause, 15.2
Written English, and contractions,
   p. 3(list)
   and *neither . . . nor,* 4.8
   prepositions and relative
      pronouns, 16.22
   punctuation for adverbials, 9.2
   relative clauses in, 16.30 to
      16.35
   verbs following reporting
      verbs, 5.23
   who and *whom,* 16.16, 16.20,
      p. 201*n*
   (*see also* Bibliography;
      Footnotes; Paraphrasing;
      Punctuation; Quotations)

Yes/no questions, 1.1 to 1.23
   and *if-*clauses, 15.15, 15.19
   use of *ever,* 9.17
   use of *still* and *anymore,* 9.22
   and *whether-*clauses, 15.15,
      15.19
   yet and *already* in, 9.20

WORD INDEX

References are to section numbers unless otherwise specified: footnote information is indexed by page number plus *n*, as p. 160*n*; shaded areas at bottom of text pages are indexed by page numbers plus (list), as p. 3 (list). Section numbers in the text can be quickly found in the margins.

a/an, as indefinite articles, 10.1 to
10.16
vs. no article, 10.6 to 10.8
before nouns referring to a
group, 10.20
vs. *the,* with proper nouns,
11.11, 11.12
a basket of, 10.4
a box of, 10.4, 10.14
a carton of, 10.4
accuse of, 12.12
a couple of + plural count noun,
10.40
a cup of, 10.4
admit, with *that*-clause or verb-*ing,*
18.17, 18.25
admittedly, as additive signal, 9.7
advice, as singular noncount
noun, 10.13
advise, with *that*-clause or
to + verb, 18.5
a few of (the), 10.24
a few + plural count noun, 10.36
after, in adverbial clauses, 13.2,
13.3
in participial phrases, 13.44
after that, as sequence signal, 9.4
ago, vs. *during* and *for,* 9.25, 9.29
with time expressions, 9.27
a great deal of + noun, 10.34
a large number of + noun, 10.34
alike, in comparisons, 14.3
a little (bit of) + noncount noun,
10.36
a little while ago, with simple past,
7.13
all (of the), 10.26
allow, with *to* + verb or verb-*ing,*
18.21
almost, before a contraction, 9.15
as intensifier, 14.5
a lot of (the), 10.24, 10.33, 10.34
already, with present perfect, 7.8
vs. *yet,* 9.20
also, as additive signal, 9.6
as comparison signal, 14.45
although, in adverbial clauses,
13.2, 13.34 to 13.40
as contrast signal, 14.48
used in place of *but,* 4.10
always, as adverbial of frequency,
9.1, 9.14
after a contraction, 9.15
and, and punctuation, 19.2, 19.16
and . . . either, in attached
statements, 4.4, 4.5
and neither, in attached
statements, 4.4, 4.5
and so, in attached statements, 4.1

and . . . too, in attached
statements, 4.1
announce . . . to + indirect
object, 6.1
another (one), 10.47
answer, in reported statements,
15.26, 15.28
answer . . . for + indirect object,
6.1
a number of + plural noun, 10.40
any, indicating indefinite quantity,
10.3
anymore, vs. *still,* 9.22
any(one) of the, 10.27
a pair of, 10.14
a piece of + noncount noun, 10.9
appreciate, with verb-*ing,* 18.17
approve of, 12.20
as . . . as, in adverbial clauses,
13.11
in comparisons, 14.16 to 14.38
as follows, and punctuation, 19.16
ask, in reported speech, 5.21,
5.23, 15.13, 15.26, 15.28,
15.30
with *that*-clause or *to* + verb,
18.5
ask . . . of + indirect object, 6.1
as soon as, in time clauses, 13.3,
13.6
at, vs. *in* and *on,* 9.31, 9.32
at that time, 15.13
at the present time, 7.3
avoid, with verb-*ing,* 18.17

barely, at beginning of sentence,
9.12
in negative sentences, 9.18
be, after *and so,* 4.1
in contractions, p. 3 (list)
+ past participle, in passive
sentences, 6.6
see also Be (forms of) in
Subject Index
be able to, in expressing ability,
8.9
be accustomed to, with verb-*ing,*
18.18
be afraid of (or **that**), 15.35
be an authority on, 12.23
be aware of (or **that**), 15.35
because, in adverbial clauses,
13.2, 13.13, 13.14, 13.19,
13.25, 13.29, 13.31, 13.34
omitted in participial phrase,
13.42
be certain, with *that*-clause or
to + verb, 18.11, 18.13
be certain of (or **that**), 15.35

be combinations, 12.23
be delighted with (or **that**), 15.35
before, in adverbial clauses, 13.2
in participial phrases, 13.44
with present perfect and past
perfect, 7.18
beg, with *that*-clause or *to* + verb,
18.5
begin, with *to* + verb or verb-*ing,*
18.21
be in charge of, 12.23
believe, in paraphrases, 15.30
in simple present to express
perception, 7.1
believe in, 12.20
be likely (unlikely), with
that-clause or *to* + verb,
18.11, 18.13
be looking forward to, 12.23
be opposed to, 12.23, 18.18
besides, as additive signal, 9.6
be used to, vs. *used to,* 3.3, 18.18
with verb-*ing,* 12.23, 18.18
blame for, 12.12
both . . . and, in comparisons,
14.8
both (of the), 10.24, 10.26
bring . . . to + indirect object, 6.1
build . . . for + indirect object, 6.1
but, in attached statements, 4.10,
4.12
in clauses of contrast and
concession, 13.36
as contrast signal, 14.46, 14.48
and punctuation, 19.2
buy . . . for + indirect object, 6.1
by bus (car, etc.**),** 9.38
by (someone), adverbial of agent,
9.9, 9.37
by the way, and punctuation,
19.10

call back, 12.10
call off, 12.6
call on, 12.1, 12.14
call up, 12.2
can, in expressing ability, 8.9
in permissions, 5.10, 8.7
in *yes/no* questions and
responses, 1.11, 1.12
can/can't, in tag questions, 3.2
can't bear, 18.21
can't stand, 18.21
carry . . . to + indirect object, 6.1
cash . . . for + indirect object, 6.1
cause, with *to* + verb, 18.15
certain, with *that*-clause or
to + verb, 18.11, 18.13
check (something) out, 12.18

cheer up, 12.10

close . . . for + indirect object, 6.1

come across, 12.14, 12.20

come along (with), 12.15

command, with *that*-clause or *to* + verb, 18.5

comment, in reported statements, 15.26, 15.30

consider, with *that*-clause or verb-*ing,* 18.17, 18.25

continue, with *to* + verb or verb-*ing,* 18.21

conversely, as contrast signal, 14.46

could, in expressing ability, 8.9
in expressing probability, 8.1
in permissions, 5.10, 8.7
in *so (that)* clauses, 13.29
in suggestions, 8.13

count on, 12.1, 12.14

decide, with *that*-clause or *to* + verb, 18.1, 18.3

declare, in reported statement, 15.26, 15.30

deliver . . . to + indirect object, 6.1

deny, with *that*-clause or verb-*ing,* 18.17, 18.25

describe . . . to + indirect object, 6.1

deserve, with *to* + verb, 18.15

different (from), in comparisons, 14.1, 14.3

dislike, with *to* + verb or verb-*ing,* 18.21

do, for emphasis, 5.1, 5.15
+ (pro)noun + simple verb form, 18.40

do/does/did, in *wh*-questions, 2.2
in *yes/no* questions and responses, 1.14 to 1.16

do/don't (does/doesn't), in tag questions, 3.1, 3.2, 3.3

do . . . for + indirect object, 6.1

don't, in affirmative suggestions, 5.25
in negative commands and requests, 5.6, 5.8

do you mind . . . , in requests, 5.1
with verb-*ing,* 18.19

do you mind if . . . , in permissions, 5.10 to 5.14

dread, with *to* + verb or verb-*ing,* 18.21

drop in (on), 12.1, 12.15

during, vs. *since/for/ago,* 9.25, 9.26

during the time (that), in adverbial time clauses, 13.6

each (of the), 10.24, 10.26, 10.29

either, in attached statements, 4.4, 4.5
in rejoinders, 4.14

either (of the), 10.29

either . . . or, and subject-verb agreement, 10.31

encourage, with *to* + verb, 18.15

endeavor, with *to* + verb, 18.15

enjoy, with verb-*ing,* 18.17

enough, as intensifier, 9.47

enough (of the), 10.26

escape, with verb-*ing,* 18.17

essential, with *that*-clause or *for*-phrase, 18.7

even if, in adverbial clauses, 13.37, 13.40

even so, as additive signal, 9.7

even though, in adverbial clauses, 13.34 to 13.41

ever, after a contraction, 9.15, 9.17
special usage, 9.17

every day (week, etc.), expressing repeated activity, 7.3, 7.11

everyone/everybody, for emphasis, 5.1

every one (of the), 10.29

everywhere, in adverbial clauses of place, 13.9

exactly, as intensifier, 14.5

expect, with *that*-clause or *to* + verb, 18.2

explain . . . to + indirect object, 6.1

extremely, as intensifier, 9.45

feel, in present continuous to express process, 7.1
followed by *like* + noun, 14.12
in paraphrases, 15.30
in simple present to express perception, 7.1
with verb-*ing* or simple form, 18.38

few/a few + plural count noun, 10.36

fewer (of the) + plural count noun, 10.38

finally, as sequence signal, 9.4

find . . . for + indirect object, 6.1

finish, with verb-*ing,* 18.17

first, as sequence signal, 9.4

first of all, as additive signal, 9.6

fix . . . for + indirect object, 6.1

for, vs. *during/since/ago,* 9.25, 9.29
in expression of purpose, 9.43
with indirect objects, 6.1
and punctuation, 19.2

for an hour (a day, etc.), 7.6

for example, and punctuation, 19.12, 19.14

forget, with *that*-clause or *to* + verb, 18.1

for-phrase, after *essential, possible, impossible, necessary,* 18.7
vs. *that*-clause, 18.7, 18.9
+ verb-*ing,* 18.31

frequently, expressing repeated activity, 7.3

from time to time, expressing repeated activity, 7.3

fully, as adverbial of manner, 9.1

furthermore, additive signal, 9.6, 9.7
and punctuation, 19.3, 19.4

get, with *to* + verb, 18.15

get behind (in), 12.15

get . . . for + indirect object, 6.1

get someone to do something, 18.35

get something done, 18.35

get (something) through, 12.18

get through (with), 12.15

get . . . to + indirect object, 6.1

give . . . to + indirect object, 6.1

give up, 12.10

granted, as additive signal, 9.7

had better, in suggestions, 8.13
in tag questions, 3.5

half (of the), 10.26

hand . . . to + indirect object, 6.1

happen + *that*-clause or *to* + verb, 18.11

hardly ever, at beginning of sentence, 9.12
with negative attached statements, 4.5

have, in contractions, p.3(list)

have combinations, 12.23

have confidence in, 12.23

have/has, in *yes/no* questions and responses, 1.11, 1.12

have someone do something, 18.35

have something done, 18.35

have to, in expressing necessity, 8.5

have you?/Have you? tag vs. contrastive questions, 3.13

hear, in simple present to express perception, 7.1
with verb-*ing* or simple form, 18.38

help + (pro)noun + simple form, 18.40

hers, as subject in *yes/no* questions, 1.9

his, as subject in *yes/no* question, 1.9

homework, as singular count noun, 10.13

hope, with *that*-clause or *to* + verb, 18.1
vs. *wish,* 17.1 to 17.7

hope that, 5.17

how, in *wh*-questions, 2.10

however, in adverbial clauses, 13.36, 13.37, 13.40
as contrast signal, 14.46, 14.48
in noun clauses, 15.10
and punctuation, 19.3, 19.4
used in place of *but,* 4.10

how many, 2.18

how much, 2.14, 2.18

how old (how long, etc.), 2.14

how's (the weather), 2.26

I, in responses, 1.3

if, following *asked* in reported dialog, 5.23
in conditional sentences, 17.8
in noun clauses, 15.15, 15.19

imagine, with *that*-clause or verb-*ing,* 18.17, 18.25

immediately, as adverbial of time, 9.1
I'm not, 1.4
impossible, with *that*-clause or *for*-phrase, 18.7
in, vs. *at* or *on,* 9.31, 9.32
in a car (taxi, etc.), 9.38
in addition, as additive signal, 9.6
inasmuch as, in adverbial clauses of reason or cause, 13.18
in contrast (to), as contrast signal, 14.46, 14.50
indeed, and punctuation, 19.10
information, as singular noncount noun, 10.13
in ink (pencil, etc.), 9.36
in order that, in purpose clauses, 13.30, 13.31
in order to + verb, in expression of purpose, 9.42, 13.30, 18.31
in practice, as additive signal, 9.7
instruct, with *to* + verb, 18.15
intend, with *to* + verb or verb-*ing,* 18.21
in that, in adverbial clauses of reason or cause, 13.18, 13.19
in time, vs. *on time,* 9.34
into, vs. *in,* 9.32
invite, with *to* + verb, 18.15
is/isn't, in tag questions, 3.2, 3.3, 3.4
isn't she?/Is he? tag vs. contrastive questions, 3.13
it, as direct object, 6.13
in responses, 1.8, 1.9

just, as adverbial of time, 9.1
before a contraction, 9.15
with present perfect, 7.8, 7.13

keep, with verb-*ing,* 18.17
know, in simple present to express perception, 7.1

last night (week, etc.), with simple past, 7.10, 7.20
learn, with *to* + verb, 18.15
leave . . . for + indirect object, 6.1
leave . . . to + indirect object, 6.1
lend . . . to + indirect object, 6.1
-less, as suffix, 14.41, 14.43
less (of the) + noncount noun, 10.38
let + (pro)noun + simple form, 18.40
let's/let us, in requests and suggestions, 5.1, 5.17, 8.13
like, in clichés, 14.27
in comparisons, 14.12, 14.14, 14.27
+ noun, as adverbial of manner, 14.12
in simple present to express perception, 6.1
as suffix, 14.14
with *to* + verb or verb-*ing,* 18.21

likely/unlikely, with *that*-clause or *to* + verb, 18.11, 18.13
likewise, as comparison signal, 14.45
listen to, with verb-*ing* or simple form, 18.38
little/a little + noncount noun, 10.36
look, followed by *like* + noun, 14.12
look down on, 12.1
look forward to + verb-*ing,* 12.23, 18.18
look into, 12.1
look on, 12.1
look over, 12.1, 12.2
look up to, 12.1

mail . . . to + indirect object, 6.1
make . . . for + indirect object, 6.1
make + (pro)noun + simple form, 18.40
many (of the), 10.24
many + plural count noun, 10.33, 10.34
may, in expressing probability, 8.1, 8.3
in permissions, 8.7
mean, with *to* + verb, 18.15
mention . . . to + indirect object, 6.1
might, in expressing probability, 8.1
in *so* (*that*) clauses, 13.29
in suggestions, 8.13
mine, as subject in *yes/no* questions, 1.9
miss, with verb-*ing,* 18.17
moreover, as additive signal, 9.6
and punctuation, 19.3, 19.4
more than, in comparisons, 14.16 to 14.37
most . . . (of all), in comparisons, 14.22, 14.25
most (of the) + noun, 10.38
Ms., for *Miss* or *Mrs.,* p. 260*n*
much + noncount noun, 10.33, 10.34
must, expressing necessity, 8.5
expressing probability, 8.1

naturally, and punctuation, 19.10
necessary, with *that*-clause or *for*-phrase, 18.7
need to, in tag questions, 3.3
neglect, with *to* + verb or verb-*ing,* 18.21
neither, in attached statements, 4.4, 4.5
in rejoinders, 4.14
neither . . . nor, in comparisons, 14.8
with compound subjects, 4.8
and subject-verb agreement, 10.31, 14.8
neither (of the), as prearticle, 10.29
never, as adverbial of frequency, 9.14

at beginning of sentence, 9.12
expressing repeated activity, 7.3
with negative attached statements, 4.5
special usage, 9.18
nevertheless, in clauses of contrast and concession, 13.36
and punctuation, 19.3, 19.4
news, as singular noun, 10.13
next, as sequence signal, 9.4
next week (month, etc.), as time expression in reported speech, 15.13
no, indicating absence of quantity, 10.3
no matter how, in clauses of contrast and concession, 13.40
no more than, in comparisons, 14.29
none of the, 10.27
not, in negative questions and responses, 1.21
not any, indicating absence of quantity, 10.3
not as (so) . . . as, in comparisons, 14.16, 14.18, 14.20
notice, with verb-*ing* or simple form, 18.38
now, with simple present and present continuous, 7.2, 7.6, 7.11, 7.20
as time expression in reported questions, 15.13

object to + verb-*ing,* 12.20, 18.18
oblige, with *to* + verb, 18.15
observe, in reported statements, 15.26
occasionally, as adverbial of frequency, 9.14
before a contraction, 9.15
and punctuation, 19.10
of course, as additive signal, 9.7
and punctuation, 19.10
offer . . . to + indirect object, 6.1
often, as adverbial of frequency, 9.1, 9.14
expressing repeated activity, 7.3, 7.11
on, vs. *in* or *at,* 9.31, 9.32
once, in time clauses, 13.6
once in a while, expressing repeated activity, 7.3
one/ones, with *the other,* 10.45
on foot (horseback), 9.38
only once, at beginning of sentence, 9.12
only + **a few/a little,** 10.36
on the other hand, as contrast, signal, 14.46, 14.48
on time, vs. *in time,* 9.34
open . . . for + indirect object, 6.1
or, and punctuation, 19.2, 19.16
order, with *that*-clause or *to* + verb, 18.5
others/the others, 10.50
ought to, in expressing obligation, 8.11